ONE TRIP TOO MANY

A PILOT'S MEMOIRS OF 38 MONTHS IN COMBAT OVER LAOS AND VIETNAM

C-130 Hercules ☆ F-105 Thunderchief ☆ A-1 Skyraider

Copyright © 2011
Wayne A. Warner

All rights reserved. No part of this book may be reproduced in any form whatsoever, except for the inclusion of brief quotations in review, without permission in writing from the author/publisher.

ISBN-13: 978-1467931557
ISBN-10: 1467931551

Printed in the United States by CreateSpace
An Amazon.com Company
Published by Independent Publisher

Acknowledgements

Special thanks to Lauren Cole who transformed the manuscript to print-ready format and to William Landsberg for his editing effort

Cover Photo

15 March 1969, A-1H 52-134562 immediately after aborted takeoff.
Nakhon Phanom Royal Thai AFB, Thailand.
(USAF photo)

Theater of Operations

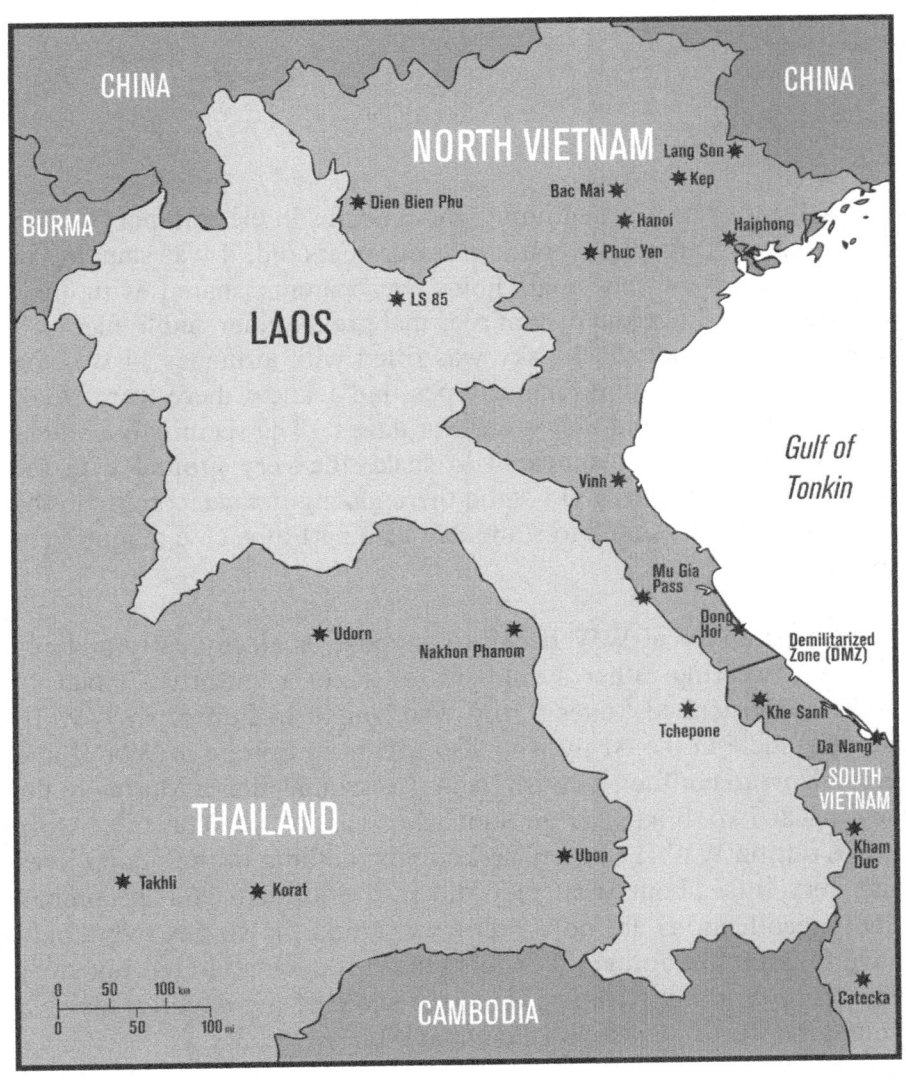

INTRODUCTION

All stories have a beginning; mine begins in the summer of 1945 in Lexington Kentucky when I was four years old. I was standing in the front yard of the small house my parents shared with their landlord when I heard a distant roar that grew louder and louder as it approached. Suddenly the sky was filled with airplanes. I was too young to know anything about types, but I knew there were small ones and big ones and they were warplanes. The seemingly endless procession of aircraft appeared to shake the very ground with the sound of their engines and I stood there gazing in awe, coming to the realization that I wanted to some day be a part of such a magnificent spectacle.

I was a typical WW II child I suppose as all my early pictures have me wearing either a soldier's or sailor's uniform. I had an uncle in the United States Army who fought in Europe in WW II; another uncle in the Army who also fought in Europe in WW II and in the Korean conflict; a cousin who was wounded as a Marine in the landing at Iwo Jima; and an aunt who was in the Women's Army Corps during WW II. I grew up knowing nothing of their daily lives and very little about what they did in the military and in combat. Their recollections are now irretrievable and the stories they could have told are lost forever. For this reason, I decided to tell my story and share with my wife and daughter some of my experiences as a young Air Force officer and a combat pilot.

This story is not about the politics of the events in Southeast Asia or about how the war should have been fought differently considering the rules of engagement imposed upon the fighting men and women of the United States military. It is simply about my personal involvement in those events, including some details of my daily life during that time period. I will say that I had no doubt as to the morality of my own involvement in the conflict and that I had nothing but disdain for the hippies and peaceniks protesting at home in the United States, a contempt that has eased with the passage of time but has not been erased. In hindsight, considering the ultimate sacrifice made by many of my closest friends, I suppose that particular war was the wrong war, in the wrong place, at the wrong time.

On one of my first flights in the C-130 over the Pacific en route to Vietnam I predicted that the people of the United States would eventually grow weary of the conflict as there was no crystal clear advantage to be gained by our country in its pursuit and we would withdraw our forces from the area, not in defeat as some describe it but in recognition of the futility of the effort compared to the sacrifices that were being made. Years passed and my prediction proved correct.

The primary source for these memoirs is, of course, my memory. Those recollections are supported by my official flying record, the Air Force Form 5; by reference to multiple sources to corroborate the events as I recalled them; and, through the memories of friends who shared some of the events described. I have used names only where I absolutely remembered them: if memory did not serve me well I omitted names and, in some cases, I did not include names to protect the innocent. Photographs are either official United States Air Force photographs that are in the public domain or pictures that are in my own private collection. This, then, is my personal story set against the backdrop of the turbulent decade of the 1960s.

Right: In 1945, Air Force Blue did not exist, so I wore Olive Drab.

Dedicated to:

My lovely and talented wife who looked past the scars and accepted me for who I am and is my best friend for life; to my equally lovely and talented daughter who followed in her dad's footsteps to become an attorney; and to the newest member of our family, my son-in-law, a Green Beret who has adventures of his own in Iraq and elsewhere in the Middle East;

Jon Ewing, Grady Allen, and Stuart Silver: without their selfless and heroic actions in March 1969 I would not be here;

My former roommates and other comrades in arms who made the ultimate sacrifice in the skies over Laos and Vietnam.

TABLE OF CONTENTS

1. THE FUTURE BEGINS IN COLORADO 1
2. FOUR YEARS IN THE ROCKIES...........................5
3. PILOT TRAINING: PRIMARY (T-37) 14
4. THOMAS CHARLES PIERSON 22
5. PILOT TRAINING: BASIC (T-33).........................30
6. ADVANCED SURVIVAL TRAINING 36
7. C-130 TRAINING: THE HERCULES 40
8. C-130 IN OKINAWA & VIETNAM 46
9. BLINDBAT & LAMPLIGHTER 64
10. TRANSITION TIME: C-130 TO F-105 81
11. F-105 TRAINING: THE THUNDERCHIEF 91
12. PACAF JUNGLE SURVIVAL SCHOOL 103
13. TAKHLI ROYAL THAI AIR FORCE BASE 106
14. MISSION # 1: COMBAT, THUD STYLE 112
15. DESTINATION KEP: MIGS 'N MORE 120
16. FOUL-UPS, SAMS, & RIVER RATS 129

17. AIR ABORT & THE DOUMER BRIDGE 140

18. MORE MIGS, IRAN, & USS PUEBLO 150

19. KHE SANH, SKYSPOTS, EDSELS, & VINH 155

20. BOMBING HALT & IN-FLIGHT REFUELING 165

21. KHAM DUC & MU GIA PASS 173

22. 100 MISSIONS NORTH 183

23. FUNCTIONAL CHECK FLIGHTS 187

24. THE END OF MY AFFAIR WITH THE THUD 196

25. A-1 TRAINING: THE SKYRAIDER 203

26. NAKHON PHANOM: FIREFLY & SANDY 212

27. HOSPITALS 238
    CLARK AB; 106th GENERAL HOSPITAL; BROOKE ARMY
    MEDICAL CENTER; WRIGHT-PATTERSON AFB

28. EPILOGUE 251

THE FUTURE BEGINS IN COLORADO

There were several ways to achieve my goal of flying for the United States Air Force. I decided during junior high school that a good way would be to go to the United States Military Academy at West Point and then apply for a transfer to the United States Air Force for flight training. That would have been a risky way to go as there would have been no guarantee I would do anything other than be an infantry officer, which was not very high on my list as a potential future career. My last year in junior high I was ecstatic to read that a new military academy had been established to meet the needs of the Air Force with the future location of the school to be near Colorado Springs, Colorado.

As early as 1925 General Billy Mitchell, a legendary air power advocate, pushed the idea of having an air academy to become the backbone of the air service just as West Point does for the Army and Annapolis does for the Navy. Support for a separate academy gained much-needed momentum with the enactment of the National Security Act of 1947 which split the Army Air Corps from the Army and established the United States Air Force as an entirely separate service. At that time, as a compromise to meet Air Force requirements without an air academy, an agreement was negotiated to allow up to 25% of West Point and Annapolis graduates to volunteer to receive their commissions in the newly established branch of the military. That was the agreement I was initially going to rely on to achieve my goal of flying for the Air Force.

In January 1950, the Service Academy Board, headed by Dwight D. Eisenhower, decided that the needs of the Air Force could not be met by the two existing service academies and that a third service academy should be established. Legislation was passed by Congress in 1954 to begin the construction of the United States Air Force Academy (USAFA) and President Eisenhower signed it into law on 1 April of that year. The original 582 sites considered were gradually reduced to the winning site of Colorado Springs. That decision was announced on 24 June 1954 just five years before the first class would graduate from the new school.

I began the process of seeking admittance to the Air Force Academy during the fall of 1955, my freshman year in high school, by writing to Senator William E. Jenner expressing interest in a future competitive nomination. Over the next three years I read any article I could find on the new school with great interest. I even joined the Civil Air Patrol so I could get a ride in a Piper Cub. That ride just fueled my desire to fly.

Our family doctor had flown B-17s during WW II and took note of my desire to attend the academy with the express goal of eventually earning my wings. The doctor was a close friend of Senator Homer E. Capehart and I felt that relationship presented my best opportunity of obtaining the coveted appointment. In October 1958, much to my joy, I received a letter from the Senator authorizing me to take a preliminary medical exam prior to his making any decision to grant my nomination request. On 24 Nov 1958 I underwent that medical exam at the USAF dispensary in Bakalar Air Force Base, Indiana. The results of the exam were absolutely disheartening as the written report stated, "Distant vision defect in right eye: not qualified for further testing." I returned home with my dreams absolutely dashed.

To my surprise I received a letter the following day from Senator William E. Jenner saying, "I am pleased to inform you I have nominated you to compete for my one cadet vacancy at USAFA." Senator Jenner served from January 1947 to January 1959 and, as he had not been re-elected in November 1958, I did not think he could any longer make such appointments. I had not contacted Senator Jenner since my freshman year and I guess he was simply filling the last squares in his duty box.

In December I received the dreaded letter from Senator Capehart stating he would not nominate me as I could not qualify for pilot training. I still had my appointment from Senator Jenner; however, and I visited two separate eye doctors to see what could be done, if anything, about my eye problem. The news was not any better as both doctors said I needed glasses.

On 30 December 1958 I received a letter from the USAFA Registrar that notified me to report to Wright-Patterson Air Force Base (WPAFB) in Ohio on 19 January 1959 for three days of testing (flying aptitude, mental exams, and physical aptitude) as a candidate for admission. With the support of my parents, I decided to continue the process for admission hoping there was still a slim chance that something good would eventually happen. I passed the battery of tests administered by WPAFB and scored well on my college entrance boards which were also part of the overall process.

On the 9th of February 1959 I received a letter from Representative Winfield K. Denton saying, "I am happy to advise I have nominated you as a candidate for the USAFA." All right, now I had two chances to gain admission as both nominations were competitive in nature. A competitive nomination simply meant that each Congressman could nominate up to ten candidates for admission with the highest scoring candidate getting the prize.

At the end of February the USAFA Registrar notified me that I had been officially recorded as a dual candidate for admission. On 19 April 1959 a Western Union telegram arrived from USAFA telling me to report on 29 April to WPAFB for final processing and medical exam. The moment of truth had finally arrived: I had to somehow jump the final hurdle of another dreaded eye exam. The day progressed rapidly with a multitude of medical personnel poking and prodding me. The eye exam actually seemed to present little problem and I thought, "Have I really made it through successfully?" The final act of the day was for a flight surgeon to go over the results of the exam and ask me any additional questions he thought necessary. He seemed to be quite interested in my desire to attend the academy and why I wanted to fly. My stomach felt queasy when he said, "Can you stay overnight for an additional eye exam? Perhaps you were tired today and I would like to check you after a good night's sleep."

I reported to the flight surgeon the following morning and he sent me into a room with a corpsman to check my eyes. The only part of the exam they wanted to repeat was where a slide rule looking device was placed against your nose and you had to read letters on a movable slide as it was moved away from your nose. The corpsman returned to the flight surgeon and said the results were the same. The flight surgeon replied that could not be right as the rest of the exam had gone so well. The flight surgeon then took me back into the room where he proceeded to open all the blinds covering the windows saying, "No wonder, the room is too dark for you to see." In the meantime, I was trying to rapidly memorize the letters on the device that was left on a table in front of me. The flight surgeon returned saying, "I want you to read these letters when you think they should be read." I repeated the exam and the flight surgeon said, "Great, I knew you could do it."

Thanks to a gracious and understanding doctor I had passed the final obstacle on my quest. I returned to my home in high spirits knowing I had opened a great door of opportunity for the future. On 29 May 1959 I received a congratulatory letter from the Superintendent stating my acceptance of the offer of appointment and confirmation of medical qualifications had brought me to the final step of admission which would occur when I reported on Friday, 26 June 1959, as a member of the Class of 1963 at the United States Air Force Academy.

FOUR YEARS IN THE ROCKIES

I was part of the fifth class to enter the Academy with 754 other basic cadets. We were the first full-sized class during the early years of the Academy when the total enrollment was set at 2400 cadets. (Current level is set at 4400 cadets.) The first graduating class in 1959 of 306 cadets received their diplomas and commissions just about three weeks prior to our arrival. Our class was the first class to spend all four years at the permanent site in Colorado Springs. The earlier classes had spent all or part of their time at the temporary site established at Lowry Air Force Base in Denver while construction was taking place on the new facilities.

I made the serious error of wanting to report in early and caught the first bus from the Colorado Springs Greyhound bus station to Vandenberg Hall where we took our oath and were then handed over to the eagerly awaiting upperclassmen. I should have waited until later in the day when they were getting tired from hazing the new arrivals. With the continued harangue and barrage of verbal abuse piled on by the first cadet to get hold of me, it took at least 30 minutes for me to learn how to salute, and give my rank, name, and serial number by saying, "Basic Cadet Warner, two zero five three K, reporting as ordered."

Summer training was not exactly what one would refer to as fun and there were times I wondered whatever possessed me to want to attend the Academy. We endured endless hours of marching, running, physical training and military training, all the while enduring that verbal abuse - the First and Second Classmen certainly knew how to induce stress in their young and immature trainees. We marched to meals where we sat at attention while eating, when we got the chance to eat. A favorite form of punishment in those early days was to withhold food - a practice that was eventually abolished but not during our summer of torture. The Academy dining hall baked a birthday cake for each of the new first year cadets - on the 10th of July that summer I received my cake at the noon meal. I hope the upperclassmen enjoyed it because I never got to taste it. The only thing that came close to being considered enjoyable during that time was getting an orientation flight in a T-33 which was a great reminder of my reason for enduring the never-ending harassment.

I survived the summer but my roommate did not. He was from Eugene, Oregon and decided he would much rather be there than in Colorado Springs. At the conclusion of summer training we were accepted into the cadet wing and given the title of Cadet Fourth Class. I was assigned to Cadet Squadron 14. There were only 16 squadrons in the 1959/1960 academic year. The following year I would move to the 18th (out of 20) and my last two years I would be in the 23rd (out of 24). The moves were necessary to have upperclassmen in the new squadrons created by the gradually increasing enrollment.

To say the least, it was an interesting four years and I was given the opportunity to visit a lot of new places and do a lot of things the normal college curriculum doesn't include. Our Third Class summer in 1960 we embarked on our Continental United States field trip. We spent a week with the United States Army at Fort Benning, Georgia where we jumped from the static towers with the airborne troops; we ran the obstacle course and tackled the officers confidence course; we rode on M-113 armored personnel carriers; we fired the M-1 rifle, the 38 handgun, the M-14 rifle, the Browning automatic rifle (BAR), the M-60 machine gun, and the 105 mm recoilless rifle; and, we watched all kinds of firepower and tank demonstrations.

We spent a week at sea with the United States Navy sailing from San Francisco Bay and passing under the Golden Gate Bridge. I was aboard a 15,000 ton Suribachi-class ammunition resupply ship, the USS Mauna Kea, AE-22, and watched as the Mauna Kea replenished the Fletcher-class destroyer USS Twining, DD-540, while underway in the Pacific. The Navy has the interesting habit of naming ammunition ships after volcanoes. At first I was disappointed to see that some of my classmates were on the Twining, a battle-hardened WW II (8 battle stars) and Korean War (5 battle stars) veteran and a real fighting ship, so I thought. That disappointment soon turned to glee when I realized the constant pitching and rolling of the 2,100-ton destroyer had stricken some of the cadets aboard with a severe case of sea-sickness: that explained why they were hanging over the rail and eating saltine crackers. The Mauna Kea later earned 12 campaign stars for service in Vietnam and was eventually sunk as a target ship off Hawaii in July 2006. The Twining was sold to the Nationalist Chinese in 1971 and served until 1999. I also spotted her in a cameo appearance in the 1957 sci-fi movie, The Monster that Challenged the World.

We were introduced to the future world of "Buck Rogers" through the laboratories and research facilities at Wright-Patterson AFB, Ohio and we viewed endless miles of conveyer belts at the logistics and resupply operations at Tinker AFB, Oklahoma. We spent time at the Air Force Flight Test Center in the desert at Edwards AFB, California where I saw my first F-105, and at March AFB, Riverside, California where we were introduced to the B-47 and B-52. While at March some of us tried to rent a car in Riverside to go to Disneyland but, despite our pleas, the rental agencies refused as we were too young by their rules.

First View of F-105 at Edwards AFB

7

As part of our social training we had to attend a mandatory formal dance dressed in our mess dress uniforms at each of the bases we visited. Those uniforms, like the parade uniform, were the design work of Cecil B. DeMille, the Hollywood director. Young ladies of the appropriate age range from the local area were invited to participate in those functions as our dates. The dating process involved gathering the girls in one room and the cadets in another room. A dance representative would pair the cadet and his date by size by looking at the girl and then saying to the cadets, "We need a short cadet, or a medium cadet, or a tall cadet." At Wright-Patterson the dance rep called for a short cadet and my buddies immediately started pushing me to the front. I rounded the corner into the adjoining room where I saw a bright red dress and the largest and tallest female I had ever seen: attractive yes, but definitely not within the dancing reach of a cadet of my stature. I froze and very indiscreetly exclaimed, "No! No! You do not want a short cadet!" To my relief (and I am quite sure to the relief of the lady in red) the dance rep escorted a very petite lady who had been hidden from view behind the red dress and introduced the two of us.

At Fort Benning, my close friend and Academy classmate, Bob Storms and I were walking to the Officers Club for the affair when a two-seat Thunderbird convertible driven by an absolutely stunning blonde pulled into one of the reserved parking spots in front of the club. We both agreed that it was never to be our good fortune to be paired with a girl like that and decided she probably was not there for the dance anyway. Surprise, surprise: she turned out to be my date for the evening. Unfortunately she was there solely because her father, a Colonel at Fort Benning, insisted on it and she continually reminded me of that fact throughout the evening. The hours spent with her were so miserable that later when the occasion arose to introduce her to some friends my memory banks had blocked the pain and I could not even remember her name. If looks could actually kill I would not be here today.

We found a way to alleviate some of the burden of attending those mandatory formal events by creating the ghoul pool. All of us would contribute a dollar to a kitty which the winner would collect by having the homeliest date as agreed to by the members of the pool. That decision was made by a vote taken while we were traveling to our next destination. The worst blow of all was to come in second in the pool as there was no prize for place or show. Somehow the news media learned of our game and printed some articles about it before we reached March Air Force Base. The ladies at March then created their own pool and publicly announced the winner while still at the dance - all I could say was I thought the public announcement was not exactly in keeping with the spirit of the game but I was very glad I was not selected the "winning" cadet as he was ribbed about it for years.

The summers of 1961 and 1962 were partially spent with basic cadet training as our class introduced the classes of 1965 and 1966 to Academy life. I was assigned to the physical training unit both summers and stood on a platform leading the doolies (as the new trainees were politely known in the 60s although they were usually addressed as Mister and referred to as a "Dumb-Squat") in repetitive exercises. Allegedly "Dooly" came from the Greek word meaning slave.

The summer of 1962 included Operation Third Lieutenant where we spent two weeks with an active Air Force unit to get a glimpse of what we could be doing when we graduated. That summer was also the first time that our class could own personal vehicles and I took possession of a brand-new, black with red interior, 1962 MGA. During Operation Third Lieutenant I was one of five cadets assigned to Columbus Air Force Base in Mississippi. It was a Strategic Air Command (SAC) base at the time and home to B-52s and KC-135s. My mentor was a squadron maintenance officer, a former F-102 pilot who had lost his wings for medical reasons. I had my first ride in the big bomber with the eight jet engines during that time: it was a ten-hour flight and I rode in a jump seat behind the navigators in the cave-like bottom section of the crew compartment. I did get a short time to visit the pilots' deck but for the most part the ride was rather boring and I was happy to get back on the ground. That flight may have had some influence in the selection of the aircraft I wanted to fly following undergraduate pilot training.

As was par for the course, we had numerous social functions to attend, one of which was to be honorary judges for a beauty pageant in Columbus. Such pageants seem to be a vital part of southern tradition and we happily agreed to participate. Following that difficult task we attended a formal dance at the local country club where the club dance committee arranged blind dates for the five of us; each young lady selected was, you guessed it, a beauty pageant winner and my date was Miss Watermelon Queen. She was quite a beautiful blonde southern belle attending Mississippi State University but she also had a boyfriend so our interaction was limited to that one evening.

That summer concluded with the best of all extra-curricular activities: our field trip to Europe where we visited Spain, France, Italy, and Germany. We flew C-130s to Dover Delaware where we boarded a C-118 for an eighteen-hour flight, including a refueling stop in the Azores, to Torrejon Air Base outside Madrid. Our typical activities included one or two days of military briefings and base tours then we had two or three days to see the local sites on our own. We stayed in civilian hotels and wore civilian clothes when we were not on a military installation. In Spain we visited Toledo and Burgos as well as Madrid. As usual we had a formal dance at Torrejon and, since I was able to speak a little Spanish, my date was the daughter of the Spanish base commander. We spent time at the Spanish Air Force summer encampment with our counterparts and played basketball against them in an impromptu get-together.

In Paris we climbed the Eiffel Tower, visited the Louvre and Notre Dame, and took a trip to the palace and gardens at Versailles. In Rome we walked through the Roman Forum and the Coliseum, and took a bus to visit Pope John XXIII in his summer residence where we attended a Papal audience.

In Germany we visited Munich, Wiesbaden and Garmisch. In Garmisch we had a great time at a beer festival where Bob Storms and I met a young German wanting to practice his English. He was the son of a vice president for Mercedes Benz and became our unofficial tour guide for the remainder of our time in that city.

Our final stop was Berlin. We had accommodations at Templehof Air Base, the airfield made famous in the Berlin airlift in 1948. On the 13th of August 1961 the Soviets and East Germany closed the border and started the construction of the Berlin Wall. When we were there a year later it was still just a wire fence but the communists were already busily improving it. It gradually evolved into the permanent concrete wall with guard towers that was finally torn down at the end of 1989.

In 1962 there were specific vehicle and pedestrian checkpoints where limited passages between East and West Berlin were allowed, the most famous of which was known as Checkpoint Charlie. That checkpoint was restricted to Allied personnel and foreigners other than Berliners or Germans. Allied military personnel and civilian officials of the Allied forces could enter and exit East Berlin without submitting to East German passport controls, purchasing a visa or being required to exchange money.

We crossed the border in uniform in two Air Force blue buses to visit East Berlin. We went to the Soviet war memorial and the Soviet cemetery. We drove past the site of the underground bunker where Adolph Hitler shot himself but the Soviets would not allow us to actually enter the site. The most remarkable aspect of the visit was the stark contrast between West and East that was apparent immediately upon crossing the border: West Berlin was filled with activity; throngs of people were happily bustling about their daily lives and the city was alive with lights and sounds; construction was booming and there was little evidence of the catastrophic war that had occurred just seventeen years earlier. On the other side of the border we saw few people and no young people; there were blocks and blocks of destroyed buildings and rubble lining the streets. Most telling, we did not see anyone smile and eye contact between people was definitely avoided. We returned to the American zone with a feeling of great relief and with a definite respect and appreciation for our way of life.

Brandenburg Gate in Berlin: Taken from the Soviet Sector

Although the daily routine at the Academy was stressful and demanding we had plenty of time to actually enjoy ourselves. During the third class year I found refuge in the archery club and spent quite a bit of free time shooting the bow and arrow in the surrounding hills. I had my picture appear on the front cover of Bowman Magazine, a national publication, when the magazine did an article on archery at the Academy. Gil Merkle, Curt Preston, Al Ragsdale, and I formed a rock-n-roll band that performed at many of our social functions and parties: none of us could sing so we copied instrumentals such as Limbo Rock, Green Onions, and songs created by the Ventures. Although we never actually had an official name, we called ourselves the Half-Fasts. Our class was treated to two chartered train trips during our time at the Academy: one from Colorado Springs to Los Angeles to attend a football game between our Falcons and UCLA and the other from Colorado Springs to Dallas-Fort Worth to march in the Texas State Fair parade and then attend our football game with SMU.

We loaded into C-130s at Peterson Field in Colorado Springs to march in President Kennedy's inauguration parade in Washington D.C. but bad weather prevented some of our aircraft from landing and we spent the night at Fort Campbell, Kentucky instead. The last off-base ceremony I participated in as a cadet was the 1963 Memorial Day parade in New York City just before we graduated. We were lodged in the United States Army barracks on Governors Island and visited Times Square in Manhattan. Three years after we stayed on the island the Army transferred control of the post to the United States Coast Guard. My first and only association with the Coasties was to spend a long weekend at the United States Coast Guard Academy in New London, Connecticut on an exchange visit during my second class year in the spring of 1962.

Spring 1963 had arrived, graduation was in sight and we were preparing to select our undergraduate pilot training bases. The only obstacle left was the final flight physical that of course included an extensive eye exam. I approached that exam with a lot of trepidation as I knew from prior experience my eyes did not always reach the 20/20 requirement needed to fly. My squadron classmates spent very little time in the exam room but I spent what seemed like an eternity - once again another flight surgeon took the time to talk to me and asked how badly I wanted to go to pilot training. I responded that flying was the reason I had endured the previous four years. He sighed and said, "Your eyes are so borderline but I am going to pass you. The next time you have an eye exam you will have your wings and they will not take them away from you." Needless to say, I was elated with his decision and walked out of the exam room on cloud nine.

On 5 June 1963, 499 cadets, including me, graduated from the United States Air Force Academy. After four long, stress-filled yet also exhilarating years, we were now the fifth class of graduates. Diplomas were presented by President John F. Kennedy and commissions as Second Lieutenants were presented by Air Force Chief of Staff, General Curtis E. LeMay. I had reached the end of the journey required to get me to the goal of attending flight school. Undergraduate pilot training at Craig Air Force Base, Alabama was my next destination.

Cadet Captain Warner (1963 Polaris)

Graduation (1963 Polaris)

PILOT TRAINING: PRIMARY (T-37)

I arrived at Craig Air Force Base on 20 August 1963 eager to learn how to fly jet-powered airplanes. I was one of 43 Second Lieutenants assigned to class 65B with the 3615th Pilot Training Wing. Thirty-nine were classmates from the Class of 1963 at the United States Air Force Academy; one was from the Class of 1963 at the United States Military Academy, West Point; one was an ROTC graduate that started with class 65A; and, one was a member of the Hawaiian Air National Guard.

During the year we would lose two members of our class: Tom Pierson would perish in an aircraft accident and Jerry Driscoll would graduate with the following class. Jerry would go to F-105 training after graduating from Craig AFB and would be shot down in his F-105D over North Vietnam on 24 April 1966. He became a prisoner of war in Hanoi and was repatriated to the United States on February 12, 1973.

Craig Air Force Base was originally named Selma Army Airfield and was built in 1940 to provide additional pilot training facilities that would be of use during WW II. As the original name implies, the base was built near Selma, Alabama in the heart of the south. The name was changed to honor a Selma native who was killed in 1941 in an aircraft accident. The barracks that were constructed in 1940 to house the trainees were single story, concrete block structures that featured a screened porch that ran the length of the building. The suites were comprised of two large bedrooms sharing a bath between them. Those WW II facilities were the same facilities we used in 1963 and 1964 as our living quarters. In 1977 the base was closed and became a civil air field and an industrial complex for the town of Selma.

The airplane used for our primary flight training was the T-37B, also known as the Tweet, and the call sign for White Flight was Little Jug. Our flight commander was Captain R.C. Roberts and my instructor was First Lieutenant Lyle Mitchell. Tom Pierson, Joe Schuchter, and I shared Lieutenant Mitchell's time.

The Cessna T-37 was a small twin-engine jet aircraft used as a beginning trainer for the U.S. Air Force and in the air forces of several other nations. In the 60s the Air Force wanted its training to be all jet-propelled as it considered props to be a thing of the past. The aircraft featured side-by-side seating facilitating communication between instructor and student. 1,269 T-37s were built with the T-37A being delivered to the U.S. Air Force beginning in June 1956 although training using the T-37A did not begin until 1957. The first T-37B was delivered in 1959. The airplane handled well, was forgiving of mistakes, and was agile and responsive, though it was definitely not overpowered. It was capable of all traditional aerobatic maneuvers including intentional spins. The last T-37B was officially retired from active USAF service on 31 July 2009. As it had been in service for over 50 years it was replaced by the T-6 Texan II which is a turboprop with more power, better fuel efficiency and more modern avionics than the Tweet.

Our flying training curriculum centered on transition including basic aerobatics, instrument flying, and navigation. I easily adapted to flying and had no real difficulties during pilot training other than I was a definite slacker when it came to studying for academics. Time quickly passed and on 16 October I took my first solo flight and received the traditional dunking in a water tank placed in front of the flight shack. The first solo flight occurred when the instructor believed the student capable of completing a takeoff, flying around the traffic pattern, and returning for a landing. I was elated at the end of my 12th flight when Lieutenant Mitchell told me to taxi to the departure end of the runway instead of returning to the ramp. With the engines running he climbed out of the cockpit, secured the right seat by fastening the restraining straps and seat belt, and wished me good luck. I taxied on the runway and started that momentous flight.

The takeoff occupied all my thoughts so I did not notice all the strange noises I had never paid any attention to before until I leveled off for the trip around the traffic pattern. What was that weird noise? I did not remember that particular sound. Was I about to suffer a catastrophic engine failure? In fact everything was quite normal and I made my turn to final and placed the Tweet on the runway without crashing. I had arrived - I was actually a pilot, or so I thought at that moment. In actuality I was a very long way from reaching that status.

Navigation was a breeze for me and I was graded nothing but excellent on all my navigation training flights. Individual flights were graded by the instructor as failure, fair, good, or excellent. It was time for my check ride to conclude the navigation phase and I was scheduled to fly with the flight commander, Captain Roberts, as my check flight pilot. I was elated to fly with Captain Roberts as he was very easy to get along with and I knew he thought I was a good student. Everything went as smooth as glass from preflight, takeoff, and through the low level portion of the ride. I was right on my planned flight path and all my checkpoints were hit within a second or two of the flight plan. I climbed from 500 feet to 22,000 feet to enter the high altitude portion of the flight. My next check point was Jackson, Mississippi.

The upper level winds turned out to be significantly stronger than what the weather briefing predicted and I arrived over Jackson two minutes ahead of schedule. That could not be right and I thought I must have been mistaken in my identification of Jackson. True, the river was there, running through the town, the highways looked like my map said they should, but the time was way off so I concluded there must be another town and river that looked the same. Was I ever wrong - after two minutes passed, there was no town and no river within sight. There was nothing but green countryside in view. I suddenly realized I was lost, not hopelessly lost but there was no way to backtrack and salvage the check flight and my pride. Captain Roberts took the airplane and we returned to Craig in silence.

When I walked into the flight shack and sat down at our table, Lieutenant Mitchell said, "Well, did you ace it?" I replied that I had in fact flunked it. Tom, Joe, and the instructor all said you are kidding aren't you? I said I was dead serious and the table erupted in gales of laughter. I had to repeat the check ride with another instructor that I did not care for; furthermore, he was known as a very stern grader who rarely gave anything above a "fair" rating. For once I was quite concerned about my next flight but the ride went fine and I was successfully through the navigation phase.

While flying and academics consumed the majority of our time, there was plenty of time left to enjoy ourselves in and around Selma and the beaches of the panhandle in Florida. I traded my MGA for a 1959 Thunderbird, the four-seat model, during the summer before I reached Craig. I liked the car but it was like the Tweet, definitely underpowered, with the standard 352-cubic-inch engine. I was interested in drag racing and occasionally visited a local automotive repair shop where the owners raced a hemi-powered, slingshot-type, rail dragster. They had a high performance Ford 406-cubic-inch motor for sale and we worked out an engine swap for my T-Bird. I also had the automatic transmission modified so it would shift like a standard shift by using the shift lever.

I thought the car was awesome but I still needed something else to ride. Joe Palazzolo from our class rode a Triumph Trophy 650cc motorcycle and that caught my eye. Motorcycles seemed like flying in two dimensions instead of three so I decided I needed a motorcycle, especially since I did not have one. Joe told me he spotted a Triumph 650cc Bonneville for sale in Montgomery and I talked Joe into taking me to Montgomery to check it out. When I started talking to the owner, it was soon apparent that I knew nothing about motorcycles and had never been on one in my life. The owner said to hop on and he would show me how to start and shift it and then I could go kill myself on it. We concluded our transaction and I hopped on the Triumph to return to Craig.

Of course I purchased the motorcycle on the east side of Montgomery meaning I had to ride completely through town to get back to the relatively deserted highway from Montgomery to Selma. I managed to do exactly what everyone does when they first climb on a motorcycle. Everyone has seen home videos where the hapless rider knows how to twist the throttle and hang on but no one seems to know how to work the clutch or brake. I headed for my first intersection where I quickly realized I was not going to stop so I cut through a service station driveway and merged into a small hole in the stream of traffic. By the time I reached the next stoplight I had collected my thoughts and managed to engage the brakes and come to a controlled stop.

I cautiously proceeded through the downtown traffic and had almost reached the west side of town when I suddenly came upon my first right hand turn. For some reason (something about gyroscopic action known only to physics majors) it is always easier to turn left than it is right on a motorcycle. I started around the corner and knew immediately I was not going to make the turn within my lane. I was headed straight for the car on the far side of the street so I cut the handlebars hard left and ran into the curb.

The motorcycle stopped but I did not: flying over the handlebars I hit a stone retaining wall head first. That is why helmets are life savers. My helmet had a big gouge on the very top but my head was fine. The driver of the car asked if I was OK and I responded that nothing was hurt but my ego. Traffic was very light at that locale and I pulled the motorcycle up on the sidewalk to take stock of the entire episode. I was fine and the Triumph only had a cracked headlamp and a small tear on the left side of the seat. I never did fix that tear on the seat nor replace the headlamp as it still worked. They served as a reminder of the need to exercise a little caution when riding a motorcycle. I finally decided that if I was ever going to ride that motorcycle, I had to get back on it. Besides, Craig was almost 45 miles away and I had no other way to get home.

One of the highlights of pilot training was the opportunity to fly several cross-country flights that were designed to acquaint us with navigation to another location and with the use of approach charts to safely land at unfamiliar airfields. On my first cross country I flew with Captain Anthony Shine rather than Lyle Mitchell. We were going to Homestead Air Force Base near Miami. En route to Miami and while over Jacksonville we encountered heavy icing conditions. I was amazed at how rapidly the leading edge of the wings became encrusted with thick layers of ice. We immediately descended to a lower altitude where the temperature increase quickly removed the ice buildup. After reaching Homestead several of us put on our sport coats and ties and went to the Playboy Club in Miami. I noticed one of the Bunnies was chewing gum, a flagrant violation of alleged Playboy Club rules. I thought all the Bunnies had on way too much makeup and I was overall somewhat disappointed in my visit to an American icon. The cross-country flight itself was absolutely great and I looked forward to the next one.

One weekend I decided to go to the beach at Panama City: It would be a marvelous motorcycle trip. In the meantime, after purchasing the Triumph, I learned the bike was only running on one cylinder and I had to pay more money to get it fixed. Probably a good thing since it was a lot slower than it should have been while I was learning to ride - another lesson learned the hard way. I departed Craig headed for Florida and managed to get almost to Oak Hill, Alabama just northwest of Evergreen when the bike died on me.
I was left with pushing the Triumph up and down hills to try and get to a telephone or a service station. I was almost exhausted pushing up a particularly long grade when a car pulled up beside me. The lady driving asked if she could be of assistance and I replied I needed a telephone. She said there was a small country store just over the next hill and I could use that telephone. She had two children in the car with her, a ten year old daughter and a six year old son. She and her husband owned the store she told me about. The family, including the husband, met me at the store when I arrived and unlocked the door to let me in as the store had closed for the day: it was around six PM.
I called the pay telephone on the wall right outside the suite I shared with my suitemate, Bill Ivey. Bill was the West Point graduate in our class and drove a new Jaguar XKE: he was also African-American and, to my knowledge, the first member of his race to go to pilot training at Craig. Bill answered the phone and I said, "Bill, what are you doing there on a Saturday night." I really did not expect anyone to even answer the telephone. Bill replied, "Wayne, this is Selma. Where do you think I would be on Saturday night?" "I see your point," I said. I explained my predicament and Bill said he would be happy to come to Oak Hill in his Jaguar to pick me up.
As it was going to be at least an hour or two before Bill could get there, the family invited me to eat dinner with them. Their house was located on a hill behind the store. We enjoyed a pleasant dinner (I remember fried okra) and the conversation eventually centered

around segregation, or the lack thereof in the military, once they learned my background. After dinner we went to the store to wait for Bill to arrive. I told my hosts that I felt they should be forewarned that the friend who was going to pick me up was black. The daughter did not hear that bit of information and she excitedly ran to the front door when we saw headlights flash through the windows saying, "That must be your friend." She looked out the door and turned around saying, "That is not your friend. It is just some _____ in a fancy car." I simply smiled and said, "From your description that is definitely my friend." As we left for Craig Bill said, "Wayne, I think your welcome was worn out when I drove up." I returned with my Thunderbird and motorcycle hitch to pick my bike up the following day. Although the family was still friendly, there was a distinct change in their overall demeanor.

Colonel William "Bill" Ivey was killed in a B-52G accident on 16 October 1984. He was riding as a safety observer on a night, low level training mission from Fairchild Air Force Base in Washington when the B-52 struck the edge of a mesa in a snow storm. The crew ejected with multiple severe injuries including one death when the chute did not deploy prior to the crewman hitting the ground. Bill was unable to eject or escape from the aircraft as he was not riding in an ejection seat and he was killed on impact.

Selma was definitely still caught in the prevailing attitudes found in the South during the early 1960s regarding separation of the races. There was a tradition at Selma and Craig for the local country club to extend an invitation to each pilot training class to become honorary members of the club and use the facilities such as the dining room, golf course, and swimming pool. The invitation extended to our class was that everyone could use the facilities as long as Bill understood he could not, and would not, attempt to do so. We took a class vote and unanimously told the country club, "No, thank you."
There was one decent restaurant in town called the Talley-Ho club. They did have wonderful steaks but you needed a club card to get in. The price to obtain a card was essentially the color of your skin. Public restrooms and drinking fountains were still marked "white" and "colored" and the restaurants we frequented definitely

did not serve African-Americans. It was guaranteed to draw stares when Bill was riding in a car with any of the members of our class. Selma and the Edmund Pettis Bridge would become two of the focal points the following year for civil rights demonstrations including the infamous "Bloody Sunday" episode and the march from Selma to Montgomery.

On 22 November 1963 the 35th President of the United States, John F. Kennedy, was assassinated by Lee Harvey Oswald in Dallas, Texas. I was airborne over Alabama on a training flight when the stunning news was announced over our UHF radios. It was a very terse communication saying, "The President of the United States has been shot." The instructor took control of the airplane and I was left wondering just what the implications of the message were. "Did it mean we were at war, and if so, with whom? Was the President still alive or not?" I also immediately recalled that JFK had been the featured speaker and a most-welcome and admired participant at our graduation ceremony just five months earlier.

THOMAS CHARLES PIERSON

Tom Pierson was one of my closest friends; we had developed that relationship during the previous four years of shared misery and great times together at the Air Force Academy. Some of our best times were in playing intramural football on the 23rd Squadron team and engaging in friendly games of squash at the gym. We picked Craig Air Force Base as our choice for pilot training in order to be able to attend the same base together. The base selection process was held in one of the large Academy lecture halls and the class order of merit was used to determine who would pick first. I was going to select slightly before Tom so we carefully examined the base vacancies and determined there were enough slots open at Craig for both of us to be able to safely end up at that location. The plan worked and we secured our places for the summer of 1963 at Selma in the 3617th Pilot Training Squadron.

Probably our most memorable joint undertaking occurred during our First Class year in the fall of 1962. The Academy decided to hold the annual Commandant's Ball for senior cadets during football season. In fact the decision was made to hold the Ball, which was a formal event requiring mess dress uniforms, after one of our home football games. That decision was not greeted entirely with enthusiasm by the Class of 63 as we had some of our best parties after home football games. The thought of having to put on yet another fancy uniform and attend a mandatory, non-alcoholic, social event in Arnold Hall rather than have a "spirited" informal get-together with our best buddies at an off-site location was, at the very least, somewhat disappointing.

Tom and I and our 23rd Squadron classmates were in a non-related meeting when the subject of the Ball and our general displeasure therewith happened to come up. Someone said we needed to do something different to liven the event up and someone else suggested that maybe one of us should attend dressed as a girl. That idea seemed to ignite a lot of enthusiasm and I was immediately and unanimously tagged by my brethren to be the "girl" to attend the dance. Although not opposed to the whole idea, I was not altogether complimented by the group decision but they convinced me that I was the logical choice because of my blonde hair and propensity for playing harmless but frequent pranks and jokes. The next issue to settle was to decide who would be my escort for the evening. Tom was devoted to his girlfriend Sandra (Sandy), who lived in Murfreesboro, Tennessee, and he remained absolutely faithful to her during his four long years in Colorado Springs. Tom was deemed the natural choice as he would attend the Ball in a stag capacity anyway.

Several of our other classmates in the Squadron had their girlfriends living in the Colorado Springs area and it was the plan to use those girlfriends as the sources of supply of the necessary attire and other paraphernalia common to "womanly" needs for formal occasions. At the Ball the girls would also act to shield me by keeping me surrounded and out of close proximity to other young ladies who might not see the humor in the situation.

As our plan developed and the day of the Ball approached, we had secured the necessary apparel and support staff. I had a lovely chiffon, hooped and strapless, floor-length formal with gymnastics slippers hidden underneath. The crowning glory was that the father of Jo Ann Hall (married the day after graduation to our good friend and classmate Johnnie Hall) thought the idea was so awesome that he arranged for the loan of a very expensive wig and comprehensive make-up session at the Garden of the Gods Country Club Beauty Salon. Immediately after the football game I hustled downtown to the Country Club with Tom to undergo the magical transformation from cadet to young lady for the evening. As I climbed into the chair in the beauty salon the beautician determined that I certainly could not remove my T-shirt with the wig and makeup on so she said for me to remove the shirt. There I sat, in a beauty salon with a full wig on, no shirt, and having all kinds of weird stuff applied to my face.

As I walked out into the parking lot carrying my shirt I heard the loud squeal of tires as one of the Country Club members apparently thought he had spotted a woman with absolutely no top on walking to her car. The beautician who had worked on me came running out of the salon with a towel that she quickly wrapped around my shoulders saying, "We do not want to cause any wrecks on Country Club property".

Tom and I went to Jo Ann's parents' house to meet Johnnie and the rest of our conspirators and to complete the transformation where I donned the formal, complaining that it seemed very cool in the outfit. Closer examination revealed that I had neglected to put the appropriate slip on under the hooped skirt. Dressing completed, we piled into our cars and drove to the dance.

The entire entourage swept into Arnold Hall and I successfully negotiated the steps into the ballroom. I felt like I received more than the occasional glance from the people surrounding us and was wondering if my actual gender was all too apparent. The real test was forthcoming in the form of the official receiving line where each person attending the dance was introduced to the Commandant and his wife. The first person in the receiving line was the Cadet Dance Representative: It was his task to get the cadet's name and the name of his date to introduce them to the Commandant.

Tom and I approached the receiving line: I stopped in front of the Commandant and Tom was standing in front of the dance rep. Unfortunately the dance rep, Pat Caruana, knew both of us very well and he wondered why Tom was with a date when he knew Tom's Sandy was still in Tennessee. When Pat looked at me he immediately recognized me and froze: he did not know what to do and he failed to make any introduction at all. I felt my heart sink. There was a very awkward silence until the Commandant finally spoke directly to me, "I am sorry, I did not catch your name." I tried to whisper hoping he would think I was hoarse from yelling at the football game. Instead it seemed like I shouted "Wendy Brown" in a decidedly non-feminine voice. I had decided on that name for simplicity's sake just to make sure the dance rep who would introduce us could remember it; so much for advance planning. I just knew my cover had been blown but to my everlasting relief the

Commandant smiled and said "I shouldn't have any trouble remembering that."

We breezed through the remainder of the line with no further conversation and laughingly rejoined our posse at the far end of the ballroom. After a few more minutes as word of our prank started to spread among some of the cadets we made our escape and retired to Vandenberg Hall, the cadet dormitory, and the safety of our rooms. Later, one of our classmates was overheard saying, "Did you see Tom's date? She wasn't too bad but talk about broad shoulders!"

As part of the original plan, the Rocky Mountain News was going to take pictures of the event; however, I do not believe a reporter or photographer ever showed up at the dance. Later during the evening as part of the "mission" the Commandant was informed of our stunt by Jerry Westerbeck, our cadet squadron commander. The Commandant was somewhat amused and his wife commented she thought there were several young ladies that looked like they could have been cadets.

The next Monday morning Tom and I received a "request" to report to the office of the Squadron Air Officer Commanding "immediately". The AOC, Captain Angelo Morinello, told us that everyone had had a good laugh at our shenanigans and that the Commandant was not offended but he also offered a sound bit of advice: "If any photographs of this event ever appear, or the Commandant is embarrassed in any way, the two of you are not going to see a graduation day."

The following summer, well after graduation, the yearbook for the Class of 1963 was introduced - there was a picture of the two of us in all our finery on the page covering the Commandant's Ball.

The caption for the picture read, "The Commandant's Ball that evening highlighted a new twist in cadet's dates...Wayne Warner was unanimously voted queen for a day." To this day I have classmates who do not know the meaning behind the caption.

(1963 Polaris)

Following graduation, Tom and Sandy were married in Murfreesboro, Tennessee. I was part of the wedding party. Later in that summer before we went to pilot training, Tom and Sandy visited me in Indiana. Tom was driving his 1957 Chevy and carrying a 2 gallon can of gas in the car. I asked him why he was carrying the gas can and he replied he was going to run out of gas but he wasn't sure when. I said, "Tom if your gas gauge is broken why don't you just fill up more often?" Tom said the gauge wasn't broken, he was just checking his gas mileage. I suggested he simply take his mileage numbers between fill-ups to determine how far he had driven and divide that number by the amount of gas measured by the gas pump at his next fuel stop.

We had all but completed primary flight training and I ate dinner with Tom and Sandy at their home outside Selma on a Thursday evening, the 12th of March. Sandy had fixed a wonderful meal and had strawberry shortcake for dessert. Tom and I agreed we had eaten too much to really enjoy the strawberry shortcake so we all agreed to finish off the dessert the next evening, Friday the 13th - a date that would prove to be very unlucky for Tom and Sandy. On that Friday, I was scheduled to fly my last dual ride with our instructor, Lieutenant Lyle Mitchell, while Tom was scheduled for a slightly earlier takeoff on his last solo flight.

It was a typical Alabama March day, weather was good and I was ready to get the last flight done and move on to basic in the T-33. As we approached the airfield at the conclusion of my flight, Lyle took the airplane and told me that Tom was overdue on his scheduled return. We silently taxied into our parking spot and Joe Schuchter met us at the airplane. He shook his head and said Tom didn't make it. Joe and Lyle left me sitting in the cockpit while they returned to the flight shack. After wiping the tears from my eyes I climbed out of the T-37 cockpit and slowly walked across the ramp. As I approached the flight shack our flight commander, Captain Roberts, met me - he said Sandy was asking for me and that I should get on over to their house. My worried response was, "What do I say?" Capt. Roberts wisely told me that all I probably needed to do was listen and that I would know what to say when the need to say anything arose.

I drove to the house and Sandy greeted me at the door. She was calm and composed but I could tell she had been crying. The base mortuary affairs officer was already at the house and was explaining funeral arrangements, transportation, and a million other things. I was sitting in somewhat of a daze when the officer explained about the duties of the "escort officer"; an escort who would accompany the remains to the final burial site. Sandy asked if she had any input into the selection of the escort officer, was informed that she certainly did, and I found myself planning to make a final trip with my good friend.

Tom was prepared for his trip to Tennessee by a Selma funeral home. I met the hearse and driver at the funeral home around two A.M. on Sunday dressed in my class "A" blue uniform. It was an ugly uniform because as a brand new Second Lieutenant I had no wings or badges, no ribbons or decorations, and I looked exactly like a bus driver.

We drove to Montgomery where I was to catch a train with Tom. We arrived at the train station in Montgomery and the casket was loaded on a baggage cart. The hearse departed and I was left alone on the train platform waiting for the arrival of the train. The station was absolutely dark and deserted. There wasn't another person to be seen and the platform was eerily quiet. We waited in that lonely silence until the train finally arrived and the casket was loaded into a baggage car. I took a seat in the passenger car next to the baggage car, in the rear seat as close to the baggage car as I could get as was expected of me as an escort. I spent most of the train ride staring out the window and thinking of the times Tom and I had spent together. I was one of very few people who ever knew Tom had climbed to the top of one of the unfinished spires on the Academy chapel to hang a Tennessee flag. He had made that extremely hazardous climb in the

USAFA Chapel Under Construction

dark and in freezing weather. Tom was a bit of a daredevil but he was always silent about his exploits. It was for his satisfaction he did what he did and not for the sake of any recognition for having done it.

The train arrived in Nashville and we took another hearse to Murfreesboro. I was fortunate in already knowing Sandy and her parents and I was invited to stay with them. We managed to get through the funeral in spite of several of the elder ladies at the church repeatedly asking why the casket was closed. I responded by saying they should remember Tom the way he was when they last saw him.

Tom was buried in the Stones River National Cemetery in Murfreesboro. Stones River was the site of a major civil war battle and the cemetery was established at that time. It is a quiet, beautiful place like most national cemeteries and I have been there a couple of times since that day in March. The funeral was a military funeral and the Honor Guard surrendered the United States flag to me for presentation to Sandy. As this was my first military funeral I had never heard the phrase "On behalf of a grateful nation" so I made my own personal comments to Sandy as I handed her the flag.

My duties as an escort officer over, I returned to Craig where I was generously praised for my performance as an escort officer by all my commanders. I found that to be most ironic as I felt I undeservedly gained something by my friend's death - I was just as happy for people to disregard the fact I had performed an extremely sad and disheartening duty.

As I had been away from flying for a few days, Captain Roberts decided it would be a good thing for me to get back into a cockpit as quickly as possible. I was given an additional solo flight in the T-37 to get readjusted to flying. I was tooling around the skies over central Alabama and decided to try some mild acrobatics, like aileron rolls, barrel rolls, loops, etc., but only authorized maneuvers of course, as Tom had been killed by flying into the ground in low level flight - something for which he was sorely inexperienced. He crashed in the vicinity of his grandparent's home near Oakman, Alabama. As I attempted my first loop, I almost blacked out from the G forces exerted on my body. That gave me a little bit of a scare and it was a few minutes before I regained my composure enough to attempt another one. The second loop went off splendidly and I was happily back in the saddle again except for the fact I was now going to basic flight training minus a close companion. Who knew that exactly five years and two days later another catastrophic aircraft crash would almost end my life? Tom was the first of my closest friends to perish in connection with an airplane; unfortunately he would not be the last.

PILOT TRAINING: BASIC (T-33)

The aircraft we used for basic pilot training was the venerable T-Bird. The T-33 T-bird was produced by Lockheed and made its first flight in 1948; it was developed from the Lockheed F-80 Shooting Star. The United States Air Force began phasing the T-33 out of front line pilot training duties in the early 1960s as the T-38 Talon began replacing it in the Undergraduate Pilot Training (UPT) role. Craig Air Force Base was one of four bases in 1963 that were still using the T-33. The other four bases had already transitioned to the T-38.

During the 1960s several T-33s were also assigned to units of the Air Defense Command as proficiency trainers and practice "bogey" aircraft. The T-33 had a crew of two: instructor pilot in the rear seat and student pilot in the front seat for training purposes. The airplane was 38 feet long with a wingspan of 39 feet. It weighed 15,000 pounds at takeoff and was powered by a single Allison J-33 engine producing 5,400 pounds of thrust.

The T-Bird was a delight to fly; it was stable in formation and responded quickly to any control inputs. It did not have any nose wheel steering and taxiing was accomplished by differential braking. I found that method of taxiing to be extremely simple and had no difficulty in handling the airplane on the ground.

Part of the standard preflight of the T-33 included checking the wing fuel tanks by removing the fuel fill caps. In the heat of an Alabama day those caps would be skin-blistering hot and fuel would invariably spray out drenching your hands and flight suit; it was imperative to wear your gloves while performing this task.

T-33 navigation and all-weather procedures were accomplished through the use of the AN/ARN-6 radio compass used as an automatic direction finder (ADF). Relative bearing to a non-directional radio beacon, identified by a Morse code signal, was displayed by a pointer on the radio magnetic indicator (RMI) in the cockpit. The system was crude, difficult to use, and demanded very good instrument flying skill from the pilot.

I was not at all disappointed to fly the T-Bird rather than the newer, sexier, T-38 with its superior performance and more advanced navigation equipment. As it would eventually turn out, flying the T-Bird was greatly to my advantage in future assignments. I was initially assigned to Lieutenant R.M. Michael for flight instruction but midway through training I was shifted to Captain Gene Hartman. Our flight commander was Captain H.L. Skinner and his assistant flight commander was Captain Cecil G. Prentis. In 1967 Cecil and I would end up in the same F-105 class and we became good buddies – a relationship not shared during pilot training due to our respective positions. Our squadron call sign was "Wetback" reflecting the non-politically-correct nature of the military in the 1960s. I had a cross-country flight to Albuquerque, New Mexico during basic and the ground crews there attending to our aircraft noticed the squadron patch attached to the left shoulder of our flight suits: the squadron insignia was a cartoon character black duck drying his back with a towel, positioned over the word Wetback. The ground crew wisely suggested we not wear our flight suits into town.

Alabama was a hot bed of racial violence during 1963 and 1964. Birmingham and Montgomery were the scenes of multiple protests by blacks and angry response by whites. President Kennedy alerted Federal troops for possible intervention and warned Governor George Wallace that continued violence would bring those troops into action. Several civil rights workers were killed during the time period along with four young black girls attending Sunday School when their 16th Street Baptist Church in Birmingham was bombed on 15 September 1963.

On the 21st of June 1964 three young civil rights workers were wrongfully detained by a deputy in Mississippi and held incommunicado in jail as the jail officials lied by saying the three were not in the jail. The three were then released at night to be stopped again by the same deputy until the KKK death squad could arrive to beat and lynch the three. Their bodies were then buried in an earthen dam. I was sitting in a bar in Selma watching the news coverage of this particular event as troops searched for the bodies. I was astounded that a patron in the bar volunteered his opinion that if he was in the military he would disobey any order to search for those bodies. I then expressed my opinion that if I gave that order and it was refused by anyone, I would simply shoot that person. Following this exchange of personal opinions my friends convinced me it was probably a good time to depart those premises to avoid further confrontation.

There was not really a lot to do in Selma during our off-duty hours so I spent quite a bit of free time riding my motorcycle around the countryside. (I should have spent some of that time studying.) I soon learned that riding shirtless and colliding with a big Alabama Junebug at sixty miles an hour hurt.

Another close friend at Craig was Norman Pfeifer: Norm and I would get together to go eat at the Chicken Shack on the south end of town or the Dairy Queen on the north end of town. There wasn't much else in between. As Second Lieutenants we earned $222 per month plus an added $100 for flight pay. Needless to say, towards the end of the month cash on hand would get somewhat scarce. Norm and I would check with each other to see which of us had enough money for the two of us to go to the Chicken Shack for lunch. Dinner trips to the Tally Ho for steaks were not nearly as frequent as trips to the Chicken Shack or the Dairy Queen. Norm was with me one night when an Alabama state trooper decided I was driving a little too fast in my T-Bird and pulled us over. Fortunately he let me off with a stern warning and I did not have to report my transgression to the authorities at Craig. The trooper also casually commented the car had a very noticeable exhaust and engine sound to it. I should have listened carefully to his veiled advice as his more lenient view was not shared by a second State Trooper who stopped me about a month later and told me to replace the straight-thru glass-packed mufflers as the car was definitely too noisy. The second Trooper commented at the end of that discussion that I appeared to be driving a little over the speed limit. I did not get stopped again for either offense as I replaced the offending mufflers and started viewing the speedometer readings as specific driving limitations rather than goals to be achieved.

I had completed my instrument flying and formation flying and was scheduled for my last cross country that would be a solo flight to the Memphis Naval Air Station with a return after dark for a night landing. The flight went very smoothly until I initiated my turn to final. I could tell I did not roll out on final exactly where I wanted to so I decided to go around rather than try to salvage a poor approach. I notified the mobile control that I was going around and mobile wanted to know if there was a problem. I responded, "No problem; just a shitty turn to final."

I landed and taxied in where I was greeted with a radio call to report to the assistant flight commander at once. I checked in to the flight shack and Captain Prentis proceeded to give me one whale of a butt chewing. I had no idea what I could possibly have done to deserve the tongue lashing I was getting and I finally said, "Captain, I have no idea what this is about and I am totally confused." Captain Prentis stopped momentarily to see if I was actually serious. He realized I was and said. "What did you say on the radio on your go-around?" I thought for a moment and then it dawned on me. I had violated FCC regulations by using profanity on the air: a violation that could have resulted in the suspension of the FCC license I needed to operate radios. I apologized and said it would not happen again. The tongue lashing was over and I headed to my quarters. I later learned the instructors in mobile control thought my radio transmission was the greatest thing since sliced bread and they howled with laughter about it for hours.

2nd Lt Warner, Call Sign Wetback 9-3

Basic was over - all that was left was to discover our assignments. The selections were made based on the needs of the Air Force and the graduation ranking of the student. The Air Force provided a complete listing of each aircraft that had available pilot positions and the number of those positions that were available. I had a great ranking in flying and military bearing and conduct but not so great a ranking in academics.

The conflict in Laos and Vietnam was just starting to grow and the only aircraft that were really involved in the fighting were a handful of propeller-driven aircraft like A-1s, T-28s, and C-47s that were not on the selection list. I looked at the list and decided my choice would be either the F-105, of which there were a total of only two spots available for Craig graduates, or one of the four C-130 slots in the Pacific Air Forces. I wanted to get to Vietnam as I said to my buddies, "That is where the flying is going to be fantastic - lots of flying time and little in the way of additional ground duties involving paper work." I also thought about the two F-100 slots but definitely did not want any of the multiple B-52, KC-135, C-124, F-4, or T-37/T-33 instructor slots.

The results were posted and I was assigned to C-130 advanced flight training at Sewart Air Force Base in Tennessee before reporting to Okinawa. Norm drew a C-130 stateside assignment. I knew the activity in Vietnam had to be supported by aircraft stationed somewhere in the Far East even if those aircraft were not actually assigned to Vietnam so I was very happy with my luck of the draw. I had little idea where Okinawa was, except that it was in the Pacific close to Japan, and had to look at a globe to see exactly where I was going to spend the next year or two.

On 11 September 1964, in keeping with Air Force tradition, my instructor Captain Gene Hartman presented me with a set of his wings. I was indeed a pilot and about to embark on a real adventure. Out of the forty-three of us that began the journey to get those wings, forty-two would reach that goal. Jerry Driscoll would receive his wings a couple of months later with the following class but, sadly, Tom Pierson would never pin on that coveted badge. Less than a year later on 7 April 1965 Dave Small, who remained at Craig as an instructor pilot in the 3617th PTS, would die in an aircraft accident near Centerville Alabama. On 20 December 1965 David Wax would be killed in South Vietnam near Tuy Hoa. He had one of the other

C-130 assignments allotted to our class. Leo Thomas would remain in the 3617th PTS as an instructor in the T-33 and then received an assignment to fly the F-4: he would be killed in action over Laos on 19 December 1971.

Undergraduate Pilot Training (Basic)
3617th Pilot Training Squadron, Class 65B. Craig Air Force Base, Selma, AL.
Bill Ivey is seated fourth from the left in the front row. Norm Pfeifer is in the flight cap kneeling just behind Bill's left shoulder. I am kneeling second from the left.
(USAF Photo)

ADVANCED SURVIVAL TRAINING

Following graduation from pilot training we had to report to Stead Air Force Base near Reno, Nevada for advanced survival school with the 3635th Flying Training Wing. We had leave between graduation and reporting to Stead and Norm went home with me to Indiana where we spent a few days. We then climbed into Norm's Chevy and left Indiana for Norm's home in San Francisco. On the long drive to California I fell asleep at the wheel somewhere in Illinois, crossed the centerline and awoke to the sound of the car running into gravel on the opposite side of the road. I guess the old saying is true that God looks out for drunks and fools - as I had not had anything to drink I knew which category I was in. I drove safely back to the right side of the road, missing culverts and trees in the process, and noticed a rather disapproving but well justified scowl from Norm who then went back to sleep. We arrived in San Francisco and had a great time visiting the usual tourist haunts in that city and eating at restaurants in China Town and at Fisherman's Wharf. We then drove to Reno, Nevada where Stead Air Force base was located.

Reno was a quiet little town in 1964 - it consisted of basically a main drag where about a half dozen casinos were located and not much else. While in Reno, I borrowed Eric Aspelin's two-seater Alpha Romeo for a side visit to Lake Tahoe, driving through the infamous Donner Pass on the trip. At Stead we had a delightful time playing prisoner of war in the stockade and traipsing about Squaw Valley in the Sierra Nevada Mountains for a week in the snow. The mock prison compound was manned by personnel, many of whom were originally from Eastern Europe, who spoke either Russian or

English with a Russian accent to us for realism. At the time the cold war was still of more interest to the United States military than was Vietnam.

We first had to negotiate an obstacle course in the cold, dark night to induce exhaustion; then we were placed in the prison compound as prisoners of war (POWs). The guards were allowed to mentally berate us but physical contact was limited to pushing and shoving. Physical stress could also be created by having us kneel on our knees on broomsticks which could become very painful in a short period of time. After being placed under guard we were blindfolded and stripped and forced to endure that humiliation. We were then placed in solitary confinement in individual concrete cells with no lights and very low ceilings that kept one from being able to stand upright. We were fed a canteen of very salty broth that was intentionally designed to create more thirst. Although recognizing the perverse reason for being given the broth, I went ahead and drank it as I was also hungry, finding it to be quite acceptable in flavor as I have always been somewhat addicted to the taste of salt.

One at a time we were taken into an interrogation room where we had to kneel on the floor facing a bright light and undergo questioning purposely designed to be stressful and intimidating. I was amazed at the details in our private lives that were revealed by the interrogators during these sessions. My captor told me in a heavy Russian accent that it would be very easy to arrange for a traffic accident to kill my younger brother Steve on the corner of Court Avenue and Wall Street in Jeffersonville, Indiana where his high school was located. During the debriefing at the conclusion of the training exercise, I was told to "be careful of responding to an actual interrogation with smart-ass answers."

Following the interrogation sessions we were then placed in the "box" for several hours. The box was exactly that: a wooden box approximately fourteen inches wide by thirty inches deep, and thirty-six inches tall. It was just big enough to kneel in with your shoulders touching the walls and your head forced down between your knees by the top. The final touch was we were enclosed in a laundry bag that covered us completely from our head to our waist prior to shoving us into the box. I was lucky - I was small enough that I was able to wiggle out of the bag and twist around in the box until I was lying on my back on the bottom of the miniscule chamber with my feet and legs drawn up over my stomach. In spite of the fact the guards beat on the sides of the box every few minutes, I managed to intermittently sleep for about two hours in the fetal position. After a rude awakening from my stolen slumber we were herded en masse into the general confinement area where we could talk with our comrades and walk around some.

I was "selected" (through the luck of a draw) by a mock "escape committee" to attempt an escape from the compound and was given a "smuggled" map showing a tunnel leading from the latrine. As could be expected the tunnel was supposed to have been dug from the pit under the wooden urinals and I dutifully climbed into the large hole in the ground. While I was searching for the tunnel in the gloom, carefully watching where I stepped, I heard the sound of running water on the back of my heavy parka. I looked up to discover someone was relieving himself on my back. I uttered an exclamation and the guy was quite startled to see someone was in the hole.

Exiting the latrine after discovering the tunnel had been filled in with dirt, I noticed there was an area directly behind the latrine that was hidden from the searchlights and the view of the guard towers. Not only that, the barbed wire fence had a gap high enough for me to slide under. I quickly looked for a guard - seeing no one in sight, I rolled under the fence and crawled into the surrounding desert.

My task was to escape from the compound and make my way to a fire tower that was about two miles away avoiding contact with the roving patrols that would be searching for me. I crawled through the dirt and cactus being thankful it was too cold for rattlesnakes and made my way to the tower where I retrieved a plastic chip as evidence I had made it. I returned to the compound where I enjoyed some cake, coffee, and pleasant conversation with the guards for a short period before I had to return to the confinement area. By the time I returned to the prison the three-day POW training session was almost over and I did not have long before I returned to our quarters to take a hot shower, removing the dirt and grime that had accumulated over the past few days.

For the final week of training at Stead we were transported to the wilds of the Sierra Nevada Mountains to practice the survival skills we learned in the classroom sessions. Snow covered the ground and fell frequently during the week. Although temperatures were tolerable during the day, it was bitterly cold when the sun went down and we were issued two sleeping bags to try and keep warm. At night we removed our flight boots, placing them between the two sleeping bags but the boots were still frozen stiff when we put them back on in the morning.

Our rations for the week included two tins of survival rations, a carrot, a potato, an onion and a rabbit split between two of us. I figured that amount of food was enough so that we would not have to resort to eating human flesh as the ill-fated Donner party had done in 1846. Bob Storms was my partner for the seven days in the survival exercise: he got very sick on the next-to-last day of the trek from eating jerky we had not completely cured in our attempt at smoking the rabbit and I had to navigate the night hike of around eight miles to our final rendezvous point without his assistance. Bob was seriously ill but he soldiered on in the snow, and together we learned the survival lesson of bonding in misery to complete escape and evasion training.

Another square had been filled in our journey to become fully qualified aircrew members. On the 21st of October our class graduated from advanced survival training and four of us climbed into a car to drive non-stop from Reno, Nevada to Nashville, Tennessee where I caught a Greyhound bus back to Indiana and a few days of leave before setting out for C-130 flight school.

Survival Training, Stead AFB, Nevada. Bob Storms and me in Squaw Valley.

C-130 TRAINING: THE HERCULES

I had survived survival school and reported to the 4442nd Combat Crew Training Wing at Sewart Air Force Base near Smyrna, Tennessee in November 1964 for advanced flying training in the C-130A Hercules. On 22 December 1941 Smyrna Army Airfield was created in response to the need for WW II training facilities. The field was renamed Sewart Air Force Base in 1950 in honor of a Nashville native who died in a bombing mission over the Solomon Islands in 1942. In 1958 Sewart was the only operational C-130 base in the United States. In 1965 the Department of Defense announced the closure of several military bases in the United States, including Sewart. On 9 March 1971 the last Hercules departed Sewart and the base was officially closed. Like many other bases it was turned into an industrial complex and air park for the local community.

My quarters at Sewart were absolutely miserable – the worst I had to endure my entire time in the Air Force. I truly believe the building I was in was one of the original 1941 buildings that had never been repaired, much less renovated. The weather was cold as it usually is in middle Tennessee in December and the only source of heat in the room I had was a steam radiator. I had one small room with a much smaller bathroom and the quarters were either blazing hot, requiring an open window, or they were freezing cold. When they were hot the heat was accompanied by the loudest clanking you can imagine emanating from a radiator. Sleep was almost impossible to find and there was no way to adjust or control the temperature. Thank heavens my time at Sewart was to be very brief.

The Hercules I would fly was a four-engine transport aircraft designed and built by Lockheed. The engines on the "A" series were Allison T-56 turboprops developing 3,750 horsepower each. The "A" aircraft were readily identified by their three-bladed propellers and outboard 450-gallon fuel tanks. The aircraft could operate from dirt fields (with liftoff in 900 feet) and was originally designed as a troop carrier (92 combat-equipped), medical evacuation, and cargo transport aircraft. The empty weight of the "A" series was 69,000 pounds and maximum takeoff weight was 125,000 pounds. Normal cargo capacity for supply missions in Vietnam was 25,000 pounds. The "As" were so agile and responsive that an unofficial aerial demonstration team known as "The Four Horsemen" was created at Sewart and performed at air-shows from 1956 to 1960. The Horsemen (named either after the four horsemen of the apocalypse or the four horsemen of the Notre Dame football team depending on whom you talk to) performed close formation maneuvers such as diamond, trail, arrowhead, and echelon. They executed formation takeoffs and even did a "bomb-burst" like the Thunderbirds using standard C-130As that were available for the flight. Their demise was prompted by a variety of reasons including political considerations, more pressing needs for the aircraft, and the fact the follow-on variants of the 130 were not quite as agile as the "A".

The airframe has since found use in a variety of other roles, including gunship, carrying paratroopers and heavy equipment, search and rescue, research support, hurricane hunter, aerial tanker, maritime patrol, and firefighting. The C-130 family has the longest continuous production run of any military aircraft in history – in 2006 the C-130 marked 50 years of continuous use with its first customer, the United States Air Force. (The aircraft has also been purchased by a multitude of foreign countries.) It remains in production today as the C-130J and its latest variant is the C-130U gunship, a modified C-130H.

Sewart received the first of its C-130s in 1956. As the C-130A became operational, it suffered from a lack of range and the 450-gallon fuel tanks were added to the wings outboard of the outer engines. A radome was also added to the aircraft changing the original "slick" nose to the readily recognizable profile of current aircraft. The "A" series continued in service throughout the Vietnam War with the airplanes from the squadrons at Naha, Okinawa and

Tachikawa, Japan. In 1964 C-130 crews from the 6315th Operations Group at Naha commenced flare missions over the Ho Chi Minh trail in Laos supporting USAF strike aircraft. In 1965 that mission was expanded to North Vietnam where the C-130s were accompanied by B-57 bombers on night reconnaissance missions against communist supply routes leading to South Vietnam from North Vietnam. In early 1966 Project Blindbat/Lamplighter was established at Ubon Air Base in Thailand and the flare mission also became a four-engine forward air controller (FAC) mission with the C-130 crew searching for targets then calling in and directing strike aircraft. I would become intimately familiar with that mission during my brief Air Force career.

    I arrived at Sewart in my Thunderbird towing my Triumph behind the car. When I first bought the motorcycle I had a custom hitch attached to the rear of the frame on the car: the hitch was very small and scarcely noticeable. It consisted of two L-shaped brackets welded to the frame with a short rod welded between the top of the brackets. The rod was the same diameter as the front axle on the motorcycle. I would remove the retaining bolts on the bottom of the fork that held the front wheel axle in place and remove the front wheel, tossing it in the trunk of the car. I would then place the front fork of the motorcycle on the rod and replace the retaining bolts. In effect the car became the front wheel of the motorcycle. All that was left was to remove the chain from the sprocket on the rear wheel of the motorcycle, making it free-wheeling, and the Triumph would docilely follow the car wherever the car went.

    I passed through the front gate and the Air Police on duty obviously did not even see the motorcycle as it trailed along. I had a day or two before classes started and I decided to ride the Triumph around the base to check things out. I had no sooner started riding until an airman flagged me down asking how in the world I had a motorcycle on base. I said no problem as I had my decal from Craig and I would get a Sewart sticker right away. The airman told me that was not going to happen as the base commander had very strict orders that absolutely prohibited motorcycles on Sewart. I found that hard to believe and decided to go for a ride to Smyrna.

    As I approached the gate the Air Police came swarming out of the guard shack waving their arms and yelling for me to halt. From their attitude I almost expected to see weapons drawn. They immediately demanded to know how I got that devilish machine on base and I replied that I pulled it on with my car. The Air Police then informed me I could not operate that motorcycle on base and that I had to remove it from the premises at once. I said, "OK. I'll take it back and hook it back up to my car to remove it." The Air Police said, "Oh no, you won't, you can not take that machine back on the base." I was incredulous as the front gate was at least three miles from my quarters. The Air Police finally agreed to call for a base taxi but I was steaming mad at this point and told the Air Police that I would walk. A couple of miles down the road I had cooled off to the point I thought maybe I should have accepted the ride offer especially as the weather was around 40 degrees and it was now dark and cold.

Sandy Pierson had returned to Murfreesboro after Tom's accident and worked as a librarian at Middle Tennessee State College (now Middle Tennessee State University). Murfreesboro is only a few miles southeast of Smyrna. I had already been in contact with Sandy and I knew she would let me keep the motorcycle at her apartment.

I went back to the front gate the following morning to pick up the Triumph and once again the new shift of Air Police came swarming out to my car demanding to know if that infernal machine belonged to me. I admitted I was indeed the guilty party and told the APs I was removing the motorcycle for good. They appeared greatly relieved and revealed the base commander had noticed the motorcycle at the gate and reminded the APs in no uncertain terms of his edict. I was quite happy I never had to meet that base commander as I am sure we would not have seen eye to eye on much of anything. I towed my bike to Sandy's place where it remained until I departed Sewart.

On 5 December 1964 I flew my first C-130A training flight. I was also promoted to First Lieutenant on that date. There was no promotion party as the training schedule really did not permit one and I did not know anyone close enough to share that event with. At least I would not have to report to my new assignment on Okinawa as a butter bar, slang for the lowest of the officer ranks. Unlike pilot training, the only purpose of the training at Sewart was to familiarize the new pilots with the flying characteristics of the aircraft: training in tactical operations such as formation flying, troop and heavy equipment drops, parachute extractions, assault landings and takeoffs, and so forth would take place with the unit of assignment. I was somewhat surprised to discover weather approaches in the A series 130s (including those I would eventually fly in the 21st TCS on Okinawa) were flown using the antiquated ADF system I had learned in the T-33. That made transition to the Hercules much easier as I could concentrate on the aircraft itself and not the ADF procedures which I had already mastered.

The increased demands for C-130 operations in the Far East maxed out the training capabilities at Sewart. Simulator rides were scheduled over a twenty-four-hour period as the simulator was operated day and night. I had many simulator flights between midnight and six o'clock in the morning. I had a total of ten flights in the Hercules including my final proficiency check ride with Captain Patrick F. O'Sullivan on the 22nd of December 1964 when I was officially designated a C-130A pilot. I mentally noted the birthday for the base was also the 22nd of December. The only other memorable flight during this period was the time we flew to Indianapolis, Indiana and then returned to Sewart: we flew directly over my hometown of Jeffersonville, Indiana enabling me to spot my parents' house from the air as we were only at 4,000 feet.

We had a brief Christmas vacation and I returned to Sewart to clear the base and take a couple of weeks of leave before departing for Okinawa. I took the Thunderbird into Murfreesboro to pick up my motorcycle and just as I was in front of the Ford dealer the car expired. I coasted into the dealership parking lot thinking for once I had a break where a vehicle was concerned. My muted joy was very short lived. The mechanics at the garage believed I had a valve problem with the car. In despair, I returned to my lovely quarters awaiting the estimate for repairs. For the next several days I would receive a daily telephone call from the Ford service department telling me they had found something else wrong with the engine. I started to wonder if they knew it was the Ford 406 high performance engine and not the original 352 that was in Thunderbirds and I reminded them of that fact.

After all was said and done, I believe the only parts that were salvaged were the block, the heads, and the intake manifold. I thought the good news was I had a new engine even if my bank account had been completely depleted. Finally I was able to leave Sewart and return to Jeffersonville. That new engine fell far short of expectations - in fact it should have been returned to the Ford dealer as it would refuse to turn over and start after the engine had been running for a while. Unfortunately, I was due to leave for Okinawa and the Ford dealer that worked on the engine was over 200 miles from my home.

I sold my motorcycle to a guy from Louisville, Kentucky and gave him a bill of sale as I had no paperwork from my original purchase. After I arrived on Okinawa I received a letter from my parents wanting to know if I had any paperwork at all on the Triumph as the guy who bought it was having trouble registering the motorcycle in Kentucky. The license plate that was on the Triumph did not belong to that motorcycle (it should have been on a Honda) and I had been riding it for a year that way. For all I knew at the time I could have been riding a stolen vehicle. I hope my buyer resolved his registration problems with the state of Kentucky as I had no further contact with him.

I gave my brother the Thunderbird and told him to trade it for whatever he wanted. Steve had his eye on a classic 1959 Triumph TR-3 convertible on a used car lot in Kentucky and he went to Louisville to see about a trade. He parked the Thunderbird around the corner from the used car dealer to let the engine cool down so it would start when it had to. After sufficient cooling he let the dealer drive the T-Bird (it successfully started) and Steve happily drove back to Indiana in the Triumph. Trading a car in - usually big bucks: turning the tables on a used car salesman - priceless. I left Louisville, Kentucky in late January on commercial air bound for my ultimate destination in Asia. It would be a 9,040-mile journey; 1,986 miles to San Francisco, 2,387 miles from San Francisco to Honolulu, Hawaii, and 4667 miles from Honolulu to Naha, Okinawa.

C-130 IN OKINAWA & VIETNAM

To get to my first operational Air Force unit as a brand new C-130 pilot I had to pass through Travis AFB, California located just north of San Francisco. There I met a high school classmate, Bob Brinkley; Bob was working on his master's degree at Berkeley and I spent a few days visiting with him and once again enjoying the sights in the "City by the Bay".

Although I enjoyed our brief reunion I was not feeling 100% as I was recovering from a bout of strep throat picked up while at home in the Ohio River Valley. When I checked in at Travis in early February to board my flight to the Far East it was discovered I had not had a recent flu shot; an omission which the medical personnel at the terminal quickly remedied.

By the time I landed in Hawaii I was extremely ill and feverish. I would never recommend taking a flu shot while still having active strep throat bacteria. Although I was greatly impressed with my initial sight of the Hawaiian Islands from the air, I was too sick to enjoy my very brief layover in the terminal. My seat from Honolulu to Kadena Air Base on Okinawa was between two humongous airborne troops headed to the 173rd Airborne Brigade - I was sandwiched between the two of them with absolutely no room to move and I suffered in miserable silence as my throat was too sore to talk.

By the time of my arrival on Okinawa my throat was so inflamed I could not swallow and I worked very hard at trying to hide just how badly I felt. I was met at Kadena by my sponsor who drove me to the BOQ at Naha where a room had been set aside for my projected eighteen-month stay.

I had been assigned to the 21st Troop Carrier Squadron (TCS) under the control of the 315th Air Division at Tachikawa Japan. The 315th was the parent command of the 6315th Operations Group, consisting at the time of the 21st TCS, the 35th TCS, the 817th TCS (all stationed at Naha Air Base Okinawa) and the 815th TCS (located at Tachikawa). The 21st had moved from Tachikawa to Naha to support CIA operations resupplying Tibetan guerillas in the 1959 to 1962 time frame. To execute those missions the C-130s were temporarily stripped of their Air Force markings at Takhli Air Base in Thailand and flown to Tibet by CIA crews: at the completion of the mission the Air Force markings were re-applied and the aircraft returned to Naha. In the early 1960s a separate flight of the 21st TCS, known as "E" Flight, was created to fly classified supply missions to support the Laotian forces resisting communism.

My quarters on Okinawa were on the second story of a modern concrete block structure and consisted of a bedroom and a bathroom. Some of the housing at Naha consisted of Quonset huts left over from WW II and I was glad I escaped living in those facilities. It was dark when my sponsor dropped me off and I stumbled into the room, throwing my bags on the floor and collapsing into bed. I was so ill the following day I could not move and lay weakly in bed sweating profusely. I spent several days in the same condition. I had nothing to eat as I was too sick to get up and there was no such thing as take-out delivery to be had. My sponsor had to fly the next morning after delivering me to my room and he was gone for over a week. He was the only person who even knew for sure I was on Naha. Someone at the squadron finally asked about the new Lieutenant and the duty officer then wondered where I was. Fortunately, to resolve the mystery of the AWOL officer, someone appeared at my door to see why I had not reported to the squadron. I was then quickly visited by a doctor who injected me with some antibiotics and someone in the squadron brought me something to eat. I was able to report to the squadron in a couple of days although my uniform was quite loose as I had lost a lot of weight. I figured I had made a less than favorable first impression on the 21st TCS.

After receiving that medical attention I recovered quickly from my return bout with the strep throat bug and completed in-processing over the next few days. On 24 February 1965 I participated in my first C-130 flight as a co-pilot in the 6315th Operations Group with the 21st Troop Carrier Squadron. It was an airborne-troop-carrying training flight over water and around the island. It was quite a change to fly 50 feet above the wave tops with a load of paratroopers from the 173rd in the back end. As we approached the drop zone we would climb to 1,000 feet, slowing to 125 knots while opening the rear door and ramp and the side troop doors. The co-pilot would turn on the green light on command from the navigator or the ground-based drop zone controller and 64 combat-equipped paratroops would exit the aircraft. We also trained for heavy equipment drops where 25,000-pound M-113 Armored Personnel Carriers, 13,000-pound ten-wheel (deuce and a half) M-35 trucks, jeeps, wheeled water tanks, 5,000-pound 105mm howitzers, and other such items would be dropped. Those drops took place at 1,250 feet and the load was released simply by unlocking the restraints on the pallets to which the equipment was attached, pulling up the nose of the airplane and allowing the pallets and equipment to slide out the open door and ramp.

    Events in Vietnam during my first month of flying started to have a dramatic impact on the course of the conflict. By the first of February 1965 the United States actually considered reducing our involvement but the 7 February Viet Cong attack on the United States advisory compound in Pleiku and the 10 February attack on the Army enlisted barracks at Qui Nhon led to the decision to instead increase both troops and air power to the war. On 2 March 1965 Operation Rolling Thunder, the aerial bombardment of North Vietnam, was authorized. The campaign resembled the geographically limited aerial bombing used in the Korean conflict rather than the unlimited bombing used in WW II. The purpose of the operation was to raise the morale of the South Vietnamese; to limit the flow of supplies from North Vietnam to the south; and, to punish North Vietnam for the escalation of the conflict. At the same time the United States wanted to avoid antagonizing China and the Soviet Union enough to prompt them to enter the fight. On the 8th of March the 9th Marine Expeditionary Brigade was deployed from Okinawa to Da Nang Air Base for base defense as many of the early Rolling Thunder sorties originated from that location.

On 11 March 1965 I flew my very first combat flight as a C-130 co-pilot from Okinawa to Da Nang, South Vietnam. It was a 2,800-mile round trip, a supply run in support of the Marine landing at the base, and was a combat flight because we landed in a designated combat zone. Sometimes combat flights in cargo/transport aircraft could appear to be a misnomer as we did not get fired on that often and we could not offer any resistance when we did receive hostile fire. As we often said in flying tactical airlift missions, "Flying is 95% boredom and 5% sheer terror." On the other hand, flying in and out of landing strips surrounded by hostile forces was not always the safest occupation in the world. The United States Air Force would lose a total of 55 C-130s in Vietnam, including 34 directly from combat.

In May the 173rd Airborne Brigade was airlifted from Okinawa to Bien Hoa Air Base in approximately 140 flights using C-130s. The 173rd was the first United States Army unit to be permanently assigned to South Vietnam and I participated in several of those flights. One of my trips during this time period was to transport a team of Marine Beachmasters to plan for the landing of the 3rd Battalion, 3rd Marine Division at the newly constructed air base at Chu Lai about 56 miles southeast of Da Nang. That base attained operational status in June of 1965.

After returning from that first trip to South Vietnam, I continued my indoctrination process to operational flying and started sea survival school under the tutelage of the 313th Air Division at Naha. We had a day and a half of academics followed by a half-day of using flares and other signaling devices. We then went to the training basin in the East China Sea where we went for a swim in the R1A anti-exposure suit and later boarded an LCM (Landing Craft Medium) where we were towed on our face and backs in a parachute harness attached by 25 feet of risers to the stern of the landing craft. We then had to simulate a parachute jump from the 14-foot tower on the rear of the moving LCM into the water where we clambered into one-man life rafts. We were hoisted out of the water by helicopter after spending several hours alone in the ocean in our rafts. We also spent time in a six-man life raft after being dumped into the sea in six-man groups. Of course our raft had a large tear in the rubber fabric that had to be repaired in the water before we could climb aboard. The seven days of training was certainly well invested as we would spend many long hours flying over the vast Pacific Ocean. For example, it was 1,700 miles one way over water from Naha to Saigon, South Vietnam. On the 19th of March I completed sea survival training.

The center of social activity at Naha for the 21st TCS was the Naha Officers Open Mess, the NOOM club. There were four new First Lieutenants, all single, in the 21st and we attended a squadron function at the club where we were rounded up by several of the younger wives and taken to a corner of the main ballroom. We were then instructed, in no uncertain terms, that we were never to bring a local girl into the club. It was all right for them to work as our waitresses and maids but we were not to consider them as dates. A few days later, we hung a sign made from a bed sheet over the name of the club changing it to read Naha Officers Wives Club.

I was still living in my one room in the BOQ but I really wanted to move off base. I was friends with one of the housing officers and he called me one day to say, "If you can find a place to live off base in the next two days, I can authorize non-availability and you can draw quarters allowance." I heard a navigator from one of the other squadrons was looking for a roommate and I found him in the club at lunch. I introduced myself to Bill "Rocky" Edmondson and told him to stop looking for a roommate as he now had one.

Our two-bedroom apartment occupied the first floor of a three-story house located on a hilltop overlooking the harbor at Naha City. Steve Sutton and Bill Quinn, two of the other new Lieutenants in the 21st lived on the second floor. The house sat on a corner lot and was surrounded by a high concrete wall. Shortly after moving in, Rocky and I decided we needed a television so we drove into downtown Naha City to find a used set. Successful in our search on the local economy we returned home to view our new purchase - apparently Japanese sets did not pick up the local Armed Forces broadcasts and our television would only speak Japanese. We watched a lot of sumo wrestling and nothing else.

I continued flying missions in and out of Vietnam until expanding airlift requirements reached the point where C-130s were needed on the ground in South Vietnam. We started doing two-week rotations in country, flying out of Da Nang, Tan Son Nhut in Saigon, and Cam Ranh Bay, another newly constructed airfield using an aluminum matting runway. On those two-week trips we would fly from field to field in Vietnam, living in temporary quarters at the base designated as our home base.

C-130E Low Altitude Parachute Extraction (LAPES) Drop at An Khe (USAF Photo)

Although we did not have any armor plating or flak vests during our flights, our loadmasters improvised a unique method of obtaining a small amount of personal protection during portions of the flight. They would take an empty 55-gallon steel drum and remove the top, partially filling the bottom with tie-down chains. During takeoffs and landings they would climb into the drum and hope they would be protected from the small-arms fire we received during our time of close proximity to the ground.

While flying from Saigon we lived at the Mai Loan Hotel in downtown Saigon. Rooms were in such demand we often had to wait in the lobby for current occupants to vacate the premises. That was especially true when we arrived at the hotel after midnight. We would sit in the dark with our feet propped up on our B-4 bags while rats were scurrying about the lobby: every once in a while you could feel one run into your bag. Rooms had so many beds crammed into them that interior doors would not close and bed linens were rarely changed. We slept in our flight suits for the most part which was not the cleanest or most comfortable way to rest.

Vietnam was not our only destination: we also pulled two-week temporary duty (TDY) tours in Bangkok, flying the Thailand shuttle mission. We would depart Don Muang Airport in Bangkok and make a day-long tour of Thailand, stopping at Korat, Ubon, Nakhon Phanom, Udorn, and Takhli before returning to Don Muang. We always stayed at the Federal Hotel on those TDYs and the shuttle was a great mission to fly. Flights to Kunsan, Korea and Tachikawa and Itazuke, Japan were also on the agenda.

We also traveled to Taipei and Tainan, Taiwan. On one of my early flights into Tainan we contacted the ground control approach for a radar-controlled landing. The controller told us to make a left turn for identification, which we did and he started giving us directions. After a couple of turns he directed us to descend to 3,000 feet. My aircraft commander told me to radio compliance with the order indicating we were level at 3,000 feet but to remain at 10,000 feet. It was becoming obvious the controller had mistaken another aircraft for us. We were then turned to a heading directly towards the mountain range lying east of the airfield. We passed directly over the tops of those mountains and my aircraft commander made a radio transmission announcing that we were all dead to inform the controller of his error. If we had been in weather we would most certainly have flown directly into the side of that mountain range as we would not have had visual aids to indicate the directions transmitted to us were in error.

Taiwan was somewhat rough on our squadron as on one stop a forklift operator at Kung Kuan stuck the forks on his machine through the side of our fuselage. That resulted in an unscheduled overnight stay at a downtown hotel where I do not believe the locals had ever seen an American. The entire staff gathered in the dining room of the hotel restaurant to curiously watch us eat. We finally managed to order chicken soup but it was quite different from what we expected as the chef had simply taken a chicken, de-feathered it, and then chopped the entire bird into pieces before boiling it. We could see pieces of beak, legs, feet, and eyes in the broth. As the conflict continued to expand, Kung Kuan was renamed Ching Chang Kuan, or simply CCK, and C-130Es were eventually stationed there.

The IRAN, or Inspect and Repair/Replace as Necessary, facility for our C-130As was in Clearwater, Florida - approximately a 19,000-mile round trip from Naha. I was assigned to fly one of those flights during the summer of 1965 and we departed Naha for the states. We flew over Iwo Jima and landed to refuel and spend the night on Wake Island. Seeing those locales gave me a better appreciation of operations in the Pacific during WW II.

After Wake we spent the next night in Hawaii where, at the Hickam Air Force Base flightline snack shack, I ran into my former roommate from the Academy, Arnold "Arnie" Patchin. Arnie was a co-pilot on a C-133 that was passing westward through Hawaii en route to the Far East. The C-133 was built by Douglas Aircraft and resembled an overgrown C-130. The fleet of 50 C-133 aircraft was used by the Military Air Transport Service (MATS) in strategic or long-range airlift operations and provided invaluable service in the Vietnam conflict.

Our next stop after Hawaii was Travis AFB in California to refuel and then to Pensacola Naval Air Station (NAS) in Florida. I called the motor pool from the terminal at NAS Base Operations to obtain crew transport to a hotel, giving the name of our aircraft commander and his rank as Captain. Almost at once two staff cars driven by smartly uniformed Navy personnel appeared on the scene and inquired as to the location of the Captain they were to pick up. When our aircraft commander replied that would be him, the Navy guy observed in a rather peeved tone that the Captain was an *Air Force* Captain - without further conversation the drivers climbed back into their staff cars and disappeared. Approximately 30 minutes later a beat-up, old, grey Navy bus appeared, the door opened, and the driver, dressed in the typical Navy work uniform of blue dungarees, said to get aboard. Lesson learned was, when around the Navy, one should not create any confusion between the lowly Air Force rank of Captain and the much more prestigious Navy rank of Captain.

July 1965 started to get even more exciting - our cargo compartment was stacked with crates of fresh lettuce and tomatoes and we took off to the west from Tan Son Nhut around midnight bound for our scheduled destination. Just after we broke ground and retracted gear and flaps, tracers erupted from the pitch black darkness below us and the number three engine just to the right of my seat exploded in flames. We immediately took the appropriate action, feathering the engine and discharging the fire extinguishing agent, while the aircraft commander began a right turn to head for Bien Hoa Air Base about 12 miles northeast of Saigon. I declared an emergency on the UHF radio as we rolled out on a base leg and dropped gear and flaps for a straight in approach for that airfield. The flames subsided as the extinguishing agent worked and we began our short final approach to landing. At daybreak we made a three-engine flight to Saigon for an engine change and the cargo was left sitting on the ramp at Bien Hoa. I have always wondered what happened to that load the next day sitting on a hot, non-air-conditioned ramp in the heat and humidity of South Vietnam. I hope the troops at Bien Hoa had an extra treat at their dining halls and that the veggies did not just sit there and spoil.

In August, while flying out of Cam Ranh Bay on one of the two-week rotations, we airlifted the 173rd Airborne Brigade from Bien Hoa to Pleiku for operations in the central highlands. Although I was supposedly stationed on Okinawa, I spent very little time on the island as nearly every day of each month was spent on a field in South Vietnam or traveling between Okinawa and Southeast Asia. The hectic pace of activity was both tiring and exhilarating and we looked forward to the unknown activities awaiting in our future – it was an exciting lifestyle for those of us not married but I often wondered how our married crewmembers with families on Okinawa coped as well as they did.

In September 1965 I was elated to find out I had been selected to become a student in Class 10-65 of the Royal Air Force's Far East Survival School in Changi, Singapore as an exchange officer. I was one of two United States Air Force personnel in attendance out of the class of approximately 41 that included "Brits", "Aussies", and "Kiwis" (New Zealanders). I rode from Naha to Bangkok on one of our C-130s where I boarded a Thai Airways flight to Singapore. When I checked in with the RAF welcoming desk at the terminal I learned what my name would be for the next three weeks; I was always called "Yank" or referred to as the "Yank Leff-tenant".

The RAF BOQs featured large brick buildings with spacious verandas and covered porches sitting on hilltops just as you would have expected from watching movies of the British Empire in the Far East. The rooms had very high ceilings with slowly revolving ceiling fans and large windows with no glass, only typhoon shutters that were left open. We slept under mosquito netting that hung from the ceiling and surrounded the bed. In the morning we would always awake to the sight of the maid preparing a cup of hot tea and milk for us before we got up. In the afternoon we always had tea and finger sandwiches of cucumber and tomato and in the evening everyone retired to the club for beer, ale, and half and half (a mixture of mild ale and bitter). We ate our meals in the officers mess located in the same building as our quarters. Without exception the very civilized mandatory "uniform" for the evening meal was long-sleeved white dress shirts with black or dark blue solid color ties. We ate as a group (reminding me of my days at the Academy) at long tables covered with white tablecloths served by uniformed waiters hired from the local population. I thought, "The Brits really know how to treat their officers." In reality I would have eventually grown tired of the strict regimentation.

One evening after consuming a large amount of ale with my new-found friends one of them said he knew where to get the best fried rice you could ever eat. We stumbled out to his motorcycle and headed for Changi Village - before we departed he realized he only had one helmet so he discarded his by tossing it down the side of the hill where his motorcycle had been parked. All I can remember about the ride to the village was a white line that weaved back and forth under my legs. He was right, the fried rice was fantastic. It was prepared by a street vendor and we sat on wooden crates on the sidewalk as we tried to counter the effects of a little hunger and way too much half and half. Several days later, at the other end of the spectrum, a group of us ventured in to Singapore where we dined at the legendary Raffles Hotel just as Rudyard Kipling had done. I even had a Singapore Sling from the bar where in 1902 a tiger was killed after scaring several of the guests.

We were subjected to the usual classroom academics in a tropical setting in a large tiki hut amidst palm trees. The heat and humidity were stifling in the confines of the hut and the very graphic training movies about how to administer first aid to the victims of an aircraft crash took their toll on several of the trainees who succumbed to the urge to vomit. I had to fight the urge myself and was very happy to end that particular session.

The real training took place during the last week of school when we spent a very uncomfortable time in the jungles of Malaya. Although we did not really give it much thought, we were actually accompanied by an armed escort due to concern over Malaysian communist insurgents in the area. Most of our travels during the training were spent wading through swamp water that ranged from ankle deep to chest deep covered in floating, rotting vegetation. Snakes, turtles, and insects of every size and description were abundant and the cries of the jungle wildlife including monkeys, gibbons, and even tigers were incessant. The evening we built a large group shelter we laughed about who would have to sleep on the ends until one of the instructors told us that the only time a tiger actually grabbed anyone it was one of the guys sleeping in the middle. He never admitted whether he was kidding or not. It rained heavily every afternoon and the trees would drip rainwater all night; in the morning the air was so full of moisture it would condense on the tree leaves and drip all morning until it rained again. When the week was over, no matter how many times she tried, the maid could not wash the jungle rot out of my flight suit and it had to be thrown away. My boots were also ruined and I had to get a new pair when I returned to Okinawa.

After we completed our time in the jungle we had a couple of days to dry out before departing for our home bases and I told the other American in the class about the fried rice. He said that sounded great so let's get some for lunch. We hopped on the local bus and rode into Changi Village around noontime. It certainly did not look quite as appealing as I thought I remembered it as the streets were sparsely populated during the heat of the day and they were covered in dust and dirt. I knew we were in the right location as I found the stack of crates that served as tables and chairs during the evening hours and saw the remains in the street gutter of the charcoal fire the vendor used at night. Even more disturbing than the general dirty and unhealthy appearance of the area were the large number of three-legged dogs we saw roaming the streets. I started to wonder exactly what I had eaten during my previous trip. It did not take us long to decide we would return to the officers club for lunch - besides it would also soon be tea time. Upon my return to Naha, I was named the squadron survival training officer and established (and taught) a well-received training course for our enlisted troops who had not attended any formal jungle survival training course.

Survival training with Royal Air Force. Changi, Singapore. Class 10-65. I am standing sixth from the left in the middle row. Sept., 1965.

When I arrived on Okinawa I discovered the high concentration of salt and humidity acted in a very corrosive manner on vehicles of all types. Cars had to be heavily undercoated to try to combat the corrosion. A car that did not receive the treatment would literally have the fenders eaten through in about a year. As a result most people owned what were called island cars - cars that had been coated with the thick tar-like undercoat, were still rusting, and could never economically be shipped back to the states.

I purchased a 1957 Ford station wagon that was covered in red primer paint to hide some of the rust: it ran but just barely. I tried to drive to the base for an early morning flight and the Ford quit - I parked it about two blocks from my apartment and caught one of the ever-present taxis that roamed the streets. As it turned out my scheduled two-day trip turned into a week-long journey and I returned to find the car had been towed. I went to the impound lot where I had to pay a fine for abandoning a car. There was an airman at the lot and he asked if I would sell the wagon. I readily agreed and let him have it for $100. He never did pay me and a year later he dropped it off at my squadron saying he had been transferred back to the states. Fortune smiled on me as a sergeant in my squadron asked if he could buy it and I sold it to him for $75 - he paid me.

After selling the Ford the first time, I spotted a 1962 red Chevrolet convertible with a 327 V-8 and four speed floor shift: I had to have that car as it certainly offered more appeal for the opposite sex than did the rusted station wagon. Within the next year the weather and salt spray on the island rendered the convertible top mechanism unworkable so I removed the motor and put the top up and down by hand. The top was mostly down and the numerous rainstorms caused water to stand in the floor so I drilled holes in the floorboards to drain the rain water out.

Rocky also had a Chevy convertible, a blue 1964, and we parked the two cars on the street by our apartment. One day Rocky was straightening up his room, noticed he had a bowling ball that was never used, and wondered if it would break or shatter if it was dropped from the roof of our house. We climbed on the roof where Rocky dropped the bowling ball into the yard aiming for some concrete blocks we had strategically placed - the ball shattered the blocks but showed little sign of damage. We climbed back to the roof where Rocky decided to drop the ball on the paved road outside our concrete wall. We asked one of our house mates if there was anyone on the street and he responded that the street was clear. He did not mention any car because he thought we knew a car was parked by the wall. Rocky gave the ball a heave to clear the wall and we listened to the very upsetting sound of bowling ball on metal, automotive metal to be precise. Rocky forgot he had parked his car at the side of the house rather than where he usually parked in the front. The ball was fine but the hood of the blue convertible did not fare quite as well.

During my first summer on Okinawa I also purchased a new Triumph motorcycle at the island dealer. I had the bike about four weeks when a taxi cab made a left turn in front of me as I was riding through an intersection: he never even saw me as he made his turn. I hit the side of the cab, bending the front fork of the motorcycle and fracturing two fingers and the thumb on my right hand.

Fortunately the taxi driver accepted full responsibility for the accident as the first responders were Okinawan police who did not speak any English. I was somewhat concerned listening to them converse in Japanese and watching them point at me and the accident scene. My right hand was bleeding from those compound fractures and one of the policemen motioned for me to hold my hand out where he poured peroxide all over it. I hopped around just a little as a result of the burning, stinging sensation while keeping my colorful comments confined to my inner voice.

A friend from another squadron wanted to know if I would sell him the motorcycle in its damaged condition. I said, "Yes, I would" as my insurance settlement and his offer greatly exceeded what I had paid for the Triumph - besides, a new Harley-Davidson dealer had just opened and they had a bright blue 900cc Sportster XLCH with my name on it.

In October we hauled large fuel bladders to Pleiku and then to a dirt strip at Catecka Tea Plantation where the 1st Air Cavalry Division was conducting a relatively new combat tactic, the helicopter assault. We would land on the dirt field, turn and taxi back to the approach end of the strip while rolling the fuel bladders out the rear cargo door and off the ramp. As we reached the end of the runway we would turn and execute an assault take off. The field was absolutely covered with helicopters refueling from the bladders with their engines running. In mid-November, we continued to haul supplies to Pleiku. At that time, just 35 miles southwest, the 7th Air Cavalry Regiment of the 1st Air Cavalry Division fought the first major engagement of the conflict in Ia Drang valley from the 14th to the 18th. That battle was the subject of the 2002 movie "We Were Soldiers."

1965 was drawing to a close; the increase in hostilities in Vietnam during the year saw a tremendous increase in American airpower in the theatre. By the year's end more than 500 aircraft and 21,000 Air Force personnel were stationed at eight major bases in South Vietnam. That increase, as well as the increase in ground forces, was supported by the C-130. I had flown missions transporting ammunition, fresh vegetables, fuel bladders, Air Police and guard dogs, body bags, vehicles of all types and sizes, howitzers, troops, litter patients, dead bodies, office equipment, aircraft spare parts and engines, and medical personnel. If it could be transported by air, we hauled it in our Herks.

The year ended with me accumulating over 200 flights in the C-130, most of them over the skies of Vietnam. It had been a good first year in an operational unit with one minor exception - my Academy classmate Steve Sutton and I were always in a friendly competition to see who achieved certain goals first. We bet on who would be the first to be combat-ready, who would be the first to reach a hundred hours of flying time, who would be the first to fly into Vietnam and other similar milestones. A significant honor would be which of us would be assigned to "E" Flight, the secretive organization in the 21st. The flight commander, a Lieutenant Colonel, was also the squadron operations officer.

I was involved in a heated dispute with the local town patrol one evening in Naha City that eventually escalated to my being placed under arrest. That particular patrol consisted of a Marine Corporal and an Airman Second Class who had a nasty disposition. A friend of mine had placed a glass filled with bourbon and water on the trunk of my car and then departed the scene. Open containers were definitely against the law and the patrol wanted to know who owned the car. The Airman and I got into an intense argument over whether or not I should be charged with anything simply on the theory it was my car and he demanded that I immediately pour the drink out on the street, pointing to the pavement between his shiny boots. I complied with his "right here, right now" command, dumping the drink right where he pointed. Oops, big mistake as the two of them started whipping out their night sticks and I feared I was about to receive the beating of my life. Instead, I was placed under arrest and walked to the town lock-up where my commander was notified. The operations officer arrived to sign for my release and we left the Air Police building in silence. He then asked how much I had to drink and I told him I had not had a single drink of any kind which was the truth. He drove me back to my car that was still parked downtown with the firm advice to pick it up and go straight home. I did exactly as was strongly suggested in spite of my burning desire to at least wave to the town patrol on my way out of the night club area. Several days later the announcement was made that Steve was the newest member of "E" Flight - obviously the flight commander was not impressed with my altercation.

1966 appeared on the calendar bringing with it more hectic flying time; it seemed I was airborne about every day of the week. Twenty four hours a day, seven days a week, the sound of C-130 engines continuously running was heard at Naha. I happened to be home on Easter morning that year when I heard a knock at the front door. I thought, "Who could that be this early?" I opened the door and there stood a young girl probably around 10 years old. She was obviously American and must have lived in the neighborhood. She handed me an Easter basket with colored hard-boiled eggs and candy and a card addressed to "the man in the red car." I was quite taken aback and before I could think of anything to say other than thank-you, she disappeared as suddenly as she had appeared. I had never seen her before that day and I never saw her afterwards.

In late April we supported Operation Birmingham and the 1st Infantry Division by flying in and out of a 4,600-foot dirt strip at Tay Ninh in South Vietnam hauling troops and ammunition. In May the 1st brigade of the 101st Airborne Division was airlifted from Tuy Hoa to Phan Thiet and then to Nhon Ko to conduct search and destroy operations in the area. After Nhon Ko the brigade was moved north to Cheo Reo and then to Dak To. I was co-pilot on the last C-130 flight to land at Cheo Reo to pick up the rear guard. We landed at the 3,500-foot dirt strip that had all but been destroyed by the large number of flights preceding us. We taxied on the least cut-up side of the runway trying to avoid the water-filled muddy ruts that occupied most of the field. As we loaded the few remaining Screaming Eagles and their supplies I approached a grunt, armed with an M-60 machine gun, leaning against a few sandbags stacked under our right wing and asked where the perimeter was. He smiled and replied, "Lieutenant, you are standing on it."

It was getting late in the day and the sun was setting. We were the only airplane on the ground with our crew of five and we had about a dozen or so airborne guys aboard. The last place we wanted to be was on a dirt field surrounded by jungle with no security beyond what was right at the aircraft as we would be a sitting duck for a mortar or rocket attack if we did not rapidly get airborne. The ground troops had a jeep and a wheeled water-tank to load and our loadmaster was told the water tank was empty so to save time he accepted the statement and strapped the tank in place on the rear ramp.

Everybody was aboard and we started engines, moving to the east end of the field to take advantage of what little breeze there was. It would be an assault takeoff to the west using full power, minimum run, and extreme climb-out attitude. As we started rolling both the pilot and I noticed the aircraft wanted to pitch up and we applied forward pressure on the yokes to try to keep the nose down. There was no room to abort the takeoff and we struggled into the air. To keep from stalling, the nose of the aircraft was pushed down to gain flying speed and we dropped into the valley at the west end of the field - fortunately the runway had been built on the top of a ridgeline. We finally managed to get the aircraft out of the valley and trimmed for close to level flight. The water tank was full, not empty, and the shift aft in center of gravity almost downed the Hercules. The loadmaster took some hoses and the water tank was drained overboard through the paratroop exit doors before we attempted to land. I suspect that on future flights the loadmaster involved never accepted anyone's word regarding the potential weight of an object to be airlifted.

For some of the lieutenants, it was getting near the end of our eighteen-month tour on Okinawa and we had to decide what to request from the Air Force Personnel Office for our next assignments. In spite of his "E" Flight assignment Steve Sutton wanted to get into fighter aircraft. Steve thought that the only way to move from the C-130 to fighters would be to apply for a UPT training slot as an instructor to build up jet time. With that goal in mind, he applied for, and received, an assignment to Air Training Command as an instructor pilot flying T-37s.

I decided I would extend my C-130 tour on Okinawa an additional year as I wanted to be upgraded to aircraft commander status. I figured there would be other opportunities at some time in the future to transfer to another aircraft if that was what I wanted. Besides, I had no desire to be an instructor at a pilot training base. My decision was ultimately rewarded when I received the long-coveted F-105 assignment in January the next year. While attending Thud school at Nellis in 1967 I ran into Steve in the flight line snack bar as he was on a cross country training flight with one of his students. Upon seeing me he exclaimed, "Please do not tell me why you are here." I did not have to respond as my reason for being there was painfully obvious from the patches on my flight suit.

I received some bad news at the beginning of June while on a trip to Bangkok. On 31 May 1966 in Operation Carolina Moon, Rocky Edmondson was killed. My former roommate had departed Okinawa for the States that spring and subsequently volunteered for a special secret mission back in Vietnam.

Operation Carolina Moon was an innovative attack planned by the Air Force to destroy the bridge at Than Hoa in North Vietnam. That bridge, nicknamed the Dragon's Jaw (Ham Rong) by the North Vietnamese, had withstood a great many aerial attacks and seemed indestructible. One attack on 4 April 1965 resulted in the first two F-105 losses to MiG-17s in the war, an action that was a severe embarrassment to Air Force leaders as they did not expect to lose a supersonic front-line fighter-bomber to the much older subsonic MiG.

Large magnetic mines, that implemented a new energy mass-focusing concept, would be floated down the Song Ma River till they reached the bridge. Magnetic sensors would set off the charges, hopefully wrecking the bridge permanently. The only aircraft capable of carrying those 5,000 pound weapons was the C-130 and the operation was scheduled to take place at night to reduce its vulnerability.

On the night of May 30, a Hercules with Rocky as the navigator dropped five mines in the river but, as after-mission reconnaissance photos showed the bridge was still standing, a second raid was planned. A different crew was used for the following night but at the last minute their navigator was replaced with Rocky as he had successfully flown the first mission. The second trip was a disaster as the C-130 and everybody aboard was lost, officially due to unknown causes, but a surface-to-air missile was the prime suspect. An F-4 escort was also downed during that night attack. The bridge was finally destroyed but not until it was struck with laser-guided bombs in 1972.

BLINDBAT & LAMPLIGHTER

The die was cast: I elected to stay in the 21st TCS for another year. In addition to the tactical airlift support in South Vietnam the squadron had another mission that greatly appealed to me - dropping flares over North Vietnam and Laos and directing airstrikes against the enemy. There were only two crews at a time from the squadron that had the opportunity to fly Blindbat/Lamplighter missions and I asked the squadron commander if I could be on one of those crews. In July I was informed by Colonel Jack D. Dieckman that I would get my wish and on 29 July 1966 I flew my first flight as a Blindbat co-pilot, from the detachment base at Ubon, Thailand. The plan was for me to gain some experience in that mission while flying the right seat and then I would be upgraded to aircraft commander status and would continue flying flare drops for a six month period: the maximum time allowed for a temporary assignment.

The Blindbat mission originated in April 1965 when a C-130A accompanied by two B-57s and a Marine Corps ECM aircraft departed Da Nang Air Base, South Vietnam at night to hunt for trucks and other vehicles moving down the Ho Chi Minh trail through Laos delivering supplies to the Viet Cong and North Vietnamese troops in South Vietnam.

The C-130 would drop flares to light any targets acquired and the B-57s would attack the targets. The ECM bird provided electronic counter-measures protection against enemy radar-controlled guns known as "firecans." The mission initiated Operation Steel Tiger, an interdiction campaign designed to complement Operation Rolling Thunder, the bombing of North Vietnam.

Laos was divided into sectors similar to the way North Vietnam was split into segments called "route packages". In Laos Operation Barrel Roll, which began on 14 December 1964, covered the northern part of the country, while Steel Tiger covered the southern or panhandle part of Laos.

The first C-130 loss of the conflict in Southeast Asia was a Blindbat aircraft that crashed near Korat Air Base in Thailand on 24 April 1965. The first combat losses for the C-130 occurred in late June of 1965 when Viet Cong infiltrators destroyed two Blindbat flareships on the ground at Da Nang. In the spring of 1966 the C-130 flareship operation moved from Da Nang to Ubon Royal Thai Air Base in Thailand near the Laotian border.

On 20 July 1966, just before I reported to Ubon, Operation Tally Ho was authorized emphasizing night interdiction in route pack one of North Vietnam: the area for intense scrutiny was from the DMZ north for approximately 30 miles. That operation had a big impact on where I would fly the vast majority of my night flare missions.

On 11 August 1966 I was flying my 7th mission from Ubon using the call sign Lamplighter in the Steel Tiger area. Blindbat 02 was patrolling the area of route pack one in North Vietnam. The orders for the day indicated there were no friendly forces operating in Blindbat's assigned area. The Blindbat crew, also from the 21st TCS, was working with a B-57 using the call sign "Yellowbird." The B-57 had expended his bombs and asked Blindbat if he had any targets suitable for a strafe attack. The immediate response was negative but a U.S. Army OV-10 Mohawk carrying side-looking radar (SLAR) picked up an unidentified vessel apparently leaving the shore approximately three quarters of a mile south of the northern boundary of the DMZ and notified Blindbat.

The crew of Blindbat dropped flares illuminating what appeared to be a hostile military vessel in the water off the coast of Vietnam. (The North Vietnamese had no flareships so the US origin of the flares should have been obvious.) The role of Blindbat under Operation Tally Ho directives was to seek out targets of opportunity in route pack one and then direct strikes from armed aircraft to destroy those targets.

Yellowbird rolled in on an identification pass and received no response to that pass to indicate the vessel was anything other than hostile. Under the flarelight provided by Blindbat Yellowbird then strafed the vessel that was taking evasive action and set the vessel ablaze. Blindbat continued the attack directing a flight of F-4s, call sign "Coyote," but Coyote failed to hit the ship with its bombs and cluster bomb units.

Meanwhile the vessel under attack radioed for assistance alleging that it was under fire from North Vietnamese aircraft notwithstanding the fact the North Vietnamese did not have C-130s, B-57s, or F-4s. Unfortunately the vessel under attack was a 78-ton, 82-foot, armed U.S. Coast Guard patrol boat named the "Point Welcome."

A second flight of F-4s was scrambled in response to Blindbat's request for additional resources to continue the assault but fate intervened as they had an air abort and returned to Da Nang. In the meantime the horrible truth emerged when someone who had access to all the radio communications started putting two and two together and a message was finally relayed to Blindbat to cease and desist.

The official board of inquiry found that the incident occurred as a result of lack of knowledge and understanding of differing missions and overlapping of assigned areas of friendly forces. The board found the Blindbat pilot was not informed of any Coastal Security Service operations by surface vessels and that the Tally Ho orders were not coordinated with the Naval forces in Vietnam.

The board further ruled that all participants performed in a manner consistent with their assigned duties, that there was no dereliction, nor improper performance, of duty, and that the resulting deaths and injuries were not caused by the intent, fault, or negligence of any member of the armed forces.

The Point Welcome survived the attack although two crewmembers were killed, including the commanding officer, and five others aboard were wounded. The patrol boat was repaired, continued to serve with the USCG in the waters off Vietnam, and was eventually transferred to South Vietnam as the Ngu Yen Han on 29 April 1970.

Notwithstanding the official findings, some Monday morning quarterbacks in the Coast Guard attempted to place the blame for the unfortunate matter on the aircraft commander of Blindbat alleging that he unreasonably interpreted the rules of engagement. In fact the rules allowed strikes on a military vessel if it was in RVN territorial seas and engaged in the unauthorized landing of troops or materiale on friendly territory. In war *appearance* and *location* rather than actuality will often dictate action and all parties involved had some share in the decisions that led to the end results. What is considered reasonable while sitting at a desk well after the fact is quite different from what is considered reasonable under the stress of combat in the darkness of night!

I have often had the disturbing thought that I could easily have been involved in that unfortunate episode if my assignment for the evening had been in the Tally Ho sector rather than in Steel Tiger. I was fortunate for my role to have been one of merely listening to radio communications between the Air Force personnel actually participating in the event as a "friendly fire" incident is something no one wants to be involved in.

On the second of September I flew my last flight as a Lamplighter/Blindbat co-pilot: I had flown a total of 18 such flights, the majority in route pack one. I returned to Naha to prepare to be upgraded from a co-pilot to an aircraft commander at the ripe old age of 26. I flew two practice rides from the left seat before taking the check which would be administered in two flights due to the variety of aircraft maneuvers I was expected to have mastered.

Those maneuvers included engine-out takeoffs and landings, blacked-out landings at night with no runway lighting, and assault takeoffs and landings. Assault takeoffs and assault landings utilize extremely steep climb-outs and approaches to minimize exposure to ground fire. The landing also requires extreme braking with full engine reverse to land in as short a distance as possible (using unimproved short runways). After I made a couple of assault landings the check pilot announced that he usually bet a case of beer as to who could execute the best assault landing but he said he would not even attempt to match mine as I could have easily landed on an aircraft carrier without the aid of arresting gear.

On 20 September 1966 I completed my upgrade check to C-130 Aircraft Commander at Naha AB. I hopped a ride to Ubon to join my crew that was waiting to get into action over Laos and North Vietnam. My first flight as an aircraft commander/Blindbat mission commander was a six-hour combat mission in route pack one on 3 October 1966.

The officers on our Blindbat crew were all Lieutenants. Our navigator was Curt Newland, a good friend of mine from prior flights together, and our co-pilot had just been promoted from the rank of Second Lieutenant. We were the only all-Lieutenant crew in the outfit during our tour and, from viewing the photographs and history of Blindbat, maybe the only such crew ever. We had a Technical Sergeant for a flight engineer who was new to the C-130 and the normal complement of four loadmaster/flare kickers who labored diligently in the rear.

Blindbat Crew, Ubon, Thailand in October, 1966. Navigator Curt Newland is standing at the right. I am standing second from the left. (USAF Photo)

Our commander at Ubon was Lieutenant Colonel George T. Carr from the 41st TCS. Colonel Carr rode on one of our missions to observe and was quite disappointed to discover there was no coffee aboard our aircraft. It was tradition for the aircraft commander to pay for the large thermos of coffee if there was a charge but usually the dining halls readily provided the coffee. We soon found out that no one on our crew even liked coffee so our loadmasters always filled the thermos with fruit punch from the enlisted dining hall.

That flight with the Colonel earned us the nickname of "the Kool-aid Kids." I was always indebted to the Colonel for another reason - he said he would never ask how I got my Harley XLCH to Ubon.

Prior to my leaving Naha I had arranged for a couple of my loadmaster friends and another Lieutenant aircraft commander to bring my motorcycle to Ubon the next time they were scheduled to stop there on a flight from Okinawa. I had the Harley crated but the slats on the crate did not hide the fact that it contained a motorcycle. In the meantime the wing commander issued a letter saying that anyone caught transporting a personal vehicle aboard a 6315th C-130 would receive an immediate article fifteen: an article fifteen is a non-judicial punishment but having one in your file would probably kill any possibility of a future promotion.

I received word that my friends would be coming through Ubon the following day and I arranged for a pickup truck to meet the airplane on arrival. As I was waiting for the 130 to arrive, I received a radio call from the Lieutenant imploring me to be ready to move the motorcycle immediately as the wing commander was also on the airplane. The commander had flagged the aircraft down as it was taxiing out for takeoff and wanted to know if that was the flight going to Bangkok. When he was told that it was, he climbed aboard for the trip.

I met the airplane and we frantically tried to get the motorcycle pushed off the ramp of the Hercules and into the truck. Suddenly the wing commander walked around the tail of the aircraft and stopped for a moment to say, "Great job down here in Blindbat: we are proud of you." My heart stopped, my stomach felt queasy - there was no way he could not have seen the motorcycle but he continued on his journey and walked out of sight. We rapidly finished hiding the

Harley Davidson at Ubon

69

Harley in the back of the truck and I took it up to my hooch. I am quite sure I had the only Harley Davidson motorcycle in all of eastern Thailand if not the entire country. It was a big hit with the Thais as the largest Honda motorcycle at the time was the 305 cc version.

Our Blindbat/Lamplighter flights lasted around six hours and were flown at 4,500 feet, unpressurized and completely blacked out with no navigation lights. Prior to takeoff we were given a schedule of flights of armed fighters and attack aircraft that would join us throughout the time we were airborne and we would then direct those aircraft against whatever targets we could locate. If we could not find any targets of opportunity we would direct the armed killers from our hunter-killer team to strike known area targets such as truck parks and interdiction points.

We flew with the rear cargo ramp and upper door partially open to allow the installation of an aluminum tray from which the flares were dispensed. One of the loadmasters, also known as a kicker, would ride above the tray and kick the flares out of the airplane with his feet when commanded to do so by the aircraft commander. The arming lanyards of the flares were attached to the tray so the flares would be armed on exit. The flares were stored in wooden containers or bins secured in the cargo hold of the airplane. The aluminum trays and wooden bins were designed and built at Naha when the mission was first undertaken back in 1965. The loadmasters had a tough job: the flares weighed about 27 pounds each and they were loaded on the aircraft and transferred from bins to tray by hand. We carried around 250 flares per trip. The loadmasters had to walk around in the cargo hold handling those flares in spite of sometimes very unexpected and violent aircraft maneuvers. I often wondered why those guys did not have more broken legs and arms.

Curt navigated, following the unimproved roads running through the jungle of Laos and North Vietnam by using the radar on the C-130 which was really designed for weather penetration, not ground navigation, and the co-pilot and I stared out the cockpit windows searching for targets. I flew the aircraft and handled air-to-air communications with the attack aircraft while the co-pilot handled air-to-ground communications and kept the log that tracked each strike and the information on the attack aircraft. We did not have any night vision equipment and the flight engineer had to continually monitor the engine instruments in very subdued red lighting so as not to interfere with our ability to pick out targets on the ground.

It was October 1966 and the northeast monsoon season was settling in bringing with it fog, rain, and thick cloud layers close to the ground in North Vietnam. We could add weather reconnaissance to the multiple tasks we were already performing and we spent hours flying alone over Laos and route pack one when all the other aircraft were grounded. The 6th and 8th of October were two of those nights when the weather grounded all flights except ours and we patrolled the skies of North Vietnam with no activity to report. The ground below was completely obscured by low-lying clouds and I was very thankful the North Vietnamese had not yet received enough SA-2s (SAMs) to move any into route pack one.

We were bored and Curt located a radio station that was carrying the World Series between the Baltimore Orioles and the Los Angeles Dodgers (the O's swept it in four). We ate canned sardines and crackers with our fruit punch while we enjoyed listening to the games even though none of us was an avid fan of either team.

We were stationed at an F-4 base with the 8th Tactical Fighter Wing with our complement of multi-engine warhorses. Usually that was not necessarily a good thing as fighter pilots tended to look down on the trash-haulers. I became friends with John Robert "Bob" Pardo, an F-4 pilot, in the bar and I really enjoyed comparing notes and swapping stories with the fighter jock.

Bob knew I wanted an F-105 assignment and his counsel regarding the potential change in aircraft was quite encouraging to me. I invited Bob to fly with us one night and he readily accepted. We were near Tchepone that evening and a 37/57 gunner took a really good shot at us - the tracers looked like a fire hose spraying a stream of red in our direction. I was glad to show the F-4 jock that we got shot at too. Several days later we were returning at dawn from a mission when an F-4 flight approached Ubon at the same time. Bob recognized my voice and asked if I wanted to fly some formation with the Phantoms. I thought that sounded like a great idea and the four F-4s joined on my right wing in an echelon. We flew initial at 300 knots and I did a tactical pitch pulling three Gs in the 60-degree banked turn while the F-4s pitched out with the appropriate spacing. I then did an assault landing, turning off at the first taxiway to make room for the Phantoms that were landing behind us. The air show went off without a hitch with one small exception - the sack of sugar that was normally used for coffee drinkers was sitting on the rear bulkhead; it turned over from the sudden prop reversal inherent in an assault landing and spilled down the back of Curt's flight suit.

Bob Pardo is well known for "Pardo's Push", a maneuver that probably saved the lives of Earl Aman and his back-seater – it certainly kept them from bailing out near Hanoi and being captured. (Earl had been an upper classman in our squadron at the Academy.) On 10 March 1967, Bob and Earl were attacking a target in North Vietnam when both of their Phantoms were hit by flak. Earl's fuel tank was hit and he lost most of his JP-4. Bob decided to try "pushing" Earl's Phantom to keep that crew from bailing out over territory where no rescue could be attempted. Bob first tried to put his nose into the drag chute compartment of Earl's F-4 to push the aircraft; however, the turbulence was too great and he had to discard that idea. Next Bob tried to use Earl's tailhook to push the F-4 by placing his windscreen against Earl's lowered tailhook. That required Earl to shut down both his engines which he did. It also resulted in cracking Bob's windscreen. Bob was actually running on only one engine as the other had caught fire and had to be shut down. Eventually Bob's second engine caught fire and failed but his daring maneuver had worked just long enough, as it allowed both aircraft to reach an uninhabited area of Laos where the two crews bailed out of their fatally crippled Phantoms to be rescued by the Sandys and Jolly Greens.

I had a truly memorable flight on the 13th of November when we received a radio call from a Nimrod, one of the prop-driven, twin-engine A-26Ks stationed at Nakhon Phanom. The A-26s were an absolute delight to work with as they carried a huge load of ordnance, were fast enough to keep pace with the 130, and were extremely accurate in delivering that ordnance load. A-1s were also very accurate and carried a large load of ordnance but they could not match our airspeed and could not rapidly follow us from target area to target area. B-57s were the best choice for fast-movers and also performed excellent work in the night-attack role. On the other hand, F-4s were usually a total waste of time - they were lucky to even hit the ground and when they did it seemed like it was never where we had directed them to drop.

Nimrod said he needed flare assistance as he had located a large truck convoy way north in the Barrel Roll area. We soon found out the convoy was actually on the border of North Vietnam, just northwest of Hanoi. I said we would be there as fast as we could and we hustled from the Tchepone area in Steel Tiger to the designated rendezvous point.

We quickly joined forces with Nimrod and dropped flares lighting up the surprised convoy that consisted of 27 trucks. Nimrod dropped a 250-pound general purpose bomb on the lead truck and then covered the last truck with napalm. The convoy was now helplessly trapped on the narrow mountain road and Nimrod made pass after pass under our flarelight, dropping cluster bombs, firing rockets, and strafing, until all 27 trucks were burning or destroyed.

It had been a good night and the Nimrod and Blindbat departed the area headed for Thailand. I was running very low on fuel and decided we needed to land at Nakhon Phanom to pick up enough JP-4 to get back to Ubon. I called Nimrod on the UHF and said. "Do you think you guys have a little extra fuel to spare? I do not believe I can get home on what I have left." Nimrod said, "Sure, after tonight's work you can have all you want."

A few minutes later Nimrod called and said they would pick us up at the airplane and take us to breakfast at the club. We landed with three out of four tank-empty warning lights glowing and taxied in to refuel. I checked with our flight engineer and loadmasters to make sure they were going to be fed and waited for the Nimrod crew to show up. The Nimrod crew arrived in a jeep and got out to greet us. The pilot was a Lieutenant Colonel and the navigator was a Major. I immediately introduced myself saying, "Hi, I am Lieutenant Warner." I used my rank as I flew the Blindbat missions in jungle fatigues that were devoid of any rank or insignia. I then introduced our navigator and our co-pilot and waited for the Nimrods to say, "Let's go eat." The Lieutenant Colonel kept looking at the flight deck of the Hercules and finally said, "When is your aircraft commander getting off?" I was a little taken aback and

Curt laughingly responded before I had a chance to recover, "Sir, you have been talking to the aircraft commander ever since you drove up." Their instant look of disbelief quickly disappeared and the Lieutenant Colonel said, "Well, you could have fooled me. Lieutenant, let's go get some breakfast – it will be on us."

December arrived bringing with it the golden opportunity I had been waiting for. The Air Force was losing so many F-105 Thunderchiefs over North Vietnam that it was having trouble filling the training slots for the aircraft as everyone knew what awaited them upon graduation from that training. Each major air command was directed to provide two "volunteers" for F-105 school. Of course I immediately placed my name in the pot hoping to score what I believed to be a real coup. While waiting to see the result of that action, December provided a few other exciting moments; one of which was again caused by a lack of communication between operating units although this time the screw-up involved only the Air Force. We were patrolling in route pack one just north of the DMZ around Dong Hoi and the night had been relatively slow with no targets of opportunity acquired. We were waiting for our next scheduled fighters to arrive and planned to put their ordnance on a suspected truck park just northwest of Dong Hoi. The night was clear for once and the ground well lit by moonlight. We were cruising on auto-pilot at our usual altitude of 4,500 feet when I sensed, more than actually saw, something falling all around the Hercules. I thought what am I seeing, or am I just imagining things?

At that moment the ground directly beneath us started exploding in burst after burst of bright flashes. My co-pilot exclaimed, "Somebody just released a load of CBU under us." I quickly said, "That is not CBU, those are 500-pound bombs going off." At once our entire crew came to the awful realization that we were in the middle of an Arc Light strike. A cell of B-52s, probably a three ship formation, was making a bombing run from around 30,000 feet directly on top of the Blindbat. Each B-52 was dropping 84 500-pounders and those bombs were falling all around our airplane.

Curt started yelling, "Break, break, break!" I sat bolt upright, cutting off the auto-pilot and tried to decide which way was the best way to break as we were surrounded by bombs. One bomb of any size on the top of the C-130 and we were definitely toast. I made a hard left diving turn to build airspeed and try to escape out over the water - the maneuver was successful and we got out of the area that was now covered in massive explosions from at least 252 500-pound general purpose bombs.

I immediately got on the UHF radio and contacted 7th Air Force in Saigon where our daily orders originated. I described in no uncertain terms, using what could be considered colorful language, how upset we were with the events of the evening. My ire was not directed at the B-52s that were just doing their job, but at the personnel responsible for coordination of effort. The fragmentation orders identifying the targets for the day arriving the following morning apologized for the previous lack of notification regarding the route pack one Arc Light mission. That would have been little comfort for my crew if one of those bombs had impacted the top of our C-130.

A few nights later we were once again roaming the skies near Dong Hoi and I was beginning to feel like route pack one was my back yard. It had been another boring evening as we had few fighters assigned to join the party. We received a radio call using an unknown call-sign asking if we would do some spotting for him (we thought at the time that it might be a surface vessel belonging to the U.S. Navy). We readily agreed and the desired coordinates of the pending barrage were given to us; Curt led us to the area and we watched in anticipation as the first rounds impacted directly on the designated position. We said, "No correction needed, you guys were right on target." The next rounds completely obliterated the target area and the unknown comrade said, "Thanks Bat, see you around." I did ask him at that point if he had his feet really wet and he responded in the affirmative. In pilot-speak, feet wet meant the aircraft was over water. By his response, I figured the vessel had to be either a Navy Destroyer or Cruiser as I knew they were operating in the coastal waters off Vietnam but I never discovered the exact identity of our new friend.

For many pilots and crews, one of the most dreaded targets in Laos was Tchepone as it was the location of many US aircraft losses during the war. It was initially a sleepy village almost due west of Khe Sanh, South Vietnam but it quickly grew into a major road junction and transshipment point for the flow of North Vietnamese equipment and supplies to the south. As such, it was heavily defended and widely considered to be a very dangerous target area to overfly.

During the course of the conflict Tchepone had more bomb tonnage dropped on it than was dropped on any German city during WW II. Oddly enough, in spite of the reputation of Tchepone we never had any close call in the area (except for the flight with Bob Pardo as our passenger) even though we flew over it on almost a nightly basis. Even if we were headed into pack one we would overfly Tchepone just to see if we could spot any enemy activity as that was a good choke point and we could relay the information to one of our other flareships.

For my crew, Dong Hoi, NVN was our "Tchepone" as several events made us quite leery of flying over that seacoast town. We were scouring route pack one in late December in the Dong Hoi area without a lot of luck in finding good targets. We had made several north and south passes over the area just slightly inland from the coastline when a 37/57mm gunner just could not take it any longer. (We grouped the two different caliber guns together as we could not tell the difference from the air.)

In either case they fired extremely dangerous shells easily capable of taking down an aircraft, especially when the aircraft was at 4,500 feet. The gunner figured he had us dead in his sights and opened up on us. The anti-aircraft guns usually left us alone as by ourselves we posed no immediate threat and firing on us not only resulted in revealing the gun's location but it could also indicate there was a worthwhile target in the vicinity. Furthermore firing on us would result in receiving the return favor as soon as we had any strike aircraft at our disposal. That night was almost the gunner's night to remember.

The Blindbat was on auto pilot and I was sitting in my seat with my feet propped on the footrests enjoying the scenery. The co-pilot was studying his log sheet and Curt was standing behind me looking out the cockpit window. All at once the sky just to my immediate left was absolutely full of angry red tracers. The stream was just a couple of feet in front of the number two engine propeller and about two feet from the left side of the fuselage and my seat. The cockpit was brightly illuminated with a frightening red glow and the stream of fire was constant. Curt started beating me on my left shoulder telling me to break; the co-pilot dropped his logs and I frantically disengaged the auto-pilot while pushing hard on the left rudder to keep the prop behind the stream of tracers. I then broke hard left to get over the water and went to maximum power to leave the gun behind.

A single shell in the left wing would have resulted in a huge explosion as the C-130 carried its fuel in the wings - we were lucky that night as I suppose we were lucky on many nights. Today I listen to the commentary of football announcers when they quite often use the tired old cliché that football is a game of inches. Believe me; you do not know what a game of inches is until you have been in combat.

We had a very happy bunch of fighter pilots at Ubon on the 2nd of January 1967. That was the date of Operation Bolo where the 8th TFW F-4 Phantoms suckered the North Vietnamese Air Force into combat by acting like F-105 Thunderchiefs. The North Vietnamese Air Force had an advantage over the U.S. Air Force during that time period as bombing air bases in and around Hanoi and Haiphong was prohibited. U.S. forces could not fire on the MiGs parked on airfields and the MiGs would attack the F-105 fighter-bombers causing them to drop their bombs in order to defend themselves against an air threat. If the Thuds dropped their bombs the MiGs would then retreat to the safety of their airfields.

The MiGs also avoided confrontations with the Phantoms that were designed for aerial combat. With these tactics in use by the enemy, MiG kills became few and far between. The 8th decided to trick the North Vietnamese into committing their MiG-21s against F-4Cs armed for air-to-air combat. The Phantoms would simulate F-105s by flying at the same altitude, speed, and route as the Thuds normally used. The F-4s would also use F-105 call signs, tanker rendezvous points, and would even make false radio calls to trick North Vietnamese ground controllers. To complete the deception, the F-4s would fly the inflexible line-abreast pod formations used by the Thuds and they were modified to carry electronic countermeasure pods used only on F-105s.

The mission was also planned so that no other friendly aircraft would be present, allowing the first three flights of F-4s to initiate a missile attack without having to first identify the target. The North Vietnamese fell for the trick, hook, line, and sinker and took to the skies to jump the incoming aircraft. Much to their surprise, it was not bomb-laden Thuds they could take shots at, it was missile armed F-4s, ready to rumble.

The ruse was a resounding success and the 8th TFW was credited with seven MiG-21 kills during the operation. The actions leading up to that very successful day made me all the more convinced that I wanted to fly the F-105 as I knew the United States would eventually bomb those MiG bases. Two days later I felt I had won the lottery when I was informed my slot in F-105 Thunderchief training had been approved and I was ordered to report to Nellis Air Force Base in February.

On the night of Friday the 13th of January 1967 we were working in the Steel Tiger area over Laos northeast of Nakhon Phanom. During my brief Air Force career in the cockpit, I had come to the conclusion that there must be a lot of truth to the superstition that Friday the 13th is an unlucky day. That night we had a two ship flight of Navy A-4s scheduled to join us: they checked in and found all we had for them to do was one of the never-ending road cuts. We kicked out our flares and gave run-in directions for the two Skyhawks.

As they were confirming target and release parameters their radio transmissions became very garbled and then silent. We tried and tried to raise the two A-4s on the UHF radio to no avail. There was no sign of serious trouble and we had no indication anything was wrong other than the silence.

Suddenly the voice of one of the Skyhawk pilots broke that silence saying, "Bat, we had a mid-air collision. I am on the ground." We contacted search and rescue and were told that a pick-up would not be attempted until first light. In the meantime we located the exact position of the downed pilot by fixing on his radio transmissions and transmitted that information.

We had no indication more than one pilot had survived the collision. We maintained hourly radio contact with the survivor and dropped single flares near his position to keep up his spirits; we would also move several miles away and drop multiple flares in other locations just to keep the enemy in the dark as to where the downed pilot was hiding. I had the flight engineer calculate our fuel load to see how long we could remain in the air and I made a decision to shut down the two outboard engines on our Herk to conserve fuel. I also had the loadmaster count our remaining flares to see how long I could keep up a continuous light source saving enough flares if a night pick-up was attempted.

It was getting near dawn when the downed pilot called and said, "Bat, I hear voices: they are coming after me." I relayed that information imploring someone to risk a night rescue. A Huey chopper belonging to some unidentified detachment at NKP launched to pick up the survivor: as he arrived in the area, we gave him directions to the guy on the ground and I called on the radio, "Pop your smoke now." At once the blackness below us was broken with not one flare but two.

The second pilot had also survived but had remained silent on the radio. The chopper successfully picked up the pilot we had been talking to and we provided directions to the chopper pilot regarding the location of the second Navy pilot. The chopper went into his hover, dropped the penetrator, and the second pilot seated himself waiting to be hoisted out of the jungle.

The chopper began hoisting the pilot from the jungle floor when the penetrator became ensnarled in the tree tops - the pilot was being crushed between the penetrator and the tree limbs when the cable snapped plunging the doomed aviator to the ground. While this was happening the pilot had an open mike and every scream and agonizing plea for help, including the prolonged scream as he fell to the ground, was being transmitted.

We sat in the Blindbat in stunned silence as what had been such a joyous moment seconds before was replaced with a profound sense of helplessness. The survivor was taken to NKP where I also had to land to refuel and we were asked if we could fly him to Da Nang where he could catch a ride back to his carrier. I readily agreed and we took off for South Vietnam after I called the Ubon command post by landline to inform my commander, Colonel Carr, what was happening.

As I was expecting a junior grade officer or enlisted troop to answer the telephone, I was quite surprised when the 8th TFW commander, Colonel Robin Olds (All-American football player at West Point, triple Ace in WW II and Vietnam, and later

Commandant of Cadets at the USAFA) answered the telephone and readily agreed to relay my message to Colonel Carr, graciously asking if there was anything else he could do to assist me.

The second pilot's body was recovered the following day by a ground team. We finally landed back at Ubon twenty-three long hours without sleep or eating after our takeoff the preceding day. I broke every rule there was regarding crew duty time but we had assisted in the recovery of at least one Navy pilot. I received an unexpected Distinguished Flying Cross for that mission - one of which I was very proud as I earned it as a C-130 aircraft commander. The fact was, trash-haulers did not collect medals like the fighter jocks did.

I did not fly on the 14th, except for the early morning flight from Da Nang back to Ubon, and on 15 January 1967 I commanded my last mission in the Blindbat role. I had racked up another 176 flights in the C-130 during the past year, including 84 flights (69 over North Vietnam) as a Blindbat pilot and mission commander. We were fortunate not to lose any aircraft while I was at Ubon but later in the war two Blindbat C-130s, both from the 41st Tactical Airlift Squadron (TAS), were shot down over Laos killing the crews, one on May 22, 1968 (piloted by an Academy classmate) and one on November 24, 1969.

I dismantled my Harley and, with the assistance of my loadmasters, shipped it back to Naha crated and boxed in several different containers hoping to say it was just spare parts if I got caught. I packed my bags and handed the 45-caliber Thompson submachine gun, obtained by trading a fifth of whiskey to an Army Sergeant in Vietnam and carried with me on the night missions, to our detachment maintenance officer as I knew I could not take that weapon back to the states. I then caught a ride back to Naha on the C-130 that brought my replacement to Ubon and anxiously awaited the start of my transition to the awesome F-105 Thunderchief.

TRANSITION TIME: C-130 TO F-105

I was ready to make the big step from multi-engine to fighter aircraft and was waiting for my port call date to arrive. My possessions had been packed and shipped to Nellis AFB, Nevada; the individual boxes and parts of my motorcycle that had been transported back to Okinawa from Ubon had also been crated and shipped. I was given the traditional "farewell" party by the 21st TCS at the Officers Club but it was a rather strange affair as I had been in Thailand for almost six months so I did not know any of the squadron members that were living on Okinawa. All my friends and acquaintances had already departed for other assignments. I commented that it seemed very odd to say "goodbye" to people I had never had the opportunity to say "hello" to. I sold my Chevy convertible to a high-school-age Air Force dependent for $600. He asked to test drive the car and I warned him that the clutch would not stand any abuse from hot-rod starts: he promptly went out and destroyed the clutch. I told him he had to replace the clutch and the price was still $600; he gave me the money and I watched the car being towed to the nearest mechanic. All that remained was for me to pack my clothes in my B-4 bag and board the commercial flight back to the States.

The day before my scheduled departure I received an urgent telephone call from the squadron - my orders had been cancelled. I was stunned, wondering how to either resolve the apparent screw-up or to get my worldly possessions returned that were already on their way to Nellis. My personnel officer told me the reason my orders had been cancelled was someone at Tactical Air Command (TAC) noted I was not currently qualified in jet aircraft as I was a C-130 aircraft commander. The personnel officer, Major Chet Beverly, was also assigned to the 21st TCS and we had flown together at times. Chet asked me, "How badly do you really want to go get yourself killed in a 105?" I responded that I definitely wanted to fly the Thud, not get killed in it.

Chet played golf with the commander of the base operations flight: that flight flew a few T-33s, primarily to act as intruders to train the Air Defense F-102s stationed on Okinawa in interception tactics. Using superior skill and cunning, Chet somehow arranged for me to fly with the base ops pilots under the following arrangement: the commander of the base ops flight said they would take me up for seven dual flights in a two-week period and subject me to a check flight on the eighth flight; if I passed the check ride, I would be certified as current in jet aircraft and TAC would be so notified.

The agreement required permission from my squadron commander, Lieutenant Colonel Dieckman, who had to agree to release me from my primary duties for the two week period. Colonel Dieckman readily agreed and I flew my first T-33 flight on the morning of 8 February 1967 to try to get my F-105 orders reinstated.

The good news was I flew the T-33 in pilot training to get my wings. As previously mentioned Craig was one of only four bases that still flew the T-33 rather than the newer T-38 that was just entering the Air Force inventory as the basic flight trainer. It took very little time for me to familiarize myself with the T-Bird again and the check lists even reappeared in my memory banks. The biggest difficulty I had in transitioning back to the T-33 from the C-130 was my initial tendency to round out too high in landing because of the physical size difference in the two aircraft. That minor flaw was quickly overcome in the next few flights and on 15 February 1967 I successfully completed my check flight in the T-33 with flight examiner Capt Roger T. Chesson to complete the jet qualification process.

Tactical Air Command was notified and my orders to F-105 training were reaffimed. My future plans were once again on track and I happily departed Naha for Nellis even if the flight back to the States was a couple of weeks later than originally scheduled.

I arrived at Nellis Air Force Base at the end of February. Nellis is located in North Las Vegas approximately seven miles northeast of the central business district of Las Vegas and due north of Sunrise Mountain. The base was originally named Las Vegas Army Air Field during WW II and it was the primary source of training B-17 gunners at the time. When the Air Force became a separate entity after the war the base was renamed Nellis Air Force Base and became an advanced single-engine training base. That role continued through Korea and into Vietnam where it was one of two F-105 training bases.

Although my brief training session in the T-33 at Naha managed to get me to Nellis, it still did not get me into F-105 training course 111506E. There were four of us reporting to Thud school that had multi-engine experience rather than previous fighter or single-engine experience. The commander of the 4520th Training Wing decided that the four of us would not be admitted to class 68A for which we were scheduled: instead we would be moved back to class 68B and placed in the 4524th training squadron for the two months before the next Thud class would begin.

The 4524th flew AT-33s, T-33s with two fifty-caliber machine guns in the nose and bomb racks under the wings. Their primary mission was to train pilots from South American countries in ordnance delivery tactics. I flew my first flight in the AT-33 on 3 March 1967. Over the next two months, from 3 March to 20 April I would fly 28 training flights learning how to deliver weapons, strafe, and fly formation again. As I was already current in the T-33 from my Naha experience I would get to fly a large number of those flights solo, usually tagging along in the number 4 position.

On the 10th of March great news; I was promoted to Captain from First Lieutenant. Of course that promotion was primarily based on time served and was not the result of achieving any great accomplishments; all that was required was not to really mess something up - which, in retrospect, I had flirted with more than once. To celebrate my promotion I enlisted the aid of my good friend and fellow former multi-engine pilot, Major Byron Black. We went downtown to Fremont Street where we found a small go-go bar that had a juke box for the girls to dance to. Our favorite song on that juke box was entitled "The Egg Plant That Ate Chicago." We played that song over and over while we enjoyed our beer. About two weeks later we decided we would make a return visit to the same place: to our chagrin the juke box had been replaced and our song was gone. I commented to one of the dancers that they had a new juke box and she said, "The old one had terrible songs on it, especially one about an egg plant that two jerks insisted on playing over and over a couple of weeks ago." We did not admit to being the jerks.

Returning to flying after my promotion party, I was on my very first attempt at dive bombing. The instructor in the back seat was telling me my dive angle was wrong, my airspeed was wrong, my roll in was wrong, and my release altitude was wrong. As I pulled out of the run the range scoring officer said, "You have a shack." A shack was a direct hit; to qualify a hit within a 300 foot circle around the target was all that was required. The instructor said, "It is very difficult to try and tell someone they did everything wrong when the end result is perfection."

My last flight in the AT-33 would be on the 21st of April when I took part in a 4520th Training Wing turkey shoot. A turkey shoot is a competition between fighter pilots to judge weapons delivery competence. The turkey shoot included two dive bomb passes, two skip bomb passes and two strafing runs. The competitors for the day included instructors and students from the two F-105 training squadrons and the AT-33 squadron. Once again I rolled in on my first dive bomb pass and again scored a shack: my second bomb run was a forty-footer and I hit both of my skip bombs. I concluded the day with a 75% strafe score.

The end result was I was the winner of the turkey shoot and the training wing commander had to present the plaque to a former multi-engine pilot. He graciously acknowledged that fact when he presented the award saying, "A couple of months ago I thought we had some multi-engine pilots that could not possibly fly fighters and today I have to present this plaque to one of them." When I accepted the award I said I was the worst pilot of our AT-33 group and that the others just had an off day. According to the Nellis newspaper I was the first student to win as all prior winners were instructors and I posted one of the highest scores ever achieved.

Nellis and Las Vegas were simply wonderful places to spend a few months. I knew I had to spend as much time as I could in Sin City and there was no good way to get to town from the base. My motorcycle had not yet arrived from Naha and I decided I needed some wheels to facilitate some interaction between me and the local population.

I had fallen in love with the thought of owning a 427 Cobra: not the wimpy Mustang by that name but the true fire-breathing, road-hugging, original snake conceived by Carroll Shelby. I called the local Ford dealer to see if they perhaps had one of the aluminum-bodied wonders since it was, after all, Las Vegas. The salesman I talked to said yes, they did have one locked up in the back of the dealership where it could be approached only by appointment.

I reiterated the object of my search was a real 427 Cobra and the salesman assured me that it was indeed what they had. I arranged a time and called a taxi to take me to see the snake. When I arrived the salesman took me to the back of the storage area to proudly show me a Mustang sporting 427 Cobra badges. I took one look and walked out to hail another taxi.

I asked that driver if he could take me to the nearest Dodge dealer where perhaps I could find a hemi-powered Mopar. The driver took me to Henderson, Nevada, which I later learned was not the closest Dodge dealer, where I did find a hemi. The salesman at the Dodge dealer showed me a desert gold 1967 Dodge Coronet RT convertible powered by the imposing 425-horsepower, 426-cubic-inch elephant motor. He said the car was a mistaken order and they would make me a real deal. The car was supposed to be a coupe with a hardtop as the buyer intended to drag race it in super stock and he would not accept the convertible.

We quickly agreed on a price, I told the cab driver he could leave, and I drove home a couple of hours later in my new convertible. For entertainment I took the car to the Las Vegas drag strip where I collected quite a few class trophies because I had the only SS/EA in the area. Forty years later I would discover from Barrett-Jackson collectible car auctions the car was the rarest muscle car ever made as there were only two 426 Hemi-powered Dodge Coronet R/T convertibles produced in 1967 by Chrysler - too bad I sold it in 1969.

Not long after I bought the hemi my motorcycle was delivered to my quarters. F-105 school was considered temporary duty (TDY) and, as bachelors had to have some place to live, we were given rooms in the BOQ on base. I thought it extremely unfair that the married officers in our class were already drawing housing allowance at their home base and then given non-availability status at Nellis increasing their TDY pay over what the unmarried officers received. I approached the housing office several times seeking non-availability funding to live off-base but was continually denied.

Ever hopeful in spite of the negative responses to my requests, I made several trips into town to check out possible places to live and found there was apartment complex after apartment complex offering one and two bedroom apartments at dirt cheap prices, prices that were affordable even for Air Force Captains. Not only that, the apartments were chock full of single women: cocktail waitresses, show girls, dancers, blackjack dealers, bartenders, all of them absolutely gorgeous and friendly. But no, I had to share my living space with a roommate in converted World War II barracks.

Oh well, I went to work reassembling the Harley in the living room of my lavish accommodations with Byron's assistance. The chain was soaking in some warm oil on the stove and I was reattaching the engine to the frame on a make-shift lift in the living room while Byron was in the bathroom scrubbing the fenders in the tub trying to remove the salt-buildup accumulated during the ocean passage from Naha. There was a knock on the door and there stood several Air Police demanding I immediately remove the motorcycle from the inside of the quarters. Apparently the maid had reported my activities and the base fire marshal took tremendous offense at my project. I was able to get the motorcycle reassembled and out of the room before the Air Police made the return inspection they promised and I now had two ways to explore the environs of Las Vegas and Nevada.

Although there was a large percentage of the population in the United States that openly disapproved of our military involvement in Vietnam and wrongfully vented their displeasure on the troops, the people I met in Las Vegas were absolutely super in their treatment of all of us at Nellis.

I started going to a little bar called Gelo's Lounge off the strip where I soon became a regular. There were only a few folks in the bar one night and someone started buying rounds for everyone. I reciprocated and was invited to join the group. They were all employees of various casinos and I revealed I was a pilot going through Thud training at Nellis. After that, I could not buy a drink in that place no matter how often I tried: not because they would not serve me but because my drinks were always paid for by the lounge. I started feeling like a free-loader and I avoided the bar for a couple of weeks.

One afternoon I stopped in to have a Jim Beam and water and I did not see anyone in the bar I recognized. The bartender was new and accepted my money without question. We chatted amiably for a while with me carefully avoiding why I was in Las Vegas and I thought perhaps I could return to my regular patronage without feeling guilty about mooching. I was amazed when the bartender abruptly asked me if my name was Wayne. I replied that it was; the bartender immediately reached into the cash drawer, pulled out the money I had just given him and said, "I was told that if you ever came in here that you could not pay for a drink, it is on the house." I accepted my fate and continued to patronize the lounge, just not as often as I did when I could pay.

One evening I decided to go for a drive west of Las Vegas to Beatty, Nevada. It was a typical star-filled night and I spotted a small sign off the side of the main road pointing across the desert to Beatty. It looked passable, even for a car, though it was a gravel road. I decided to take that route as I could see the lights of Beatty in the distance.

The road soon turned into a very narrow gravel path that then turned into basically two ruts in which the car had to stay to maintain any traction. I crossed a couple of dry stream beds and the road seemed to be disappearing entirely although I could still see the faint outline of the ruts. I was bottoming out on the extremely rough and rocky surface and beating the tailpipes and exhaust pipes under the car to a pulp. It seemed like the last mile the road had completely disappeared but I could see the lights in Beatty were very close and I continued in my quest. I finally bounced out into a lit parking lot near a drugstore in Beatty. Two cowboys in a beat up truck asked where in the world I had come from. I told them from the main highway leading into Vegas and they could not believe it.

I decided I would take the highway back to Nellis as I could no longer even find the path I had taken to Beatty. The following day I surveyed the car for any possible damage and discovered I had to replace the dual exhaust pipes as they had been badly dented.

I took the car to Mac's Muffler shop where a huge, tattooed employee named Pete, according to his shirt, was given the task of replacing the exhaust pipes. We engaged in conversation and he learned I had been to Vietnam in the C-130 and was going back in the F-105. Pete gave me a ride back to the base as it took a couple of days for him to do the repairs. Months later, just before I was to graduate from my Thud training I was told by the squadron duty officer I had a visitor in the lobby. I went to the lobby to discover Pete who asked if I would go outside with him for a minute. I was wondering what was happening and why Pete was asking to see me as I had no contact with him after the repair work on the Dodge. When we got outside Pete handed me a small package and said to open it. I did and found a money clip with pilots' wings and Captain Wayne A. Warner engraved on it. Pete had looked at the auto registration while he was working on the car to get my name. I was absolutely speechless for a minute and Pete said he did not really know why he did it but he just wanted me to know he appreciated and admired the fact I was returning to Vietnam. I asked if I could at least give him a tour of the Thud and he said he had already seen them at air shows and static displays. Pete then said "goodbye and good luck" and vanished as quickly as he had appeared.

The owner of the Thunderbird casino showed his support for the military by throwing a party at the officers club on base for the fighter pilots at Nellis. He was a fighter pilot in WW II and knew from experience what we would be going through in combat. He provided all the food and drinks and brought with him one of his lounge shows - two lovely ladies who danced and sang for the event.

One of the dancers kept watching me and Byron was giving me a good-natured ribbing about my apparent interest but ridiculously shy reluctance to actually speak to her. She finally walked over, stood in front of me, extended her hand, and said, "Hi, my name is Fran." I was convinced from her speech that she was British and I later asked where she was from. "Nebraska" was the response. Fran explained that dancers were a dime a dozen in Las Vegas and something to set her apart from all the other girls was necessary to get a job. She said she was usually picked by the show producer saying, "Take the good looking blonde that talks with the accent."

I finally got up the courage to meet her one night at the Thunderbird where she suggested we go to Lake Mead the next weekend on my motorcycle. We went to a party on a mega-yacht with a lot of high-rollers where I felt pretty much out of place but Fran always made me feel better by enthusiastically introducing me saying with an obvious amount of admiration, "This is Wayne, he's a fighter pilot."

One of the partiers arrived by float plane and wanted to know if anyone wanted a ride. Fran was the first to volunteer the two of us and we climbed into the rear seats of the Cessna. I had no view of the instruments or controls and wondered about the experience level of our host. The answer to that unspoken question soon became apparent. The pilot applied power and we started across the lake, attaining speed as we bounced across the relatively flat and calm surface of the lake, but no lift. At least he did not have to keep the airplane on a straight and narrow runway as he meandered around the lake. After two such failed attempts and the pilot wondering aloud why the airplane would not get airborne, I asked him if the Cessna did not use flaps for takeoff. That did the trick - he put the flaps in the takeoff position and we soon became airborne.

I wondered if the landing would go any better: fortunately it did (perhaps because a float-plane always has its gear in a landing position and I gently suggested the flap setting for landing be double-checked) and we were soon safely enjoying ourselves on the yacht again. When I returned to the base late that night I had a heck of a sun-burn from riding the motorcycle to Lake Mead and back and spending all the time on the water. I saw Fran a couple of more times but not long after we met she was offered a job in Los Angeles, California and we lost touch with each other. Her desire was to be a big-time success in show business. I hope she made it.

F-105 TRAINING: THE THUNDERCHIEF

Finally, after several minor setbacks, I was in the 4520th Combat Crew Training Wing, with the 4526th Combat Crew Training Squadron Cobras, preparing to fly the F-105 Thunderchief. To my surprise one of my 18 classmates was Cecil Prentis, the assistant flight commander of my UPT basic training flight.

The Thunderchief, built by Republic Aviation of Farmingdale, New York, was a supersonic tactical fighter-bomber that was known as the biggest single-seat, single-engine combat aircraft in history. The concept for the aircraft originated during the Korean War and it first flew in 1955. It entered the Air Force inventory in 1958. Plans for the production of 1,500 aircraft were eventually cancelled in 1961 by Secretary of Defense Robert S. McNamara in favor of procuring the Navy F-4, resulting in a total buy of 833 Thunderchiefs. The F-105 was originally intended primarily for nuclear strike missions and the F-4 was considered capable of a more versatile role.

The Thunderchief was notable for its large internal bomb bay and the characteristic, swept-forward engine inlets in the wing roots. In Vietnam the bomb bay was used to carry an extra 390-gallon fuel tank and all ordnance was carried externally. The wing was highly swept, incorporated low-speed ailerons and high-speed spoilers for lateral control, and had leading-edge flaps. The Thunderchief, referred to respectfully and affectionately by its pilots as the "Thud", shouldered a tremendous burden during the Vietnam War, especially during Operation Rolling Thunder, and excelled at deadly and accurate tactical bombing.

The Thud was further characterized by two unique systems: it was the only jet fighter to refuel from a retractable side-fuselage boom, and was the first jet fighter to employ the M-61 General Electric Vulcan 20mm Gatling gun, capable of firing at the astonishing rate of 6,000 rounds per minute. Other unusual design features were the use of the four-petal speed brake on the rear of the aircraft fuselage and the cooling air inlet at the base of the vertical fin.

Navigational aids installed in the aircraft were TACAN (AN/ARN-62), Doppler (AN/APN-131), a UHF direction finder, and the R-14 radar. TACAN (tactical air navigation) provides bearing and range to a ground station while Doppler is a self-contained navigator that displays direction and distance from the present position to a selected destination by using latitude and longitude readings.

The single-seat "D" series made more air strikes against North Vietnam than any other US aircraft, and also suffered more losses. During the war, the Thud was also credited with 27 & 1/2 MiG kills. Two-seat F-105F aircraft were used in training and in combat as "Wild Weasels" where they carried an electronics warfare officer known as a "Bear" in the back seat and specialized in jamming enemy radar and destroying surface-to-air missile sites.

To judge the size of the Thud, the F-105F was the same length as the WW II B-24 and only seven feet shorter than a WW II B-17. An "F" was three feet longer than a "D" to accommodate the additional seat. Although designated a fighter aircraft, the F-105 carried a greater bomb load than either of those two heavy WW II bombers that were manned with crews of ten or eleven men.

In spite of the overall size of the airplane the wingspan of the Thud was only 34 feet making it a fast, stable aircraft at low levels while sacrificing some maneuverability and increasing turning radius. The maximum takeoff weight was 54,000 pounds and that immense mass was pushed into the air by a single Pratt and Whitney J-75 jet engine that produced 26,000 pounds of thrust with afterburner. It had a range (unrefueled) of 1,500 miles and a service ceiling of 48,000 feet. Cruise speed was 350 knots but it easily and rapidly could pass Mach One and was classified as a Mach Two aircraft.

After my last flight in the AT-33 on the 21st of April we immediately started academic classes for the Thud. Before we could actually fly the airplane we had to complete several simulator rides. The simulators in the 1960s were not nearly as advanced as present-day simulators; in fact they were little more than procedures trainers as they had no movement and very little of the instrumentation actually worked as it would in the airplane.

The instructor pilot (IP) assigned to teach me to fly the 105 was Major Warren Briggs. We did not exactly become the best of friends and I believe he was out to demonstrate that my success in the turkey shoot was an aberration as he made several comments about pure luck. Just before completion of the ride in what was to be my final simulator flight before taking to the air Warren told me to make another simulated takeoff. I applied full power and afterburner with the throttle, released brakes, and nothing happened: I saw no response from my instruments. I aborted the takeoff by pulling the throttle to idle, hitting the brakes, and said there is something wrong with the simulator.

Warren said, "What is wrong?" I repeated there must be something wrong with the simulator because it did not react to my control inputs. Warren then said, "What do you mean?" I said, "Look at the instruments; nothing happens when I advance the throttle." I then pushed the throttle up and left it there. Warren then told me to look at my standby airspeed indicator which now indicated 600 knots. He said that he failed my primary instruments and I should have checked the standby.

I was incensed and said, "Come on. I identified a problem and aborted the takeoff. Do you think, even if my primary instruments had failed, that I would not have realized the airplane was moving? I certainly would have aborted the takeoff in that situation." Warren then said he had no choice but to fail me and I angrily responded that he was not screwing with a brand new pilot. True, I was not a fighter pilot yet but I had 1,500 hours of flying time and had encountered more than my fair share of material failures and combat damage over the previous two years. We returned to the flight shack without saying anything else after I told him that what he did was pure "chickens---."

I successfully repeated the simulator ride being very careful to watch for any further cheap tricks from my IP and on 3 May 1967 I flew my first training flight in the back seat of an F-105F to acquaint myself with the actual airborne characteristics of the Thud - my next flight would be in the front seat. The 105 was not an easy aircraft to land as it had one of the highest touchdown speeds of any aircraft. The "F" touched down at 190 knots with 2,000 pounds of fuel remaining which is comparable to the space shuttle touchdown speed of 195 knots. (For each additional 2,000 pounds of weight at landing, five knots were added to the 190 knots.) Although the space shuttle lands with no power, it is greatly aided by a sophisticated computer system and multiple radars.

The Thud was definitely a power-on approach and landing airplane and that rule could be violated only with disastrous consequences. Initial approach in the traffic pattern was flown at 1,500 feet above ground level at a calibrated airspeed of 350 knots. Just at the end of the runway a 60 degree bank pulling two Gs would be initiated, bleeding off airspeed to 250 knots by using the throttle. While maintaining 250 knots and 1,500 feet the gear would be dropped, followed by full flaps. Dropping the gear and flaps caused significant trim changes for which the pilot had to compensate. Prior to turning the base leg the standby airspeed indicator and the tape speed would be compared and a 45 degree turn initiated while dropping the nose of the airplane. By varying the bank the runway could be lined up and by varying the throttle the computed final approach speed could be reached.

Flying a good final approach required very close attention to airspeed and angle of attack. The angle of attack indicator, although a very sensitive instrument, was the primary aid in establishing the correct attitude for landing. The Thud landed in a nose high attitude and sink rate was controlled by the throttle. As the aircraft approached the overrun a roundout or flare was initiated requiring slightly more throttle to counteract the increased sink rate as the nose came up. After touchdown the drag chute would be deployed when speed was below 200 knots and the nose of the aircraft held in the air to approximately 130 knots to add aerodynamic braking.

The back seat of the "F" had absolutely no forward visibility and a landing could not even be attempted from the rear seat. I will readily admit the instructor on that second ride really did put his life in the hands of a pilot that had never before landed a Thud. The aircraft was so difficult to land that the rule was you had two chances to learn how to safely place the aircraft on the ground or you would be removed from the training program. A safe landing also meant landing in front of mobile control as landing in the right spot was also critical.

On my first attempt I landed short of mobile control as I did not adequately allow for the increased sink rate as I tried to roundout. Needless to say my instructor almost appeared jubilant as he said, "That is one." The next flight I had my final approach set up and I was about to touch in front of mobile control when the throttle was abruptly shoved forward from the rear seat. I quickly grabbed for the throttle to pull it back but it was too late. I landed 1,000 feet past mobile control and Warren said, "You were going to be short again." We went into the flight shack where the flight commander greeted us wanting to know what the problem was. Warren did not say a thing and just sat there with a smirk on his face. I said, "You aren't going to say a word, are you?" I thought my dream of flying the Thunderchief was going to have a very unhappy ending.

The next day another instructor walked up to me and said, "Get your gear, we are going flying." He also said he understood I was having problems landing the aircraft. I remained silent as to the real problem I had and happily accepted the opportunity to show I could land the Thud. The new instructor told me the entire trick to a good landing was a good approach paying close attention to airspeed. We tried a few practice approaches followed by go-arounds and the moment of truth arrived: he said, "Let's land." We did, and very successfully, I may add. The next day the flight commander told me that I would no longer have a permanently assigned instructor, allegedly due to a shortage of instructors, and I would fly with whoever was available for the training flight. That was fantastic news; to my great relief, I would never again fly with Warren.

Transition to the Thunderchief began with mastering the landing. We then proceeded to do aerobatics including, aileron and barrel rolls, loops, Immelmans, clover leafs, and Cuban eights. Formation flying was a requirement on every flight and we practiced close fingertip, echelon, route, trail and tactical, including fluid four, defensive spread, and fighting wing. Fingertip is just as the name implies: the aircraft are in a formation that looks like the fingertips of your right hand when the fingers are held together. Lead is in the front with two on his left wing and three and four on the right wing. Wingtip clearance was maintained and your position was judged by visually placing the wingtip navigation light of the aircraft you were flying formation on in the middle of the star painted on his fuselage. Route formation is fingertip with spacing ranging from 75 to 150 feet between aircraft; echelon formation has all three wingmen on the same side of the lead ship and is used for entering the traffic pattern for landing. As the name also implies, trail means the wingmen follow lead in a single file dropping slightly lower than the aircraft in front to avoid the jet blast.

Formation takeoffs were used in training unless ordnance was carried. The F-105 had an exhaust pressure ratio (EPR) gauge that was used to determine if engine thrust was acceptable for takeoff. Runway temperature determined the index marker setting that was dialed in as part of the preflight check. Thrust was checked before takeoff by seeing if an indicating pointer fell within the dovetailed index marker on the circumference of the gauge.

On one of my early formation takeoffs I could tell I was overrunning the flight lead and asked him to push it up. My EPR gauge was not reaching the minimums established during preflight so I increased throttle and called "taking the lead" passing my number one on the takeoff roll. On debriefing, my instructor for the flight asked why I overran lead and I explained my assessment of the situation regarding the EPR reading. He laughed and said if lead was going to fly so was I and where formation takeoffs were concerned watch lead and not that gauge after releasing brakes. That instructor was an exchange officer from Canada and his favorite drink was scotch and milk which I discovered one evening while we were being entertained at a local piano bar.

The training course included instrument flying; ground attack including dive bomb, skip bomb, rockets, napalm, and strafe; air-to-air combat; AGM-12B air-to-ground missile firing; aerial gunnery against the towed dart target; AIM-9B air-to-air missile firing; aerial refueling; and, nuclear weapons delivery. Many of our flights took us near the infamous Area 51 but, to my knowledge, I never saw any alien activity; however, it was a fact that some of the local people living in the remote areas of Nevada (perhaps future extras for the movies, The Hills Have Eyes) would occasionally take a shot at our aircraft.

Prior to firing the AGM also known as the Bullpup, a minimum of 150 simulator runs had to be accomplished. The Bullpup was visually guided by the pilot using a flare on the back of the missile to track the weapon in flight while using a control joystick mounted on the throttle quadrant to steer it toward the target using radio signals. It was powered by a solid fuel rocket motor and carried a 250-pound warhead. I was surprised to see my Form 5 flight record actually recorded the flying time of .1 hours for guiding the Bullpup on my AGM flight on the 27th of July. On that flight I did not engage the missile joystick soon enough as the Bullpup was released from my wing and it dropped very low on its flight path. I then had to pull back almost continuously on the joystick to keep the missile from impacting the ground way short of the target and I guided the missile at a very low level above the desert to finally hit the target.

The AIM-9B was known as the Sidewinder and was a 190-pound air-to-air guided missile with a 20-pound warhead that used infrared target detection to seek out its prey. We created a target for the Sidewinder by firing a five-inch high-velocity aircraft rocket from one wing of our Thud and then shooting at that rocket with the AIM-9B that was carried and released from the other wing. The only time I ever carried napalm was on a training flight at Nellis: the canisters certainly made an impressive sight when they impacted the ground with a very large fireball. Our aerial refueling flights included both probe and drogue, where the receiver uses its probe to engage a drogue (aka basket) towed by the tanker, and boom refueling, where the tanker has a flying boom to plug into a receptacle on the receiver aircraft. On one of our refueling training flights we flew to Mountain Home Air Force Base in Idaho and then back to Nellis.

The F-105 was originally designed primarily to accomplish a radar-navigated combat mission culminating in a nuclear weapon delivery on enemy targets in darkness and under all weather conditions. That mission was the ultimate test of the pilot and aircraft functioning as a completely integrated weapon system.

To simulate actual instrument conditions the student flew the aircraft from the rear seat under a hood while the instructor acted as a visual observer from the front cockpit. Successful completion of a nuclear weapon delivery mission profile required excellent instrument flying capability coupled with use of the doppler and radar to navigate and finally use of the aircraft toss bomb computer to deliver the simulated nuclear weapon.

The doppler navigation system would automatically supply the pilot with continual position coordinates, ground speed, wind direction, distance to target, heading and other pertinent information. The monopulse radar provided all-weather terrain avoidance for pinpoint, low-level bombing missions. The simulated nuclear missions were flown at 1,600 feet at 420 knots. Navigation on these flights using the R-14 radar for terrain avoidance was very difficult and safe use of the technique required experience. The scope would display all kinds of returns including natural terrain returns such as mountains, rivers, lakes, coastlines etc.; cultural returns such as buildings, road edges, railway tracks, bridges, etc.; and weather returns such as clouds and precipitation.

To provide some level of experience in using the radar we flew seven flights in the T-39 Sabreliner. The F-105 student would occupy the right seat of the T-39 and fly the airplane using the radar for guidance while the pilot of the airplane would observe from the left seat. Those flights were quite interesting in that we would get an occasional peripheral glimpse of the mountains surrounding the valleys we would be traversing. Up and down over ridge lines we flew, continually changing the radar modes from pencil beam to spoil or wide beam to try to distinguish the features displayed on our scopes.

Due to the intense pilot workload involved with flying by radar and doppler and locating the target, the Thud was equipped with a toss bomb computer (TBC) that enabled the pilot to release the bomb at the correct angle for a toss delivery. The toss delivery was necessary to provide room for the aircraft to escape the nuclear blast. The TBC took airspeed inputs from the aircraft, altitude inputs from the aircraft static and gyroscopic systems and inputs from weapons selectors signifying the type of bomb to calculate the appropriate release point of the ordnance. Instead of triggering the release directly, the pilot engaged the TBC "consenting" to release the weapon, then began a steady climb. The computer then calculated the desired ballistic path, and when that path was produced by the current aircraft attitude and airspeed, the computer released the bomb. As should be expected, the accuracy needed to qualify for nuclear weapons certification was a little more lenient than for the delivery of a dumb bomb - so what if you are a few hundred feet off with a nuke! I have always been extremely thankful that no Thud pilot has ever had to actually fly that type of mission for real.

I flew twelve flights in the two-seat "F" before I could finally fly the single seat "D": that flight occurred on 8 June 1967. My training was proceeding very satisfactorily but was abruptly interrupted in July when I was scheduled for an "annual" flying physical. Pilots in Southeast Asia were simply too busy for annual physical exams to interfere with flying duties and I had not had such a physical for four years. I was temporarily grounded when the Air Force finally realized that I had not taken an eye exam since the spring of 1963 at the United States Air Force Academy. As I was looking at the usual "E" chart, the flight surgeon administering my physical proclaimed, "My God, you are blind. You can not fly an airplane!" He sent me downtown to Las Vegas to visit an eye specialist.

The eye doctor asked what exactly we were shooting for as far as vision was concerned and my response was, "I did not know for sure, but I certainly wanted to continue to fly." The doctor gave me a complete eye exam and once again declared that my vision was "borderline" (not quite 20-20 but not exactly requiring glasses) based on the standard alphabetical charts. He said he would write a prescription for me to satisfy the flight surgeon but that glasses would not help me at all in flying as the results of my depth perception and other eye tests were perfect. Although he stated glasses might provide some assistance in reading, he also said he doubted I would ever wear them as any small benefit from using them was outweighed by the inconvenience of putting them on and taking them off. His final suggestion was to simply carry the glasses in my g-suit pocket just in case I was ever involved in an accident.

My brief "grounding" over, I happily returned to learning to fly the Thunderchief. In actuality, vision was never a problem for me in flying as I had no difficulty in reading my instruments and I could spot a tanker or a MiG in the distance as quickly as any other member of my flight. I will confess I had some difficulty reading a small tail number at a distance but that was never any kind of a detriment to my flying abilities.

Due to the complex and unforgiving nature of the aircraft, I would fly a total of 62 training flights in the 105 compared to 10 in the C-130. One of those 62 flights was memorable for the time I spent on the ground and not in the air. A crosswind over 30 knots on the runway at Nellis required us to land at an alternate field: that alternate airfield was the commercial airport at Las Vegas, McCarran Field. On one of our training flights a thunderstorm created extreme crosswinds at Nellis. As we were low on fuel we flew into McCarran for refueling and to await calmer conditions at Nellis. I was in a "D" and was flying as number four in the flight.

We landed without incident and McCarran tower called asking us to retain our chutes so they would not have to be picked up rather than drop them after leaving the active runway as was normal procedure. As we taxied in the tower radioed taxi instructions rather than send a follow-me vehicle out to our flight. I was approaching an intersection where I knew the three aircraft in front of me had turned left but the tower called telling me to make a right turn. I questioned the directions and the tower confirmed a right turn. I turned right wondering where the tower was directing me and continued to taxi dragging my chute behind me. After a few seconds I received a frantic call from the tower saying, "Black 4, hold your position; hold your position." I braked to a halt looking around and wondering what the urgent call was for. The tower then called and said, "Black 4, drop your chute right there: do not taxi with it." I adjusted the mirrors to see the taxiway behind me and saw that I was plucking the taxiway lights out one by one with my drag chute. The chute is made of steel mesh, not fabric as many people think. I could see lots of lights, PVC pipe, and electrical wiring tangled in my chute and I pulled the handle releasing the chute and the load of broken lights on the pavement. The tower's error in having me turn right resulted in the prevailing wind carrying my chute well to the side of the taxiway. The tower then asked if I had room to make a u-turn on the taxiway and apologized for the wrong directions. As I made the u-turn I wondered if McCarran would make a claim against the government for the damage to their lighting system.

On 15 September 1967 I flew my last F-105 training flight at Nellis. I sold my motorcycle to a guy from southern California and then flew home commercially for a short visit before heading back to the Far East again. I returned to Nellis to out-process and picked up my Dodge to drive to San Francisco where I would meet Cecil Prentis at the Top of The Mark at the Mark Hopkins Hotel.

F-105 Class 68B, Nellis AFB, Nevada.
Cecil Prentis is kneeling second from the right. Byron Black is standing third from the right. I am kneeling fourth from the right. (USAF Photo)

On the trip to San Francisco I was driving the typically deserted two-lane blacktop roads in western Nevada that were major thoroughfares then when I spotted a very large spider crossing the road. I was traveling about 95 miles an hour as there were never any police around and traffic was almost non-existent. In spite of my speed that spider was still large enough to be seen. I stopped about a quarter of a mile down the road and turned around to go back and take a look. I believe the spider was waiting for me to return as he was sitting in the middle of the road staring at me as I carefully approached on foot. I have yet to see a tarantula as large as that one was. Remembering that those things can really jump and that I did not want to wrestle him out there in the desert, I cautiously retreated to my car and returned to my journey.

I arrived in San Francisco after driving a circuitous route through Reno, Tahoe and Sacramento and met Cecil at the appointed spot where I had to show my ID card to prove I was at least 21, much to the delight of my companions. Cecil and I went to an Air Force vs. Cal football game and had a good time in North Beach where we spent quite a few bucks supporting the go-go dancers, bars and restaurants in the area. I spent a couple of hours arguing with one of the hippie dancers who believed all police departments and fire departments should be disbanded because they were "the Man's" way to control the people; that hospitals were where the government conducted experiments on unknowing patients; that our schools were where the government brain-washed the population; and, that the military was a bunch of mercenaries conducting genocide all over the world. I thought, "What should I expect? This is San Francisco, California."

After a few days of playing tourist, we reported to Travis Air Force Base to catch our ride to the Philippines and jungle survival school. I placed my Dodge in long term storage by leaving it at a drop-off place at the main gate to Travis.

I was scheduled to depart on a later flight than Cecil and I inquired about space available on the flight Cecil was on. The Master Sergeant on duty told me I already had a flight scheduled and that I would be reported as a no-show if I was not on that flight. I said, "What are they going to do? Send me to Vietnam?" The Sergeant was not amused and said I would be reported to my new unit commander. I replied I doubted my new commander would be upset with my wanting to arrive early and placed my name on the space available list. Cecil and I left Travis bound for jungle survival school on the same flight.

PACAF JUNGLE SURVIVAL SCHOOL

The entrance to the Pacific Air Forces jungle survival school had a sign that arched over the gate saying, "PACAF Jungle Survival School, The College of Jungle Knowledge, Learn and Return." Many of its graduates referred to it as "snake school." The school was located at Clark Air Base on Luzon Island in the Philippines and began operation in April of 1966. During 1967 the school graduated 6,734 students. I arrived at the site in early October after departing Travis Air Force Base in California with a refueling stop in Hawaii.

The first few days were occupied with classroom activity interspersed with demonstrations of the various vile booby traps our very enterprising enemy used in the jungle. We were also introduced to the school mascot, a twelve-foot python named Charlie. Charlie was fed live chickens: when the hapless bird was placed on the ground in front of the snake it was frozen in fear and would not move, making it an easy meal.

Following the classroom instruction we were transported to the jungle training site. For our class the training site was not the usual area as mudslides caused by extremely wet weather had closed the primary location. We had about a two-hour bus ride to the alternate site where we then spent time in the jungle getting acquainted with the sights, smells, and sounds of real tropical living. The first lesson to be pounded into our memories was that to survive in the jungle for any length of time you had to figure out how to create a sleeping area that was not directly on the ground. An elevated sleeping area would keep you dryer, warmer, and protect you from the thousands of things that crept and crawled on the jungle floor.

Assisting our Air Force instructors were Philippine Negritos, the original native inhabitants of the islands. They were so-named by the Spaniards, who controlled the islands beginning during the late 1500s, because of their dark skin. In the 60s the Negritos were still a nomadic people who lived in temporary huts made of vegetation that were easily vacated when food supplies in the area became scarce. They had few social rules and lived according to their ancient customs, which was most evident by their usual attire of loin-cloths. They are fierce, independent, small-statured people who, at that time, still had an intense hatred for the Japanese from the treatment they received in WW II. One of my classmates was of Japanese ancestry and the instructors took great pains to ensure the Negritos understood that he was definitely American in spite of his appearance.

I watched with a certain amount of fascination as one of the Negritos quickly and expertly demonstrated how to fashion a splendid bed from lengths of bamboo and part of a parachute canopy which could keep us from sleeping on the ground. We were then provided some parachute panels and shroudlines and sent off to prepare our own sleeping accommodations for the evening.

I was floundering away trying unsuccessfully to match the skill of the Negrito when, to my distraction, the little guy appeared at my location and proceeded to intently watch me. I glanced at him and he smiled but I wasn't sure whether it was to encourage me or to secretly laugh at my efforts. While I was continuing to struggle a crashing and thrashing sound came from the jungle ravine to our left. The Negrito immediately alerted to the noise and intently listened. To this point he had not uttered a sound: his silence was broken when he looked at me and said, "Pig!" I looked at him trying to figure out just what his utterance meant when the same noise was repeated. The Negrito again said, "Pig!" He then smiled and headed off into the surrounding dense foliage. I returned to the task of trying to make a bed for the night. Several minutes passed during which I was quite happy I no longer had an audience watching my every move. Suddenly the bushes parted and the Negrito reappeared dragging with vines a wild pig with its throat cut. He pulled the dead pig right up to where I was standing, stood with his left foot firmly implanted on the animal, pointed proudly at it and said, "Pig!"

I am sure he must have had a great time with his fellow tribesmen explaining to them how one of his trainees had never before seen a pig and had no idea what one looked like. That evening the entire group of us enjoyed an excellent dinner of wild porker roasted over an open fire, accompanied by jungle sweet potato tops and rice cooked in bamboo tubes wrapped in vines.

We returned to Clark by bus at the conclusion of the field exercise, passing a Kentucky Fried Chicken restaurant on the narrow, winding road to the base. Colonel Sanders definitely looked out of place with his red and white store surrounded by rice paddies and water buffalo. On 18 October 1967 I completed the course at the PACAF Jungle Survival School and departed the Philippines for my ultimate destination - Takhli, Thailand. Clark Air Base was one of the largest overseas US military installations to ever exist. It began as an Army Cavalry post in 1902 and played a prominent role in WW II and Vietnam. Many of our C-130 flights from Okinawa to destinations in Vietnam and Thailand included a stop at Clark. The tremendous volcanic eruption of Mount Pinatubo in June 1991 heavily damaged the base as well as the surrounding communities, leading to its eventual closure in November 1991.

TAKHLI ROYAL THAI AIR FORCE BASE

After completing the Pacific Air Forces jungle survival school at Clark Air Base in the Philippine Islands, I immediately caught a contract flight to Bangkok and then hopped on the Thailand shuttle from Don Muang Airport, Bangkok to Takhli with orders to report to the 355th Tactical Fighter Wing. There were three squadrons in the 355th TFW; the 333rd TFS, the 354th TFS, and the 357th TFS. Each squadron had approximately 16 aircraft and 20 pilots. I arrived at Takhli on the 18th of October 1967 wondering what the future would hold for me.

I was given a temporary bunk in a "hooch" near the Officers Club. Those quarters were in an open bay, single story, wooden building with partitions dividing the bay into small cubicles. Each cubicle had a bunk bed and nothing else in it that I can recall. The upper bunk was already occupied by another brand new 105 jock so I dumped my B-4 bag on the lower bed. I did not bother to unpack. I never really got to know my new "roommate" as he was assigned to another squadron and we were both busy trying to report in and get to our new jobs, that of flying the Thud into the heat of battle.

Takhli is located approximately 130 miles north-northwest of Bangkok near the city of Nakhon Sawan. The town is tied to Bangkok by both a highway and a rail line. Takhli was known as the land of the King Cobra and the snake was prominently featured on the roofs of the hangars and the noses of the Thai F-86 aircraft when they were still stationed at the base. It was not uncommon to find a cobra sunning itself in front of our living quarters or in the dust and dirt of the open air market known as the Thai BX on the base.

KB-50 tankers flew in and out of Takhli in the early 1960s to refuel the F-100s stationed there on a rotational assignment. Mel Marvel, aka Captain Marvel, a good friend of mine and a navigator in my C-130 squadron with whom I shared several flights and even more parties, was a KB-50 navigator before coming to the 21st TCS at Naha. Mel told stories of driving up and down the runways at Takhli after dark to see how many King Cobras they could run over. There was apparently very little to do at Takhli at that time.

Takhli, along with Korat and Don Muang in Bangkok, were originally Japanese Air Force Bases during WW ll. Thailand was a Japanese ally at that time and declared war on the United States. The passage of time altered the political scene and Thailand eventually became a US ally. The earliest United States Air Force personnel to arrive at Takhli were with a detachment of F-100s from Cannon AFB in 1961. The F-100 units were rotational units that were attempting to halt the Pathet Lao from overrunning Laos. The F-100 units were moved to Da Nang Air Base in South Vietnam in 1964 and rotational units of F-105s, primarily from McConnell AFB in Kansas, Itazuke Air Base in Japan, and Kadena AB in Okinawa, replaced the F-100s in 1964 and 1965. Following the implementation of Operation Rolling Thunder in March 1965 the 355th TFW with its Thuds was permanently assigned to Takhli, moving from McConnell AFB in Kansas.

The KB-50s I mentioned earlier were hose and drogue tankers and the newer tankers, KC-97s and KC-135s, were boom-equipped. Tactical Air Command fighters had to refuel behind the KB-50s because the Strategic Air Command got all the newer boom-equipped tankers. Because the 105s initially had to refuel behind KB-50s, and eventually behind KC-97s, and KC-135s, the later models of the Thud (designated —31 production models) were produced with the capability to refuel using both the hose and drogue method and the boom. (An interesting aside: although the tankers were referred to as "hose and drogue", Thud pilots referred to that method of refueling as "probe and drogue" because of the "probe" on the Thud that had to be activated to engage the "drogue".) All the 105s at Takhli were equipped to enable either method of refueling.

By the time I arrived at Takhli, the facilities were excellent. My permanent hooch was a single story, concrete block, air-conditioned, ranch-style man-cave. It had a central living area with some comfortable couches and a small kitchen area that I never once used. The walls of our "living room" were completely covered with centerfold pull-outs from Playboy Magazines. (I had to admit, they looked a lot better than the Bunnies I remembered from the Miami Playboy Club.) There were six bedrooms, with two beds to a room, sharing three bathrooms. Hot water was always available which was fantastic when you returned from a sweat-soaked, salt-stained, dirt-encrusted mission. Although furnishings were sparse, they were quite comfortable and we had absolutely no gripes about where we lived.

The hooch was quite a distance from the Officers Club which was our primary dining facility (hence Officers Open Mess) as well as the place to obtain a "cocktail" or two when the occasion warranted (which was about every night). To solve the transportation issue on base, our squadron was given two vehicles, a stepvan and a four-door pick-up. The keys were always left in the vehicles and they were always parked at either the club or the hooch. If you wanted to go someplace you simply found the pickup or the stepvan that was left at one of those two locations and took it. Trip complete, you would then leave the vehicle and its keys in one of the two designated spots.

The dining room at the club was quite large and had a slightly raised platform at one end of the room. That platform had three large round tables on it which is where the three F-105 squadrons ate. We had consistently cheerful Thai waitresses who always took care of the same tables and got to know the pilots they waited on. For the most part the waitresses were daughters of the Thai Air Force Officers stationed on the Thai side of the base. As a result they were better educated and had some command of English which was of great benefit as our command of Thai was pretty much limited to greetings and thank-yous. The meals in the club were generally more than adequate but if we wanted a good steak or rock lobster tail we had to go to town.

The reason a trip to town for steak was needed was that all our meat was imported from the US and had been frozen for an extended period of time. Fresh milk and eggs were never to be had either but on rare occasion we could get real ice cream from the states. One day ice cream was available and I was so informed by our waitress, "Nip". It was early in the day prior to a mission and my stomach was more preoccupied with knots than with the thought of eating ice cream. Mission complete, we went to the club to eat and I remembered the ice cream. I told Nip I was ready for the ice cream and Nip responded, "No have." I figured she was kidding so I repeated my order. Nip was getting somewhat aggravated at my lack of understanding and responded more firmly, "I said, no have. Ice cream same-same soup." Thinking Nip may have been misinterpreting my request I said, "Nip, we had ice cream this morning and I know we could not be out of it this early so bring me some ice cream." Nip disappeared into the kitchen and shortly reappeared with a bowl in one hand and a spoon in the other. She marched up to the table with determination, placed the bowl firmly in front of me, handed me the spoon, and said, "See. Ice cream same-same soup: You eat!" I looked at the bowl and saw melted ice cream; it seems the freezer had quit working. My table mates howled with laughter and one of them asked what I was going to do. I laughingly replied that I was definitely going to eat, or at least drink, that ice cream.

The club had a stag bar that was almost devoid of furniture as most of the furnishings had been destroyed by various drinking games. We liked to roll for drinks, a game in which the last person to complete a somersault and rest both feet against the bar had to buy a round. We also played "carrier landing" in which the object was to see how far one could do a belly slide on a large serving tray after crushed ice had been spread on the floor. In addition to the stag bar there was a real bar with actual bar stools just off the dining area where the more civilized people would congregate. I do not recall ever using that bar.

The club had a swimming pool but I never saw anyone use it except for one occasion. An Australian USO show came through Takhli that featured a rather large female singer whose girth far exceeded her talent. She very unhappily wound up in the pool after refusing to voluntarily go swimming with a very inebriated, unnamed, member of the club. He picked her up (literally, not figuratively) and jumped into the pool with her in his grasp. Our squadron, and probably the other squadrons, had to contribute to a fund to replace her wig and dress in order to avoid an international incident.

Takhli had a small dispensary which I was fortunate enough to never visit. During my tour the flight surgeon assigned to take care of medical issues at the base was Major Richard Smith. The affable doctor was attached to our squadron and attended all of our functions. The Thai word for doctor is "Ma" and I always addressed our doctor as "Ma" Smith. During the spring, "Ma" Smith was not only busy with us but with other unique situations, many of which involved the local population as he spent countless hours tending to their needs and generating good will for the US. Thais are known for eating very spicy food and we all thought they had cast iron stomachs. The doc soon dispelled that notion when he revealed that many of his indigenous patients were being treated for stomach ulcers. He was called out of a squadron dinner one evening to attend to a fatally injured airman who had been sucked into a running jet engine on one of the EB-66s. He also had to treat a Thai farmer who had a close encounter of the wrong kind with one of the resident cobras. The farmer had been bitten on the hand, and, in a tremendous feat of self preservation, took his machete and quickly cut off his hand saving his life.

In addition to the physical care provided by our flight surgeon we also had spiritual assistance rendered by the three chaplains assigned to our wing with the Catholic chaplain being attached to our squadron. They demonstrated their support on a daily basis by taking turns standing in the arming area regardless of the time or weather, giving each aircraft a "thumbs-up" signal as we took the runway. I always thought a good word to the Guy up above coming from such a reliable source certainly never hurt.

Takhli also had a gym, so I was told, but I never saw the inside of it, nor did I know any Thud driver who did. Staying in shape and gaining weight was not something any of us were concerned with. In fact, I was reaching the point where my combined flight gear weighed about as much as I did. We had plenty of physical activity and burned up lots of calories from our daily flying routine and from the number of G-forces that we pulled in a mission.

The heat, humidity, and stress resulted in sweat and more sweat: after only a few missions our flight suits developed salt stains that could not be removed by washing. Our g-suits, more properly referred to as anti-gravity suits, were so encrusted with salt that I believed they could truly stand on their own. The maids for our quarters took care of washing our clothes and you could always see flight suits drying in the sun by our hooch. The bottom line was it was not an entirely bad way to have to fight a war - at least we had very good living conditions to return to after a mission, if we returned.

MISSION #1: COMBAT, THUD STYLE

I was assigned to the 357th TFS "Dragons." To readily identify our squadron aircraft, we had a big RU painted on the tails of our Thuds and a gold stripe painted around the nose just behind the radome. I met my new squadron commander, Lieutenant Colonel Thomas "Tom" Kirk, who had been in Class 68A at Nellis. He told me that when he saw the roster of the incoming replacement pilots he had asked for me to be in his outfit because he remembered my feat at Nellis in winning the wing turkey shoot.

As the squadron was short of pilots and the flying schedule was extremely demanding, it was necessary to get us FNGs (friggin new guys) airborne as soon as possible. I was given a local area flight on the 20th of October to reacquaint myself with flying the Thunderchief. As my last flight in an F-105 had been on the 15th of September at Nellis, over a month earlier, I knew my flying skills would be extremely rusty. The Thud was a wonderful airplane: it was also very unforgiving to the novice and the speed with which things happened in the airplane meant you had to be very proficient. I was so far "behind" the airplane during that flight that the Thud had landed while I was still thinking about the takeoff. It may not have actually been that bad but I knew I had a long way to go to be ready for the rigors of combat.

I never did meet my temporary roommate as he was killed in a non-combat loss on the 23rd while I was learning the rules of engagement and getting personnel files and other paperwork squared away. I had moved into my permanent quarters on the 24th and discovered my first combat mission was scheduled for the next day, the 25th – so much for getting used to my new surroundings before setting about the task of simply trying to stay alive while figuring out how to actually fly the 105 again instead of just hanging on for the ride.

In the beginning of Rolling Thunder operations in March 1965 the Air Force and the Navy shared time over their targets in North Vietnam. Complicating matters, in carrier operations the Navy liked to recover aircraft every hour and a half around the clock making efficient time-splitting between the two services difficult to achieve. To resolve the time-splitting issue, in the fall of 1965 North Vietnam was divided into "route packages" or "packs" which the Air Force and Navy split between them, but for some reason, pack assignments were alternated every week. To make planning and scheduling easier, in the spring of 1966 the procedure was further modified by the Navy being assigned responsibility for targets in packs two, three, four, and six bravo while the Air Force assumed responsibility for targets in packs one, five, and six alpha. A buffer zone was also established along the border with China to try to prevent aircraft penetrating Chinese airspace although at times targets were attacked within that buffer zone.

Air Force pack six missions were flown by a strike force consisting of 16 bombing Thuds. The planes flew in a "pod" formation designed to thwart SAM attacks and were accompanied by Wild Weasel Thuds, whose job was to identify and attack SAM sites. Other Air Force pack missions were flown as either a two-ship or four-ship formation.

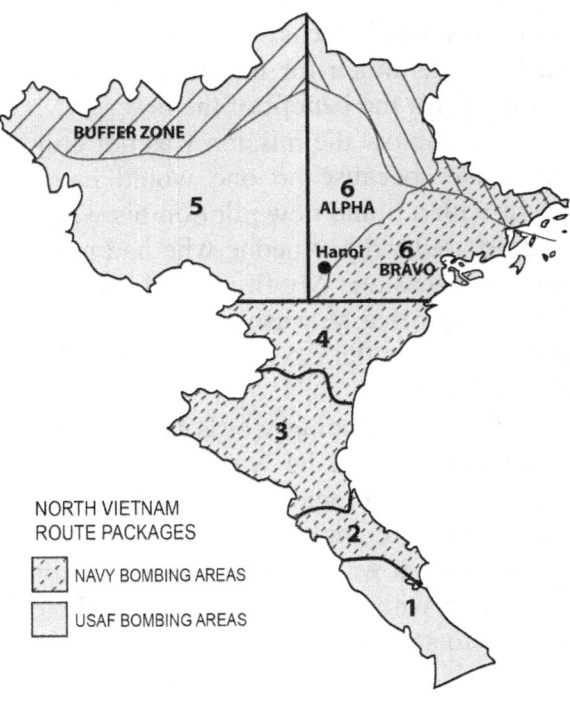

I spent a restless night, tossing and turning and thinking about the next day, wondering if I would be able to do what I was expected to do without screwing up. I thought of a million things that could go wrong but oddly enough none of my thoughts concerned being shot down. After all I had flown over Laos and route pack one many times in the Blindbat/Lamplighter mission, single ship and at night. Surely the upcoming flight would not be any worse than that.

   I reported to the flight shack for my briefing as there was no need for my flight brief to take place in the wing briefing room where the strike force was prepping for their mission. I discovered that I was going to fly my first combat trip in a two-ship with a pilot from one of our sister squadrons. He was on one of his last few flights prior to completing his 100 counters and returning to the land of the big BX.

   A counter was a mission over North Vietnam. Flights over North Vietnam were considered hazardous enough that a pilot was required to complete only 100 such flights to be given another assignment, thus the goal of every F-105 pilot was to reach that magic number of 100. The standard procedure was for Air Force pilots to fly their first 10 flights over the north in route pack one or five and then finish their tour with the last 10 flights being in the same lower-risk areas. Brand new pilots were not sent into route pack six, as much for the benefit of the pilots who had been there before as for the benefit of the new guy.

   I did know the mission was not going to be the actual 100th for my leader because no one would have flown such a momentous flight with a brand new pilot on his wing - the 100th was special, not to be shared with someone who had not yet earned the right to share such an occasion. My flight lead was none too friendly and he made it very clear that he wasn't real happy about his assignment to be my baby-sitter for the day. I do not recall whether he ever introduced himself or not.

   Without mincing words he said the last thing he needed was a lost wingman and he was going to ensure that was not going to happen: I was directed to fly on his wing in close formation for the entire mission, including the roll-in and dive pass to deliver our bomb load. It was going to be only the one pass and he expected me to be right with him the whole way. He told me that the only time he wanted to see me leave his wing was on the pitchout and spacing for landing. OK then, I knew what was expected of me and I thought, "Wonder if my entire tour will be like this." Flying down the chute at 450 to 500 knots in a 45-degree-dive delivery in close formation with live bombs was not what I expected to be doing. My formation flying skills were limited at best at this stage of my Thud career and something I had not done in well over 6 weeks.

I was quite nervous as I went to the equipment room to don my g-suit and survival vest, pick up my parachute and helmet, and walk out to the paddy wagon for the short ride to the aircraft. I managed to go through my pre-flight and get strapped into the airplane and fire up the engine. We taxied to the arming area where the arming crew scurried around our aircraft pulling the safety pins with their long red streamers from the ordnance, holding them out for us to count, while we sat in our cockpits with our hands in view of the arming crew to ensure we did not hit a switch in error. Arming complete, we then taxied onto the runway. My lead gave the signal for engine run-up, I nodded that I was ready to roll and "Lead" lit his burner and thundered down the runway. Twenty seconds later I followed and my first mission was truly underway.

This mission was flown entirely in daylight as the strike force had departed in the pre-dawn hours. Thank heavens for small favors: at least the joinup, also referred to as a rejoin, would not be in the dark. I executed a good rejoin and we silently went looking for our tanker - another thing to worry about, I thought, as I had done very well with hose and drogue refueling in training but had not done so well with refueling on a boom. That was the exact opposite of every other Thud pilot I ever talked to. I knew our tanker would be a boomer as that was by far the most prevalent method used in Southeast Asia. Worry aside; I was concentrating very hard on flying the best formation I possibly could. We rendezvoused with our refueler and Lead immediately hooked up on the boom. I watched intently, noting that the radio procedures for aerial refueling taught in training were not at all the same procedures used by Lead; in fact I soon learned that almost all refueling was done in relative silence after initial radio contact was made. Lead took on the desired amount of JP-4 and moved down and away from the boom.

I slid into position and closed on the boom to give my Thud a drink - Success, I hooked up and managed to stay in contact until I too was ready to disconnect. That little achievement bolstered my confidence and I thought, "I will be able to stay with Lead on that dive pass." We dropped away from the tanker and headed across Laos into North Vietnam and route pack one.

The target was a road cut in route pack one, we were carrying a load of six 750-pound M-117 general purpose bombs on a centerline MER (multiple ejector rack), we had two 450-gallon drop tanks on the inboard stations, and our outboard stations were empty. I was flying my close formation as I had been ordered so I had little idea of exactly where we were going (other than it was a road in route pack one) or how to get there.

Lead gave the order to "green-em-up" and I flicked on the master arm switch after flipping up the guard that prevented inadvertent arming. The term "green-em-up" originated because part of the arming sequence involved selecting the station or pylon from which ordnance would be delivered: that station was selected by depressing the appropriate station select button that would then display a green light when the master arm switch was turned on.

Lead called "burner now" and we went to afterburner, climbing and then rolling to the left. I was maintaining my wing position by doing an echelon-type turn and then we nosed over and started down, airspeed building. We were hurtling towards the ground at around 500 knots but all I saw was another 105.

Lead called "pickle now" and I pressed the pickle button. The Thud immediately felt considerably lighter, as well it should, and we pulled up and to the left. Lead again called "burner now" and we returned to military power. We eased into level flight and headed back towards Takhli. I never saw the ground; I never saw the target or bomb impact; I do not know if we were shot at or not. In fact, I did not see much at all.

We flew back to base in silence and turned on initial. Lead pitched left and I continued straight for an additional four seconds for spacing. I had not left Lead's wing until the pitch, just as he had directed. Our debriefing was just that, brief. In the paddy wagon on the way back to our equipment shack, Lead simply said, "Good job" and he disappeared to join his squadron mates at the club.

I knew that I had learned very little on that flight but at least it was the first counter; 1 down and 99 to go. I marked my bush hat or "go-to-hell" hat as we called them and thought this could be a long year. That evening in the club, the phrase "If I had 99 to go, I'd just kill myself" was repeated quite often for my benefit. No matter, I was officially a combat fighter pilot even if I was still an FNG.

Although I felt some small measure of personal satisfaction as a result of the day's events, the mood for the entire wing that evening was very somber. It had been a bad couple of days for the 355th. Two F-105s from the wing had been shot down, one on the 24th and one on the 25th, and the pilots were taken prisoner by the North Vietnamese. The F-105D Thuds of Ramon "Ray" Horinek (Ray had flown A-1s prior to going to the Thunderchief) and Richard "Gene" Smith were taken down by flak in pack six in the vicinity of Hanoi. Both would spend nearly six long years in captivity. They were released in Operation Homecoming on March 14, 1973. (As a "historical" note since I had no personal knowledge of the event at the time, Senator, and presidential candidate, John McCain was downed by a SAM on his 23rd mission in an A-4E near Hanoi and taken prisoner the following day, the 26th.) A small measure of revenge for the loss of Horinek and Smith was extracted on the 27th when Captain Gene Basel, call sign Bison 2, of the 354th TFS downed a MiG-17 with his gun on a mission to the Canal Des Rapides Bridge in Hanoi. On the 28th of October our squadron received even more bad news. The target for the day was the Paul Doumer Bridge located in the heart of Hanoi and the strike force was led by the 357th squadron commander, Tom Kirk. Tom's F-105D was hit by ground fire and he was forced to bail out, was taken prisoner and became "roommates" with John McCain in the infamous "Hanoi Hilton." Tom and John McCain were also released in Operation Homecoming.

The next day, 29 October 1967, I flew another local area checkout flight in a two-seater F-105F to reacquaint myself with that airframe. On October 30th, 31st, and on the 1st, and 2nd of November I flew four more "easy" missions to route pack one. The only memorable thing that happened during that time was due to one of my questionable personal decisions. The air conditioning system on the Thud supplied pressurized air from the engine compressor for heating, pressurizing and ventilating the cockpit. The pressurized air entered the cockpit through two tubes, or standpipes, located behind the pilot's seat. In the very humid air of the area condensation in the form of ice crystals or snow would enter the cockpit directly over the pilot's shoulders. At times the standpipes would completely freeze up with the resulting increase in pressure eventually expelling the ice forcibly into the cockpit, spraying ice shards with a very attention-getting "explosion". The temperature control panel lever manually selected cockpit temperature and ventilated the cockpit. It had six positions including a "ram" position (used during takeoff, aerial refueling, and combat) that mechanically actuated a dump valve to depressurize and allow outside air to circulate through the cockpit. On one of those early flights I decided not to switch to ram prior to making my bomb run as it got very hot in the cockpit without air conditioning and we were in pack one. That was definitely a mistake as during my dive the standpipes suddenly erupted in a loud explosion spraying those ice shards all over my neck and head. I immediately thought I had taken a flak hit. By the time I recovered my composure enough to recognize what had actually happened, I was too low to release my bombs and had to make a second pass. Although the episode was quite humorous afterwards, I can guarantee you it was not a laughable matter at the time of occurrence and I did not commit that error in judgment again.

During those flights I was also introduced to the pod formation to be used in pack six to defend against SA-2 surface-to-air missiles (SAMs). The pod formation was a box formation with a flight at each corner of the box. Each four-ship would fly line-abreast two to four aircraft widths apart. Flights would be approximately 3,000 to 6,000 feet apart. Aircraft altitudes were slightly staggered (500 feet) between and within each flight. The result was an unwieldy formation for maneuverability but it precluded the SAM radars from identifying or tracking individual aircraft.

The upcoming month of November saw the acquisition of two new friends who would "take me under their wing" and provide invaluable knowledge and encouragement in my quest to reach the magic number of 100 missions over North Vietnam: Captains Gary Olin, who graduated with the Class of 1964 at the Air Force Academy, and Cal Jewett, both former F-100 pilots who possessed true warrior skills. Gary and Cal were in the class at Nellis with Tom Kirk from which I was transferred so they arrived at Takhli a couple of months prior to my reporting to the squadron. They were cool under fire as they each possessed an abundance of courage coupled with the ability to rapidly assimilate and assess the entire combat situation and make good decisions based on that assessment. They were definitely the guys I wanted to try to emulate. Gary and "Ma" Smith were roommates and Cal was my roommate in our home away from home.

DESTINATION KEP: MIGS 'N MORE

Kep Airfield was located approximately 37 miles northeast of Hanoi on the northeast railroad that connects Hanoi to China. It was a very important transshipment point for war supplies for the North Vietnamese and a large POL (Petroleum, Oil, and Lubricant) storage area.

In 1966 the CIA identified Kep as part of a growing number of NVN air bases that could host MiG-21 fighters as well as the older MiG-17s. To counter that major threat to United States Air and Naval Forces bombing in the Hanoi-Haiphong area under Operation Rolling Thunder, Kep Airfield was placed on the list of authorized targets in April 1967. It was just as I had predicted in January 1967 following Operation Bolo. Afterwards the Air Force and Navy repeatedly bombed Kep, in addition to other bases identified as being capable of handling MiGs. The North Vietnamese reacted by dispersing some of their aircraft to Chinese bases and by greatly increasing the air defenses in the Kep area resulting in heavy losses for the attacking aircraft.

On 16 August 1967, General Momyer, Deputy Commander for Air Operations, Military Assistance Command, Vietnam, and Commander, Seventh Air Force, told a Senate committee, "We have driven the MiGs out of the sky for all practical purposes..." Those MiGs that were driven out of the sky by August certainly made a surprising reappearance a few short weeks later.

The principal aerial adversaries encountered by US forces in the sky over North Vietnam were the MiG-17 and the MiG-21. Both aircraft were single-seat Soviet fighters and presented a formidable threat to the much-larger, heavier, 50,000 pound Thunderchief in the performance of its bombing mission.

A small, stubby aircraft, the MiG-17 was 36 feet long, with a wingspan of 31 feet. It weighed 11,700 pounds and was powered by a single afterburning jet engine producing 7,500 pounds of thrust. Although its maximum speed was only in the 700 miles per hour range, it had amazing maneuverability (greatly exceeding the maneuverability of the F-105 as the Thud's high wing-loading precluded the sustained turning required in a dog-fight) and good rate of climb. It was heavily armed with a single 37mm cannon and two 23mm cannon. The flight characteristics of the MiG-17 dictated that it be used in the immediate area targeted by the Thuds and it was the 17 that engaged in the typical dog-fight scenario. The North Vietnamese received their first MiGs, 36 MiG-17s, from the USSR in February 1964 to form their first fighter squadron.

The MiG-21 was also a small aircraft with an overall length of 51 feet and a wingspan of only 23 feet. It weighed 15,650 pounds and was powered by a single afterburning jet engine producing 12,650 pounds of thrust. It could reach speeds approaching 1,400 miles per hour and was armed with a single 30mm cannon and two air-to-air missiles. The MiG-21 was designed for very short, ground-controlled intercept missions, which resulted in the type of hit-and-run tactics that it employed against its opposing forces over North Vietnam. The first MiG-21s arrived directly from the Soviet Union by ship in April 1966 and were off-loaded in Haiphong harbor before being sent to Kep and other airfields.

The North Vietnamese pilots were trained by the Soviet Union and Red China with three MiG-17 pilots and thirteen MiG-21 pilots achieving "Ace" status (destroying five or more aircraft) during the conflict. Multiple sources acknowledge 17 F-105s "killed" by MiGs during Rolling Thunder although the North Vietnamese claim several more.

On the 3rd of November 1967 I made my first trip north of the 20th parallel to pay a visit to the Hanoi-Haiphong area. It was my 6th combat mission in the Thud. Although the usual procedure was to acclimate new pilots to the rigors of combat by having them fly 10 "easy" counters in the lower route packs prior to ever sending them to pack six, I was presented the unique opportunity to see pack six up close and personal after only 5 such flights. I realized the mission was not going to be a "milk-run" as soon as the briefing officer said "Gentlemen, your target for the day is Kep Airfield" and the reaction in the briefing room was one of complete silence. There were no cheers or cries of exultation over the thought of a "real" target, only that deafening silence. The reaction was especially revealing to me as I knew the other pilots in the room had been to pack six before and they knew what to expect. That silence continued through the force briefing and into the individual flight briefing where the only voice to be heard was that of the flight lead.

We strapped on our 60 pounds of flight gear, loaded into the paddy-wagon for the short ride to our aircraft and went through the preflight, engine start and taxi to the arming area; all in an atmosphere filled with apprehension. Our loadout for that trip was six 750-pounders on the centerline, two 450-gallon drop tanks on the inboard stations, and QRC-160 pods (AN/ALQ-72) on the outboard stations. QRC was short for quick reaction capability which allegedly described the speed with which the jamming pods were developed to counter the ever-increasing SA-2 (SAM) threat.

The pre-dawn takeoff and flight across Laos was uneventful except for the fact I began the ritual of singing Tommy Roe's "Oh Sweet Pea" to myself as I sat on the tanker: a superstitious practice I would continue for the next 94 missions north. The song had no particular significance other than the fact it was the only song I could remember any of the words to at the time.

I was flying in the number 4 position of the last flight in the formation (befitting my FNG status) - my call sign was Zebra 4. As was the usual procedure for visits to the northeast section of North Vietnam, we refueled over the Gulf of Tonkin on the "Brown Anchor" tanker route. Refueling complete, the "spares" were released to go hit another target and the strike force continued its journey northward. Not long after the spares were released a Thud in the 3rd flight, Wolf flight, developed an in-flight problem and had to leave the formation accompanied by his element lead. Wolf flight was now short two aircraft which put a large "hole" in the center of the anti-SAM QRC jamming capability of the strike force. As we were headed into SAM country my flight lead told me to slide over to Wolf flight and become Wolf 3 rather than Zebra 4. I thought, "Wow, even if I do not have a wingman I am an element lead on my 6th mission as a Thud driver." I was now flying with a flight from a squadron other than my own so I had no idea who the pilots were. I am sure they would not have been overjoyed to know their new flight mate was an absolute "newbie".

The force turned inland and headed for the target area. As Wolf 3, my position was in the middle of the last two flights of the force so I was primarily looking out of the formation for any hostile activity on the left side of our inbound strike. The day was beautiful with only a smattering of puffy white cumulus clouds in sight, the sky and sea were blue and the Vietnamese countryside was emerald green. The scene was almost surreal. I thought this is not at all what I was expecting. Apparently others in the force shared my thoughts as post flight debriefings revealed that everyone had been growing concerned over the dead silence. There were no MiG calls (maybe they had left as General Momyer thought); there were no SAM calls; there was no sound but the expected and usual humming and rumbling noise emanating from the workings of my reliable Thud. It was to be the lull before the storm.

We were given the order by the force commander, Bear 1, to "green-em-up" (turn on the master arm switch) and "music on" (activate the QRC pods). We were now "hot" preparing to roll in on the enemy airfield rapidly approaching.

Up to this point the mission was unfolding according to plan and I felt that I needed to attempt to learn as much as I could in the absence of any immediate threats. Our training at Nellis had not addressed either the use of the QRC pods that were now in wide use on F-105 trips north to pack six or the use of the RHAW system (APR-25/26 Radar Homing and Warning) installed on combat Thuds.

The stick grip on the 105 incorporated multiple systems, including the trim switch, the freeze fire button also known as the "pickle button", the gun trigger, the sight electric cage/range cursor button, and nose wheel steering/range scale button. Needless to say the correct operation of all those functions with your right hand while attempting to fly the airplane in the proper formation position, watch for MiGs, SAMs and flak, operate radios, and monitor the engine instruments was a formidable task for the most experienced Thud driver. Your left hand was meanwhile occupied with the throttle, afterburner, speed brake, and mike button. The sight electric cage/range cursor button had been tied to the radar warning system and provided a "look-thru" mode to identify the immediate threat from SAMs. The RHAW gear had a cockpit display that generated strobes to identify various threats: It also generated various aural identifiers that could be heard in your headset. On this day it was strangely quiet and displayed no visual strobes.

Notwithstanding the obvious fact that there was no activity to have to "look thru", I decided to engage the system to see how it worked. That particular button was located just under the pickle button so you can probably guess which button I engaged. I immediately realized my error but to my chagrin I heard the call "Hey 3, you are dropping your bombs." The Multiple Ejector Rack attached to the fuselage had millisecond delays built into the MER to provide safe separation between the bombs as they were released and the pilot had to hold the pickle button until all six bombs were dropped. Releasing the pickle button before all bombs had separated was known as short-pickling and something to avoid. In this case I was fortunate to short-pickle in time to save three of my six 750s.

Things began to happen very rapidly from that point forward. Bear lead made a small course correction to the left and I got my first look at 85/100mm flak. The gunners had been carefully tracking our strike force and their first volley was exactly at our altitude but just a little to the right of our altered course. I was amazed at the amount of ugly brown/black clouds that suddenly erupted in the clear blue sky. We began "jinking" as we closed on our target and the flak increased in intensity. "Jinking" was making rapid, minor alterations in heading and altitude, while still maintaining your relative position within the pod formation.

As we began to pull up for our bomb delivery I spotted MiG-17s down low hugging Little Thud Ridge and tracking opposite our heading. There were two flights of four and it was apparent they were going to engage from our rear as we were preoccupied with our bomb run. I swallowed hard and mustered up my most professional fighter pilot voice; triggering the mike button on my throttle, I called out: "Bear lead, Wolf 3, we have two flights of bandits at eight o'clock, low, closing fast." I am not sure what I expected but I was impressed with the stoic response of a solitary word "Roger".

Bear lead rolled in on his bomb run immediately following his single word response. He had a lot of other things on his mind at the time other than the impending dog fight. Bison flight was right with

Bear flight headed down the chute. I had one last glimpse of the MiGs that were now climbing right behind us as I rolled into the attack with Wolf lead. I thought the MiGs would not engage as the flak guys were shooting but that did not appear to be the case; the gunners also did not stop firing until the MiGs were fully engaged. Only then did I see the flak cease or at least I was too busy looking at the MiGS to even notice any flak. As I settled into my dive run I could see the Kep runway for a split second before it was covered by thick brown/black clouds of smoke, debris, and dust as the 48 bombs from the first two flights struck their target. It was easy for me to see where to add my three 750s as all I had to do was aim for the smoke clouds.

I released my bombs accurately on the target and pulled hard to the left in a climbing turn trying to follow Wolf lead but as I was busily searching for him a MiG slid under me and positioned himself right in front of my eyes. He was concentrating on a Thud in front of him; it was probably one of either Bear flight or Bison flight as they were the first to pull away from their bomb runs. I could not believe it, my 6th mission and I was actually going to get a shot at a MiG. By this time pandemonium had broken out, the radios were overloaded with MiG warnings and sightings – a Thud driver was screaming "There is a MiG on my tail. Someone get him off." Thunderchiefs were scrambling everywhere with MiGs in hot pursuit.

I suddenly developed sensory overload, I knew my sight which was set for dive bombing was of no use in air combat but for the life of me I could not remember how to activate the air-to-air sight. In desperation I reached up and manually cranked the depression out of my sight as I knew it was of absolutely no use as it was set. I also found that I was not closing on the MiG and I was still out of gun range. I engaged the burner and tried to close but I did not think to take the time to jettison the drop tanks or bomb rack. I certainly did not want to jettison the QRC pods so I was later thankful that I did not engage the master jettison switch which would have cleaned all external stores off the airplane.

Finally my afterburner took effect, my airspeed increased, and I started to close on the MiG in front of me which was now firing at his target. Just as I was getting into range to possibly fire my Gatling gun I started to question my identification of the aircraft I was chasing; "Was it really a MiG or was it another 105?" I did not want to make such an egregious error and the thought caused me to hesitate. As I was pondering this issue, another thought crossed my already overloaded brain: "Words to the wise in aerial combat, if there is one in front of you, there is probably one behind you."

Remember, all this activity is taking place at the speed of light in a period of mass confusion and my experience level was about as low as one could get. To add to the difficulty of the situation, I was a single ship at this point as I had no wingman to watch my tail. I rolled my right wing up, kicked the left rudder hard to skid the Thud in order to get a better view of my six o'clock area. Sure enough, I was treated to the frightening sight of not one, but two MiG-17s behind me and closing fast. To make matters worse, they were already in firing position as they were well inside my turn and had a "lead" on me.

When you see an enemy aircraft behind you the first thing you assess is whether or not he is inside your turn: if you can see the top of the attacking aircraft you know he is not able to bring his guns to bear and he will be firing behind you. On the other hand, if you can see the belly of that aircraft that means he is leading you and has a good shot at you. To my great consternation all I could see was the bellies of the two MiGs. They were in a tight turn, closing with the wingman in a fine "fighting-wing" formation. I am sure the MiG pilots did not expect the sudden skid by me with the resultant small loss in airspeed and luckily they would overshoot as they fired.

I rolled back to the right, centering my rudder, and fired a quick burst at the MiG in front of me with little hope of doing anything other than perhaps diverting his attention from his intended prey. That worked as the MiG broke off his attack and broke hard right. I immediately saw tracers just slightly to the left and above my canopy and trailing off in front of me. My pursuers had caught me and I was still in dire straits. I could not break left as that would have taken me directly into their line of fire so I rolled hard right and down, following the MiG in front of me. Although not wanting to get into a "turning" fight with my pursuers, I reversed my turn hard left in a climb in a scissors maneuver to try and position the trailing MiGs in front of me.

To my surprise, I could not see either of the two that had been chasing me and with my hard left turn I had lost sight of the one I had been chasing. The trailing MiGs had apparently rolled right to follow my initial break, overshot, and then not followed my left turn. In the meantime I could still hear panicked radio calls of "I need help; there's a MiG on my tail." Very unsympathetically I thought to myself, "Big deal, doesn't everybody have one?" I rolled back to the right and leveled off, cutting off the afterburner to conserve fuel as it was rapidly being depleted.

To my utter amazement at the same time I was rolling right and leveling, a single MiG was rolling left and leveling in almost a perfect side-by-side formation with me. We were approximately 100 feet apart with identical airspeeds. For an instant time froze - The MiG pilot and I looked at each other and I could see his leather flying helmet and goggles as we each tried to figure out our next move. I knew what mine was going to be as a 105 could easily outrun the MiG-17. I lit the burner again and sprinted for the coastline joining the widespread, disorganized gaggle of Thuds as they departed the area. The MiG rolled right in a descending turn and headed for his home.

My dogfight was over and thankfully the Gulf was not far ahead. Radio chatter was decidedly quieter and I heard Wolf lead calling "Wolf 3, where are you?" He said he was doing an aileron roll so I could identify him. I spotted my flight lead about a mile to my right and slightly above me and I quickly joined on his wing. We then looked each other over for any battle damage and to our relief there was none on either aircraft.

This was my first encounter with MiGs but it would not be my last. It would, however, be the only chance I had during my tour to be on a MiG's tail rather than the other way around. The good news is the fight ended in a "draw": not nearly as good as a "win", but decidedly better than a "loss".

As we hooked up with the tankers for the post-strike refueling, I noticed some of the force had indeed dropped their tanks and were taking some good natured ribbing for it on the radio. My arms and hands were aching from the death grip I had on my throttle and stick and my flight suit and g-suit were wringing wet with sweat. I had to remove my oxygen mask as I was feeling very claustrophobic at that instant and suffered from some stress-induced dry heaves. The inflight refueling was actually a chance to clear my mind, compose myself, and practice "Oh Sweet Pea" again. The 800-mile flight from Kep back across South Vietnam, Laos, and Thailand was uneventful and we landed at home with no losses and a successful attack as the runway was severely damaged, at least for a couple of days until the North Vietnamese repaired it.

The mood on arrival at Takhli was very different from the mood at departure that morning. Everyone was still charged with adrenaline and excitedly all talking at once, comparing notes and exchanging their individual harrowing tales. In spite of my gaffe with the premature release of part of my bomb load, I felt I had in fact acquitted myself quite well under the circumstances regardless of my lack of experience. I was tremendously fired-up as I had finally faced the dreaded pack six and lived to tell about it: not only that, I had actually been in a real dogfight with our adversaries and had my own tale of a true life-or-death adventure. I had a newfound belief that I would, in fact, become a true hard-nosed, seemingly fearless, fighter pilot in the tradition of my more experienced comrades in arms. At any rate, it was a counter - 6 down and 94 to go.

16
FOUL-UPS, SAMS, & RIVER RATS

My new-found feeling of confidence in being ready to competently fulfill my role as a Thud driver did not last long after returning from the Kep strike. On the next day I flew a mission on James E. "Jim" Light's wing: Jim was the 357th squadron operations officer and chief of the Combat Analysis Branch for the 355th TFW. He was a very experienced fighter pilot long before he came to Takhli - a serious, no-nonsense type of individual who completed his 100 missions in March of 1968 and eventually rose to the rank of Lieutenant General in the United States Air Force.

On my flight as Jim's wingman, I definitely overcompensated for the mistake I made at Kep with the release of my bombs. This time, instead of hitting the pickle button at the wrong time, I failed to engage it at all resulting in my embarrassing arrival at the post-strike tanker with my bombs still on the airplane. I must have depressed the sight electric cage button instead of the pickle button as I know I pushed something.

The decision was made to return to Takhli and I was told by Jim I could elect to jettison my 750s on the jettison range or I could land with them. I was apprehensive about landing with the ordnance and elected to jettison the bombs. I could tell that was not what Jim really wanted me to do as he added there was no problem with landing with them still on the centerline. We arrived at the jettison area and I approached the bomb run with a lot of trepidation as the range procedures there called for a 20 degree dive delivery.

I was not absolutely comfortable with the sight setting for that delivery technique and worried about releasing ordnance over friendly territory. I rolled in, started my run, and realized I had not engaged the master arm switch: dry run, so I had to go around again. Of course Jim wanted to know what was wrong and I sank even lower into my state of utter shame and embarrassment when I had to admit my second serious error of the day. By this time I was absolutely stressed out, I rolled in on another pass and finally managed to release the load. I watched as the bombs fell away, getting closer and closer to the end of the range and I thought "please, please do not let them be long and overshoot." I could see my career in the 357th coming to an abrupt end.

Thank heavens the bombs finally impacted the ground within the confines of the jettison area. We returned to Takhli and Jim succinctly advised, "That is what checklists are for." He also observed that the release was quite close to the end of the range. I was definitely not in a celebratory mood that evening and pretty much hid in my room. I was determined that the day's events would never again be repeated.

I had very little time to sulk as I was on the schedule for the following day, the 5th of November; it was to be another pack six mission and the target would be Phuc Yen airfield near Hanoi. Once again that same feeling of dread filled the pilots briefing room as the target was announced. The force got airborne and we headed for our tankers. Suddenly my element lead called me and said, "4, you have a panel loose on the top of your airplane." Sure enough, someone had failed to fasten an access panel on the ridgeback of my Thud.

As it was located on the very top of the airplane there was no way anyone could spot it. It was certainly not within the sight range of my preflight inspection and no one in the revetment or at the arming area noticed it. The flight lead called and told me to go home; he said there is nothing you can do and there is no way you should be going on a combat mission, especially to pack six, potentially shedding parts of your airplane. I departed the formation and one of the spares took my place.

It was getting daylight by the time I reached the airfield. I took a little extra time to burn some of my heavy fuel load off and then prepared to land. I recalled the embarrassing events of the preceding day at the jettison range and decided that landing with my bombs was preferable to a possible repeat of those events. Furthermore, arriving at the base with my bomb load still intact was self-explanatory as the abort occurred early in the mission and prior to ever reaching the assigned target. The landing was uneventful and I taxied into the area to de-arm and then returned to the designated revetment.

I was probably fortunate that day as it would turn out to be another bad one for the squadron and the wing. Bill "Sparky" Sparks, Marlin lead, the force commander and a 357th comrade, was shot up by flak on his run. Fortunately he managed to fly his burning Thud back to the vicinity of the Red River, just far enough away from Hanoi to have a rescue attempted. An F-105F from the 333rd, with Dick Dutton and Earl Cobiel aboard, was also brought down by flak. Two F-4s were also lost in the raid. Dutton and Cobiel were captured as were the F-4 crews. Dick Dutton and three of the F-4 crewmen were repatriated on the 14th of March 1973 and Earl Cobiel died from continued beatings in captivity. Sparky was the only one out of seven airmen on the ground that day who was rescued by the Jolly Greens and Sandys. That would have been Sparky's 146th mission in the Thud - he had over 50 in route pack six, most of them as a Wild Weasel pilot. He was flying the "D" as strike lead because our squadron needed at least two qualified force commanders and we had just lost Tom Kirk, leaving only Neely Johnson to fill that role.

Sparky's tour was over: the decision was made by the Air Force that he would not be allowed to continue in his quest for 200 F-105 missions. We did greet Sparky late that evening when the base Gooney Bird (C-47) brought him home from Nakhon Phanom where the Jolly Green had taken him.

I continued flying pack six missions and flew on the 6th to hit the Gia Thuong storage facility near the center of Hanoi, and on the 7th to strike the Lang Gia rail yard northeast of Kep. I also flew on the 8th and 9th but do not recall the exact targets.

It was time to take a break and I headed off for Bangkok for a short R&R trip. As had been my practice in my C-130 days, I stayed at the Federal Hotel where I ran into a C-130 crew from the 21st TCS. Enough time had passed that none of us knew each other and the reunion of sorts did not last very long. At the hotel pool I did meet a really cute American girl who was also staying there - turns out she was with a USO show that had been touring Southeast Asia to entertain the troops. Her name was Mary Ann and she was a school teacher from Kansas. The theme of her song and dance show was to have some regular girl-next-door types for the guys to see and talk to.

She was with two other girls and a tall, arrogant, self-important guy whom I took an immediate dislike to. I noticed the girls addressed the guy as "Tarzan" when they talked to him. Out of curiosity I asked Mary Ann why they did so. She had a confused look on her face and said, "Why, because he is." My turn for confusion and my face must have betrayed that fact. Mary Ann laughed and asked how long it had been since I had watched television. I responded it had been several years except for the Japanese-speaking television Rocky and I had bought on Okinawa. Mary Ann then informed me the guy at the pool played Tarzan in a 1966 television series.

Later, as I was getting ready to go eat dinner at one of my favorite restaurants in Bangkok, my room telephone rang and Mary Ann asked if I wanted to go to dine with her and her USO group. I asked if "Tarzan" was also going and her response was in the affirmative. I weighed all the alternatives and the possibilities of ever seeing Mary Ann again and I decided that slim chance was not worth putting up with "Tarzan" for an entire evening. I politely declined even though I subsequently dined alone. A day later I returned to base from Bangkok, rested and ready to resume my journey to the 100 mark.

Adjusting to flying again after the few days off, I flew another counter on the 16th with no memorable circumstances or results. On the following day, the 17th, I was assigned duty in mobile control, a small trailer at the end of the runway where we could take a last look at the departing and arriving aircraft for safety purposes: checking for arming flags, proper position of gear, flaps, etc. On that day Ed Cappelli of the 354th was taken down over Bac Mai by a SAM and listed as KIA.

Gene "G.I." Basel, who was in the 354th with Cappelli, relates in his book "PAK SIX" that he, Tom Kirk, Gary Olin, and Ed Cappelli were in the same F-100 unit together before they went to Nellis to check out in the Thud. Of the close-knit group in G.I.'s circle (including Gene Smith) only Gary Olin, who provided priceless assistance to me, would complete his tour of duty unscathed, with 100 missions marked on his bush hat. The foreword to "PAK SIX" was written by Colonel Lawrence "Larry" Pickett, Vice Commander of the 355th TFW. When I read "PAK SIX" it was déjà vu all over again; I was not that surprised to recall some eerily similar episodes in my own tour. I would fly with Colonel Pickett later in the year when I had become one of the "old heads".

I was in action again on the 19th. It would be my 12th combat mission in the F-105. The target for the day was a concrete products plant on the outskirts of Hanoi. The SAM activity that day was unusually heavy; I suppose the North Vietnamese had received a new, very large shipment from their Soviet comrades.

As was my usual position I was on the wing as either 2 or 4, probably 4 as that seemed to be my permanent call sign. Hanoi is 480 miles from Takhli as the crow flies but, of course, we did not fly like a crow and our route was closer to 700 miles. We approached from the northwest, coming down Thud Ridge (named after the large number of mauled and burning F-105s that ended their careers on the prominent landmark after suffering critical battle damage in the Red River Valley) and emerging into the flatlands around Hanoi. The RHAW gear was operating overtime and the strobes filled the scope with absolutely no indication as to where the greatest threat was. The headset noise generated by the system was so intense I just turned it off. The bottom line was, there was no mechanical or electronic substitute for 20 sets of eyeballs and the competence, professionalism, and courage of your fellow Thud drivers to get you home safely.

As the strike force entered the flatlands the first SAM calls started. The Weasels were hard at work but there were simply too many sites to cover. We were in afterburner, increasing speed and starting our climb from around 10,000 feet to our roll-in altitude of around 15,000 feet when the barrage of SAMs started. The sky was literally filled with flak and SAMs. I thought it was like flying upside down in a rainstorm of red, punctuated with the orange flashes of uncountable explosions followed by the dirty brown/black clouds that were the result of those detonations. Add to that the numerous SAM trails that were streaking up and through the weaving and bobbing strike force formation. SAMs did succeed in downing two Thuds that day; they were from the 388th based at Korat.

The trick to evading a SAM depended first on maintaining the proper pod formation to enable the QRC-160 jamming system to work: This would preclude the acquisition radars from finding you and the tracking radars from then following you.

It was actually possible to spot the SAMs being fired and leaving their launchers if you were looking in the right place at that instant. Once airborne the SAMs and their flaming exhaust trail were large enough to keep track of visually. Pilots would then call out the threat as it converged on the force. The way to tell if a SAM was on a collision course with you would be to watch for movement across your canopy: If the SAM was moving relative to the first sight of it on your canopy then it was not going to hit you. On the other hand, if it stayed on the same spot where you first saw it and it just kept getting bigger, you knew you were in deep trouble. I saw multiple SAMs seemingly targeting others in the force and sure enough I spotted several coming at me from my left side.

Radio calls were coming fast and frequent and the strike channel was flooded with SAM calls. Gary Olin called me blurting out, "Watch it, Wayne!" As he later related he knew he did not have time to say, "You have three at ten o'clock, two at two o'clock, and one at twelve o'clock." His call did warn me of the SAM that really had my name on it, and I knew it was closing fast. I could see the SAM just above my canopy rail on the leading edge of my canopy: It just seemed to be glued in that position. I elected to climb a little faster than just trying to keep up with the force for the roll in. The SAM's relative position on my canopy didn't budge and I could start to see the guidance canards. I went to max burner and yanked the stick aft turning slightly left to keep the SAM in sight. At the last moment, just before I expected the impact, the SAM dipped just slightly in its path and slid under me missing me by inches it seemed. I looked to my right to see the burning exhaust from the SAM just above my Thud and then watched as the SAM detonated in a brilliant flash. The proximity fuze in its warhead did not function until it was too late and the shrapnel and explosive concussion traveled away from my airplane.

I pushed the stick forward to get back into my position in the pod formation just as the force started its bomb run. I had no time to stress over the narrow escape as I now had the target in sight and was concentrating on the proper release. The strike camera recorded the accuracy of my delivery, right on target, and much to my relief after the fiasco with Jim Light. Adding to all the confusion of the day were numerous MiG warnings but I have to confess, I did not see any MiGs: the SAMs (more than 30 were launched at us that day) definitely occupied most of my attention. In the end it was an unexpected, but welcome, surprise when I received a Distinguished Flying Cross for the raid on the concrete products plant - that was the second of my four DFCs and my first as a fighter pilot.

Colonel Pickett Presenting the DFC (USAF Photo)

On one of the flights heading into route pack six during the month of November I was flying on Neely Johnson's wing. Neely was another ultimate fighter pilot, a strike force commander possessing experience and knowledge essential to survival in pack six, knowledge he had the ability and desire to impart to others.

We started getting MiG warnings from Ethan, an EC-121 AWACS (airborne warning and control system) aircraft that would orbit in northern Laos searching for MiG flights on its radars. The relative position of any MiGs located would then be relayed to aircraft that could be attacked by those MiGs. The EC-121s were originally designed to warn North America of the approach of Soviet nuclear bombers but were modified to provide service in Vietnam.

We were still over Laos inbound to pack six in a loose route formation, escorted by a flight of F-4s providing MiGcap. The F-4s were using one of their usual automotive call signs, Buick flight. Buick was split into two elements with one element on each side of the two rear F-105 flights. They were positioned just about even with, but slightly higher than, the Thuds. Neely was flight lead for the rear flight on the right side of the formation next to Buick 3 and 4. I was on his right wing closest to Buick 3.

Ethan called, "Buick, you have black bandits at six o'clock, 18 miles, your altitude, closing." Buick lead said, "Roger". (Black bandits were MiG-21s) Seconds passed and Ethan again called Buick saying, "Bandits are at your six at 12 miles." I was intently watching this entire episode unfold wondering when someone, especially Buick, would give some indication they were getting ready to meet the incoming threat. It was painfully obvious to me that the MiGs were not out for a joy ride. Ethan again called with a noticeable sense of urgency, "Buick 3, bandits are your six, 3 miles and closing fast." Buick 3 then responded as had Buick lead with a single word, "Roger". I was busy watching my formation flying and trying to spot the MiGs that were now very close to not only Buick 3 but to our flight. Finally Ethan in desperation said, "Buick 3: bandits, bandits, bandits." I had twisted in my seat as far as I could trying to acquire the MiGs when I spotted the 21s just as they launched their Atoll air-to-air missiles, one of which disappeared into the rear end of Buick 3 with a sickening explosion. It happened so fast that no one in our flight had the chance to yell for Buick to break. Buick 3 meanwhile had not made the slightest move to evade the attack and was still in straight and level flight when the missile impacted. Buick 3 then transmitted, "I'm hit." The MiGs flashed up and to the right past Buick 3 and 4.

I could not figure out why the MiGs had selected the Phantoms rather than us Thuds as we were in a much more rigid formation and represented little offensive air threat to our adversaries. Furthermore the primary reason the MiGs used the tactics they did was to force the 105s to jettison their bomb load which immediately made the intended mission a failure.

Neely immediately took action. He told me to roll in with him and drop my bombs on a road that was almost directly under us. Rapidly arming my bombs and rolling in with Neely, we both dropped our 750s on the road below.

Pulling off our unexpected bomb run, I could see two parachutes open: The crew made it out of the fatally crippled Phantom as the airplane itself went into a flat spin with the tail section gone. The MiGs disappeared into the distance but there was no guarantee they were gone for good. We started an orbit around the F-4 crew as they floated towards the ground. One of the crewmen drifted towards a village and was surrounded by hostiles at once. The other crewman managed to steer his chute towards a ridgeline to get some separation from the village.

Neely was on the radio calling Crown, the C-130 rescue command and control bird, providing coordinates of the bailout and the conditions on the ground. Meanwhile the remainder of the strike force continued on their mission with the spares filling in for Neely and me. Prior to takeoff Neely had briefed me on search and rescue missions explaining that one element would go low to locate the survivors and provide necessary cover fire while the other element would go high to provide cover for the low element and to get a better overall view of the situation. As we were only two aircraft, I incorrectly thought I should go high and did so. Minutes later Neely called wanting to know where I was as he thought I had gotten lost. I told him I was above and slightly in trail and that I had him in sight. He told me to get back on his wing which I immediately did and we continued to orbit the area.

We were over the village long enough waiting for the Sandys and Jolly Greens that the strike force had completed their attack and was now coming back through the same area. The spares had assumed our call signs when they filled in for us creating even more confusion. I radioed I had reached bingo fuel meaning I had just enough to return to base if no difficulties were encountered. There was no response from Neely as he was really busy and may have thought the call came from the spare. I thought, "Well, maybe all I need is enough to just get to the tanker." Minutes later, I called below bingo as I was starting to grow apprehensive over my fuel status and still did not get a response. Finally, in desperation I said over the UHF that I was flat running out of fuel. Neely realized it was indeed his wingman calling and reacted quickly to my plight, immediately escorting me towards the tankers and telling me to jettison my MER and empty tanks to conserve what precious little fuel I had left.

The tanker headed north to meet me and I spotted him in the distance. My fuel gauge was reading 600 pounds, down to a level that was definitely not considered accurate, and I prayed that I would make a good hook-up on the boom. I drove straight up to the tanker:

the boomer had the boom run out to its maximum length and I grabbed it on my first attempt, pushing it up almost to its minimum limit before I slowed my closure rate enough to exactly match the tanker airspeed. Having successfully refueled, we dropped off the tanker and headed for home minus my rack and tanks as well as my bombs. No counter, but I learned a lot, thanks to Neely.

I flew missions on the 20th, 24th, and 27th to round out the month of November: I had now completed 16 missions, 84 to go. On the last day of the month, a Red River Rats convention was held at Takhli, hosted by the 355th Commander, Colonel John C. Giraudo, aka the Big Kahuna. (Red River Rats are aircrew members who have flown missions crossing the Red River Valley in North Vietnam.) The name of the River Rats Association has varied somewhat over time but the foreword to the 1967 River Rats song book states: "The 355th Tactical Fighter Wing takes great pleasure in dedicating this songbook to the Red River Rats Association members present, and to those who, unfortunately, cannot be with us tonight. We at Takhli have strived to make this 30 November conference a memorable one and invite you to enjoy yourselves. WELCOME." Although the convention featured a parade with floats as well as a memorable party at the club, the convention also served the purpose of allowing the many units that had to coordinate route pack six attacks to exchange ideas on how to do that more efficiently and safely.

As to the songbook, I still have it although I do not share it with many people due to the bawdy and irreverent nature of the songs contained therein. Singing was a way for us to relieve our stress and we entertained ourselves quite frequently in that manner. We may not have been good but we were loud and enthusiastic and political correctness was not even in our vocabulary at the time. Our favorites in the 357th included such memorable ditties as: We're the Boys of the 57th; Sally in the Alley; Good Ship Titanic; I Love My Wife (which I was not allowed to sing being single, and I substituted the word "your" for "my"); Red River Valley; Republic's Ultra Hog; Adeline Schmidt; and, Mary Anne Burns. It is pretty easy to see the primary themes involved. Another favorite which was used to indoctrinate the FNGs was Hail Britannia. The first verse goes "Hail Britannia, marmalade and jam, three French crackers up your asshole, blam, blam, blam." The FNG was given the first verse and then instructed to join the remainder of the group and to sing at the top of his voice repeating the verse three times counting down from three crackers to two to one. If he screwed up, he would be expected to buy a round. What the FNG did not know was, in singing the second verse, the word "blam" would only be repeated twice, representing two crackers instead of three, and he would be the only person yelling the third blam at the top of his voice. It always worked.

AIR ABORT & THE DOUMER BRIDGE

We had a new squadron commander, Lieutenant Colonel Parks M. Rea, to replace Tom Kirk. Parks was transferred to Takhli from commanding an F-105 squadron in Europe. He was another excellent commander even though he was rather quiet; he had the demeanor and appearance of a college professor and was a welcome addition to lead our squadron family.

I was given a few days off again and I decided to visit Okinawa, my former place of residence. I hopped a ride with a C-130 that was returning to Naha from Takhli: I even managed to log some more C-130 time on my Form 5. Upon arrival on Okinawa, I checked in to the VOQ (visiting officers quarters) and walked over to the 21st TCS operations and scheduling office. I recognized only a couple of names on the scheduling and roster board and the guys I did know were away from the base flying. I basically fooled around on the island for a couple of days visiting my former haunts and made it a point to "ring the bell" in the officers club bar. That bar had an outside entrance and it was very easy to walk in and forget to remove your hat. Such a grievous breach of etiquette could result in the necessity to buy a round for everyone in the bar if someone else rang the bell before you could remove your headgear. I successfully avoided that lapse in judgment while a C-130 pilot but I decided it was worth ringing the bell myself just so I could wear my new-found badge of courage, my "go-to-hell" hat with its precious markings, whilst drinking with my fellow boys in blue.

I caught a ride from Naha with a Blindbat/Lamplighter crew that was returning to Ubon where I rang the bell in the bar belonging to the 8th TFW, and still the home of F-4 Phantoms. Thank heavens drinks were ridiculously inexpensive in the officers clubs and I caught the Phantom Flyers during the day at lunch when almost all of them were airborne. After lunch I jumped on the Thailand shuttle and arrived back at Takhli ready to go flying and fighting again.

I had the one air abort during the month of November and the same misfortune struck again in the month of December. No one wanted to gain the reputation of being the guy who turned back from a mission on the flimsiest of excuses. That was not to be my fate as I had only two air aborts during my entire tour and both were absolutely justifiable. On the first abort, as already described, I was told to go home and the second abort was based on even more critical circumstances.

It was a pre-dawn takeoff with two 3,000-pounders for the bomb load. Just as I was airborne and reaching for the gear handle and flap handle, the master caution light, situated at eye level on the main instrument panel, suddenly illuminated, almost blinding me in the darkness. It had been triggered by the ATM (Air Turbine Motor) air line overheat caution light. The overheat condition was caused by a leak in the ATM hot air line that could have resulted in more serious damage, including fire, to the airplane and its equipment.

The emergency procedures required me to immediately trade airspeed for altitude and to shut down the ATM. The ATM provided power for the AC generator and the utility hydraulic system pump. Loss of the ATM meant I would have to land without leading edge flaps, speed brakes, nose wheel steering, normal brakes, and anti-skid. With AC power failure I also lost my transponder and fuel pumps and had to depend on gravity fuel feed. I gained altitude, getting gear and flaps retracted, and shut off the ATM. I notified my flight lead of my predicament and said I was done for the day. The other Thuds departed the area for the mission and I prepared for a rather hazardous landing.

As my transponder was inoperative the ground control approach radar could not acquire my aircraft. Additionally, the radar could not adequately skin-paint me because of the camouflage paint on the airplane so a GCA (Ground Controlled Approach, using radar assistance for heading and glide-path) was out of consideration. I could not risk trying to jettison the bombs on the jettison range because it was dark and I could not find it. I was forced, with little other choice, to get on the ground as soon as possible even if I had to land with my ordnance and a lot of fuel. I watched to see if the ATM warning light went out, which it did, and I reset the master caution light to get the glare out of my eyes. Although I would have liked to, emergency procedures for the situation prohibited turning the ATM switch back on. I dropped the gear, yawing and pulling positive Gs to ensure the gear was down and locked while still being mindful of the fuel feed issue - the indicators showed three in the green.

I moved the flap lever to the landing and takeoff position and thought to myself, "Please make this a soft touch as I can not afford to blow a tire." I rolled out on final carrying a tremendous increase in final approach speed, around 225 knots and well over the usual 180 knots required in a normal landing for the "D", to compensate for the extremely heavy weight of the airplane and the loss of the leading edge flaps.

I gingerly approached the touchdown, easing the stick aft to slightly flare the Thud and, much to my chagrin, the 3,000-pounders and the nearly full drop tanks had dramatically moved the center of gravity of the airplane aft. The nose pitched up, the sink rate rapidly increased, and I immediately applied power and eased the stick forward - too late, I smacked the runway much harder than I had hoped. Miraculously the tires held and I used aerodynamic braking to slow my Thud until I saw the airspeed dropping to 200 knots where it was safe to deploy the drag chute.

Emergency braking was limited to one application once you started pressing the brake pedals and without nose wheel steering I had to rely on very equal braking to keep the airplane on the runway. My final step was to stopcock the throttle and set the emergency brake. I had informed the tower of my situation and figured the tower officer, who was supposed to have pulled out the F-105 Dash-1 containing the emergency procedures to assist as needed, would know I would be stopping on the runway and shutting the engine down. As my radios were dying and I was sitting in the dark, I heard one last fading transmission from the tower, "Shark 4, will you be requiring further assistance?" I patiently waited for the tug to tow me to the hot brake area where my tires were intentionally spiked to prevent a tire explosion.

During the winter northeast monsoon from November to March, the weather over most of North Vietnam was very poor which resulted in many strike cancellations. The weather was characterized by dense clouds, and heavy rainfall, with low ceilings, fog, and continuous drizzle between the periods of heavy rain.

We had a week of uncharacteristically clear weather in the Hanoi area from around the 14th to the 19th. As a result, I found I was going to hit the Doumer Bridge on the 14th: "Downtown, where all the lights are bright and everything is waiting for you." (Everyone associated with the Thunderchief mission in North Vietnam knows of the Petula Clark song that soon became associated with trips to Hanoi.) It would be number 20 for me if I managed to get through it. The Paul Doumer Bridge crossed the Red River in the middle of Hanoi. It was the only bridge over the Red at the time and carried both rail and road traffic. It was named after the French engineer who designed it near the turn of the century but the Vietnamese knew it as the Long Bien Bridge. It was a cantilever bridge with 14 spans, about a mile long but only about 38 feet wide. Of all the targets in North Vietnam, the Doumer Bridge is perhaps the most iconic and plays a prominent role in the history of the war, both from the American point of view (especially Thud drivers) and the North Vietnamese point of view. The bridge has been immortalized by North Vietnam as representative of their struggles, sacrifices, and ultimate success in forcing the withdrawal of the American Forces from the conflict.

We had our usual "O'-dark-thirty" briefing and pre-dawn takeoff. A refueling over Thailand and Laos was accomplished with no problems. For bridge strikes, 3,000-pounders nicknamed "Baby Hueys" were slung under the inboard pylons. The proper designation for the weapon was the M-118 General Purpose Bomb. Baby Hueys were an awesome weapon: they exploded with a huge bright orange fireball followed by a small mushroom cloud. The highly visible shock wave from the explosion would radiate outward from the center of the blast leveling everything in its path. The only aircraft in the Air Force inventory capable of carrying the 3,000-pound bomb were the Thud (which could carry three if no external fuel tanks were carried) and the A-1 (which could carry one on its centerline).

Hauling our Baby Hueys, we took the Thud Ridge route into the Hanoi area and the force commander headed for the southern bank of the Red River to establish a left roll in on the bridge. The MiG calls were frequent but they stayed clear of us as the SAM launches were numerous and 85/100 mm flak was extremely heavy.

I was in my customary position as number four but I was finally starting to be aware of all my surroundings. I easily recognized the terrain navigational aids such as the big bend in the Red and of course Thud Ridge. I was starting to be able to pick out flak sites and SAM sites as we overflew them and it was no sweat maintaining my proper formation position.

As we turned into our final approach from the southwest I felt that we had traveled slightly farther from the bridge than was desirable for a good roll-in. My attention was briefly diverted to a SAM launch in my vicinity and I made sure it would not present a problem. The force commander started his bomb run and the rest of the flights followed suit. We lit our burners as usual to climb to the roll-in altitude and I came over the top and pointed the nose down, looking out the front of the windscreen expecting to see the bridge.

There was nothing in my view except rice paddies - not what I was looking for. I pulled back on the stick to shallow my dive and still had nothing but rice paddies in view; I did not even see the river much less a bridge. I decreased my dive angle even more and suddenly the Red was in my windscreen but I was well south of the bridge. Flak clouds and tracers were all around us as we drove up the river to a release point. I thought that I was going to have to skip-bomb the bridge if I had any chance of hitting it. With burner still going, I was passing 600 knots at least as I drove upriver to the target. The superstructure of the bridge was filling my windscreen when I thought to myself, this looks about right for a level flight bomb release from around 4,500 feet. Pressing the pickle button with my right hand while my left hand was poised on the jettison external stores button I released my Baby Hueys.

The reason for getting your hand close to the jettison button was a hung 3,000-pound bomb on one wing while the other bomb released would put the aircraft into a sudden roll into the hung bomb. (That precautionary advice was another tip from Cal and Gary.) At low altitudes and extreme airspeeds there was no recovery from the violent maneuver and contact with the ground was a given unless the hung bomb could be immediately jettisoned.

I could not see my bomb impact as I was pulling up and away from the target but I could see the dirty clouds of dirt and debris from the first flights' bombs surrounding the bridge. We probably did as much damage from sonic booms as we did from our bombing as we were all escaping the cauldron of fire as rapidly as possible. The force headed for Thud Ridge and back into Laos for our post-strike refueling.

That evening in the club one of the wing intelligence officers who examined all the strike camera films for the mission told me I was the only Thud driver to actually hit the bridge that day. He said one of my bombs detonated in the superstructure of one of the spans and the other impacted the roadbed. I do not know whether his assessment was accurate or not but I do know the 355th, minus me as I was not on the schedule, had to return to the Doumer in the next day or two to finish the job. They did so in fine style by dropping several spans into the river. I received my third DFC for that raid on the 14th.

The unusually good weather for that time of the year held a few more days and on 17 December 1967 we struck the Canal des Rapides Bridge in one of the last big strikes "Downtown" until the Operation Linebacker strikes in 1972. The Canal des Rapides raid would be my last venture into the city limits of Hanoi. (In Operation Linebacker the venerable Thud would be replaced in the strike role by the B-52.) Hanoi would be safe under the cover of the northeast monsoon for the next three months.

During the month of December I lost yet another former roommate. The 355th was returning from a strike in the Hanoi area and we picked up some transmissions from our sister wing, the 388th at Korat. The radio chatter indicated a Weasel "bear" had somehow been hit by something as he was slumped over the stick and non-responsive. (A "bear" was the back seater in the two seat Wild Weasel Thuds.) They were not pilots but electronic warfare officers who had the task of operating the equipment used to locate and destroy SAM sites.

The pilot was asked if he could control the aircraft and he replied he could. His wingman reported that the rear canopy over the bear was shattered. I later learned that the Weasels had been delivering cluster bombs in a strike on a SAM site and that one of the pellets from the bomblets used had penetrated the canopy while the Thud was in a steep bank, low over the target. The pellet then hit the bear in the top of his helmet, killing him instantly. Other than the shattered canopy the airplane suffered no damage: one of the "freak" accidents of war. I also learned the bear was my roommate for a short time at Nellis. Sadly, I no longer remember his name, but I remember he liked country and western music and he was not happy to be in "bear school" as he had spent his career as a navigator in multi-engine transports, primarily the lumbering and notoriously slow C-124 powered by four reciprocating engines and known as "Old Shakey". He was also just a year or two from retirement.

Enemy defenses were not the only dangers that faced the 105 crews - night and pre-dawn takeoffs and joinups were also a hazardous undertaking. As safety requirements dictated individual takeoffs by aircraft with ordnance aboard, a "joinup" was required to get the flight together again.

After the four Thuds rolled onto the active runway and lined up in an echelon formation, the final checks were made with all aircraft repeating Lead's call of, "canopy, pins, lanyard, and ram." "Canopy" was to ensure everyone's canopy was down and locked; "pins" a reminder to ensure ejection seat safety pins were removed; "lanyard" to check for proper hooking of the parachute zero delay lanyard for immediate chute deployment on takeoff if required to bail out; and "ram" to verify the temperature control lever was in the ram position in order for the water injection system to function.

Lead would manually signal for engine run-up by extending his index finger and moving his hand in a circular motion. When all four Thuds were at full mil power and ready as signified by head-nods originating with number 4, Lead would roll. The rest of the flight would allow for 20-second spacing between departures, select burner, and release brakes in turn. In training we were taught to release brakes and then select burner to preclude blowing a tire but experience in a combat environment with full loads, heavy aircraft, and hot, humid weather dictated getting maximum power as quickly as possible. The slight delay between selecting burner with the throttle and actually getting a burner light would eat up valuable runway and combat pilots learned how to compensate.

Night and pre-dawn takeoffs meant it was still black outside and visibility was severely restricted. After leaving the ground the lead aircraft would accelerate to 350 knots in a shallow climb to a point 4-5 miles away from the airfield and begin a turn to pick up a heading to the refueling rendezvous point. Number 2 joined on the inside wing of the lead's turn while 3 and 4 joined on the outside wing. To execute a turning joinup the trailing aircraft would begin a cut-off turn after their gear and flaps were up and they were accelerating. The trailing aircraft would use a steeper bank than the lead aircraft to create a tighter turning circle enabling the trailing aircraft to cut off the lead. When the trailing Thud reached either the 10 o'clock or 2 o'clock position on the lead, maintaining a position where the lead appeared just above the horizon, the trailing Thud would then close into formation.

The only visual reference for a night/pre-dawn joinup was a small pinpoint of light from the navigation lights on the lead aircraft. That small pinpoint of light would very easily blend in with stars in the sky and lights on the ground in the distance. To further complicate matters, in the blackness of a moonless night there was no visual horizon to separate sky and ground and provide any kind of a reference point. (Quite fortunately, my minor vision defect had absolutely no impact on either my formation flying ability or my night-vision and I had no difficulty at all on joinups. When I flew as number 3, I always bet number 2 that I would be in place on lead's wing before 2 ever got there.)

Although normal procedure on any joinup was to be below the altitude of the aircraft you were overtaking, during a post-takeoff joinup the lead aircraft was still obviously at a very low altitude. This meant there was very little room to "drop lower" than the aircraft you were joining on. That could lead to a disastrous error on night takeoff joinups as a pilot from one of our sister squadrons would discover.

The strike force was getting airborne on one of our pack six missions and the first couple of flights had already completed their takeoff. I was just turning on the taxiway when I saw several bright flashes on the ground south of the airfield followed by the dull thump of distant explosions. I thought someone had jettisoned their ordnance for some emergency. As I lifted off and started my joinup, I noticed many fires on the ground under me as I flew over. I did not spend any time sight-seeing as I was intently concentrating on maintaining visual contact with my lead. At night, once you spotted the aircraft you were chasing, you did not dare blink or take your eyes off that point of light - it could disappear in an instant. In spite of the need for that intense concentration, you still had to be keenly aware of your altitude.

On our return from the mission, I discovered the explosions I had seen just south of the end of the runway were not caused by a jettisoned bomb load. They were caused by a Thunderchief that had indeed flown into the ground (the pilot apparently not recognizing until too late how low he was on his attempted joinup) resulting in scattering his ordnance and a 105 across the countryside. The pilot did survive his mistake but I have no earthly idea how.

The F-105 was not the only aircraft at Takhli to suffer losses in November and December: A damaged EB-66 attempting a landing on one engine crashed and burned at the end of the runway on 17 November and a second EB-66 crashed on landing on the 6th of December. The two crashes resulted in the deaths of 8 crewmen with 5 injured survivors.

A bright spot in the month of December was that several of my comrades safely completed their 100 missions, including Neely Johnson. The bad news was Neely's expertise and leadership would be sorely missed by those of us remaining. Bob Hope visited the base for one of his annual Christmas shows, accompanied by Raquel Welch. There was a parade of floats on the flightline with Raquel perched high on a makeshift "throne". I thought she looked rather unhappy: in fact, similar to the proverbial wet hen, as the temperature on the flightline was well above 110 degrees and the humidity was stifling, resulting in a lot of running mascara. I had never before seen a face actually melt. Neely was given the opportunity to introduce Bob Hope on the stage that was set up not far from the club. The fighter pilots all enthusiastically greeted Neely and we started to watch the show. As time passed, we grew less and less enamored with the entertainment and decided to return to the stag bar in the club to continue the 100-mission celebration with our buddies. Some things in life are more important than movie stars, even ones that look like Raquel with her makeup intact.

The 19th was the last clear weather day of the month over North Vietnam and I was airborne that day, but not to pack six. I missed some excitement in the Kep area where Otter Flight, a flight of Weasels, engaged our experienced adversaries, the MiG-17s. Otter 3, Captain Philip Drew and his "bear", Major William Wheeler, from the 357th downed a 17 with their Gatling gun while Otter 2 shot-up another 17. That crew of Major William Dalton and Major James Graham was from the 333rd. That kill was shared with an F-4D so each aircraft was awarded one half a kill accounting for the ½ in the 27 and ½ kills made by the Thud in Vietnam.

A bombing pause over North Vietnam was imposed on the 24th and 25th of December and again on New Year's Eve. I flew all three days but only over Laos. Our ordnance loads for NVN missions on the 23rd and 30th did include several bombs with 24-hour time-delay fuzes just so the North Vietnamese would not forget us over the holidays. We also gaily decorated our bombs with appropriate Christmas and New Year greetings although I doubt the recipients ever had the chance to read them. By the end of the month I had completed 29 missions, with 15 in pack six.

18
MORE MIGS, IRAN, & USS PUEBLO

1968 arrived with no end in sight to either the war or the monsoon weather over much of North Vietnam and especially surrounding Hanoi. On the 5th the weather cleared just enough for the 355th to strike a bridge on the northeast railroad about 30 miles from Kep Airfield closer to the Chinese border. It would be my 31st combat mission and the 16th over pack six. Our refueling track was the Brown Anchor over the Gulf of Tonkin. After refueling we would ingress westward, tracking just north of Little Thud Ridge to our target.

As was expected Ethan started calling out Black Bandits, MiG-21s, at our twelve o'clock position --- 21 miles --- high. The MiGs were going to make a head-on pass at our formation. SAM activity was insignificant, probably because the MiGs would be in the same area as our 105s. Flak activity was also relatively quiet at the moment. The MiGs were closing very fast as our combined airspeeds would be around the 1,000 miles per hour range. Everything happened rapidly at that point. The MiGs dove through our formation firing their missiles in a head-on attack. That type of missile delivery was extremely inaccurate as there was little chance of an actual hit and no chance for a missile to track a target. The attacking aircraft were in a flight of three and the first two passed between me and the flight just to my right. The third MiG passed on the right of that flight of Thuds. The pass was made with no damage to any strike aircraft and we watched to see if the MiGs would attempt to turn and engage from our rear. They did not, using their normal hit-and-run tactic, and continued eastward out of view.

Now the flak started and as usual it was extremely heavy. We reached our target and rolled in - scratch one more bridge, courtesy of the "Bridge-Busting Professionals of the 355th". After the mad dash back to the coast we returned to our tankers listening to the distress calls of one of the strike aircraft.

The pilot had forgotten to cut his afterburner off, instead leaving the throttle in the minimum burner position, rapidly depleting his fuel supply. He frantically tried to close on the tanker as his remaining fuel supply dwindled lower and lower. I watched as the clearly stressed pilot approached within 500 feet of the tanker when suddenly his closure rate stopped and the nose of the Thud dropped towards the Gulf - so close and yet so far. As his descent increased, we saw the pilot punch out of the aircraft. The good news was he had made it back over the water; Crown had already been alerted, and the Thud pilot was quickly picked up by the Navy. That flight ended his tour as he requested a transfer from flying duties.

The mission was not only bad for the strike pilot, it was even worse for a Weasel crew from the 357th. Major James C. Hartney and Captain Samuel Fantle in a two-seat F-105F were near Kep airfield covering the strike force against SAMs when they were downed by a MiG-17. The location precluded any rescue attempt and they were eventually declared KIA or killed in action. I picked up my fourth DFC that day on my 16th and last pack six mission.

A couple of days later, I cut my hand on a broken shower handle in our hooch and had to have stitches and a splint which were taken care of by "Ma" Smith via a "house call". The decision was made that perhaps I should not fly combat when I had a chance of having to survive in the jungle for a few days and the possibility of infection setting in from the cut was a serious consideration.

Instead I would fly a Thud that was due an IRAN trip. Remember, IRAN was not the country; it meant inspect and repair (or replace) as necessary just as it did with the C-130. The closest IRAN facility for the F-105 was in Tainan, Taiwan. I was to fly to Korat where I would get a "buddy", another 105 due for the same treatment, to fly formation across the Gulf to Clark AB and then on to Tainan. On the 12th, a Friday, I approached the Thud that needed a major overhaul only to discover it had the names Major Hartney and Captain Fantle painted on the aircraft. Although pilots with seniority in the squadron had their names on an airplane it did not mean that pilot, or crew in the case of the Weasels, always flew it. We were assigned aircraft for a mission by tail number. The Thud that eventually bore my name was actually flown by me only twice.

We were a superstitious lot, and the fact the airplane had "belonged" to the crew just downed was not a good omen by any stretch of the imagination. I thought thankfully I just missed Friday the 13th by a day. We believed a good handlebar moustache would help ward off evil spirits and let you return safely home. We would not alter our established routines like my habit of singing "Sweet Pea" while refueling. One should not fly in a brand new flight suit and, heaven forbid, never ever change your gloves or g-suit. By this time my gloves no longer had any fingers left: pack six missions and other harrowing experiences made me grasp the stick and throttle in a vise-like grip that eventually wore the fingers completely out.

I flew to Korat, joined up with my buddy, and we made the journey to Tainan, stopping to refuel and spend the night at Clark. When we arrived at Tainan on Saturday I discovered the airplane scheduled for my return flight was not going to be ready for several days. The Korat bird was ready and there was another Takhli 105 ready to depart for Thailand. The Takhli bird already had a 355th pilot waiting so I was stuck with no ride.

I contacted the 357th and was told to get a voucher from the travel office at Tainan and fly back commercially. The Takhli pilot volunteered to take my flying gear with him so I would not have to lug all that gear through a commercial flight and I agreed. As it turned out, I departed Tainan before the 355th F-105 was able to leave. I had civilian clothes with me on the trip and I made reservations to return via Chinese Civil Air Transport to Taipei and Pan Am to Bangkok.

In the meantime I enjoyed a couple of days in Taipei. Once again I stayed at a hotel I was familiar with from my days in the C-130; the hotel manager remembered me and took me to dinner where we enjoyed Mongolian barbeque in a distinctly Chinese establishment. It looked like it was right out of a Jackie Chan movie as it was located on the fourth floor of a tenement building and we had to maneuver our way through hanging laundry as we climbed the stairs to reach the restaurant. I was definitely the only person with blonde hair in the place.

I arrived at Takhli to discover the F-105 carrying my flight gear had developed serious problems and was still at Clark AB. I was scheduled to fly on the 23rd and still did not have my flight gear. I was missing my g-suit, survival vest with the 38 S&W, my gloves (what was left of them), and my checklist. Fortunately I had packed my flight suit in my B-4 bag and I had carried my helmet and oxygen mask in its own bag. The troops in our equipment shack outfitted me with brand new replacement items except for a checklist. They finally located a checklist after a hasty search and happily presented it to me as I left the shack to go to the paddy wagon. Needless to say, I rode out to my aircraft with a certain amount of trepidation and dread in view of the ingrained superstitions. As I climbed into the cockpit, I opened the checklist as usual only to discover it had belonged to a pilot from our squadron who had been downed over North Vietnam before my tour started. That was the final straw as I thought, "This is it: I am going to buy the farm; kick the bucket; catch the golden BB; go down in flames; in short, I am going to die today." The only thing I really remember about the flight itself was, in spite of everything that had occurred, I actually survived.

The most dramatic event of the month also happened on the 23rd and it had little to do with the war in Southeast Asia. It was on that date that the North Koreans seized the USS Pueblo, a Navy intelligence ship plying the waters near the Korean coast. The capture of the vessel was a major cold war incident that curiously occurred only weeks before the Tet offensive. North Korea maintained that the Pueblo had strayed into their territorial waters, but the United States insisted that it was in international waters at the time of the incident. The Pueblo is still held by the DPKR today and officially remains a commissioned ship of the United States Navy. It is currently moored along the banks of the Taedong River in Pyongyang where it is used by North Korea as a museum.

The action did have an immediate impact on the F-105 units in Thailand. Fearing the outbreak of hostilities in Korea, the United States Air Force transferred almost half of our two-seat Wild Weasels to the Korean peninsula to protect the fighter aircraft stationed there in the event war erupted. The loss of our SAM protection was mitigated by bad weather over North Vietnam that precluded any strikes in the area where SAMs were most prevalent.

To compensate for the decrease in Weasel capability due to the loss of the F-series aircraft during the Pueblo crisis several strike pilots, including me, were designated to fly our Ds as wingmen to a Weasel "F". We were armed with AGM-45 Shrike missiles, QRC pods, and centerline fuel tanks. Our role was to stay in formation with our lead Weasel and launch our Shrikes on command from our lead. I flew one such mission but the weather was so bad we eventually returned to base with our missiles still aboard.

Although the monsoon prevented carrying out massed strikes in pack six, it did not stop us from planning such attacks and we continued to plan and brief for those deadly missions only to have our individual flights diverted to secondary targets in the lower route packs and Laos. At the end of January I reached a total of 39 missions with 16 in pack six.

Wild Weasel on Takeoff
(USAF Photo, Camera Operated by A1C Sheryl D. Barnett)

KHE SANH, SKYSPOTS, EDSELS, & VINH

During February and March the bad weather over North Vietnam continued, limiting our area of operations to Laos and the lower route packs - Hanoi remained safe from our strikes. In South Vietnam the weather did not inhibit the North Vietnamese and their Viet Cong comrades at all in their operations. The Tet Offensive erupted at the end of the month in January and South Vietnam was plunged into a new phase of the war, just when it appeared the United States and its allies may have been accomplishing significant strides in winning the conflict.

The village of Khe Sanh was the seat of government in Huong Hoa district, situated about seven miles from the Laotian frontier on Route 9, the northernmost transverse road in South Vietnam. The badly deteriorated road ran from the coastal region through the western highlands, and then crossed the border into Laos heading to Tchepone. The US Army Special Forces constructed an outpost and airfield in August 1962 outside the village at the site of an old French fort. The plateau camp was permanently manned by the US Marines during 1967 when they established an outpost next to the airstrip. That base was to serve as the western anchor of Marine Corps forces, which had tactical responsibility for the five northernmost provinces of South Vietnam.

The North Vietnamese siege of Khe Sanh began in earnest in February and lasted for 77 days. To support the defense of the base, Operation Niagara was implemented and called for the massive application of aerial firepower by the Air Force, Navy, and Marines. The 355th TFW and the 357th TFS Dragons flew many sorties in

Operation Niagara during February under "skyspot" guidance to assist in the Battle for Khe Sanh.

The Strategic Air Command (SAC) had been using a ground-based radar/computer unit designated "MSQ-3" to evaluate the proficiency of their bomber crews. This system, called "Radar Bomb Scoring" or "RBS", could predict the exact point of impact of a simulated bomb drop. Using this highly accurate SAC radar system, a test was conducted in 1965 to determine the feasibility of the system to deliver live ordnance. Factors such as altitude, wind speed, aircraft speed, temperature, and ordnance characteristics were introduced into the computer. The pilot was given heading, altitude, and airspeed instructions (similar to flying a GCA for landing) as the bomb run progressed. As the aircraft neared the point of bomb release, a countdown was initiated and a release was accomplished on the controller's command. In Vietnam and Laos this system was called "skyspot". A number of skyspot radar sites were placed in Vietnam and Thailand. We used primarily the Da Nang (Monkey Mountain), Ubon, and Nakhon Phanom sites to guide our skyspot missions. The missions were somewhat boring from our point of view as we simply flew in fingertip formation, straight and level, following the guidance called out by the controller on the ground. We did not have any particular defenses to worry about since we were well above the ground fire that could be generated by the weapons used by our opposing forces. In addition to the boredom, the missions were disappointing as they were flown over South Vietnam and Laos and did not count toward our goal of 100.

I was assigned a super additional duty in the month of February. I would be flying Functional Check Flight (FCF) missions as well as combat sorties for the squadron. An FCF was required anytime a Thud had an engine change or maintenance on the airframe, equipment, or systems of the aircraft that could only be checked in its intended environment in the air. I flew my first FCF in an F-series aircraft on the 13th of February. For an FCF the aircraft was in a "clean" configuration meaning no tanks, pylons, or external stores of any nature. I had about an hour's worth of fuel for such flights and I usually completed the check in about 45 minutes leaving the remaining 15 minutes to sight-see Thailand.

I would eventually revamp the FCF checklist to consolidate different system checks and to eliminate some checks that were of no use in our role in Southeast Asia. I enjoyed flying FCF flights so much I volunteered to extend my tour to a year rather than to depart Takhli at the conclusion of the 100 missions over North Vietnam. For my role in revising the checklist and in flying such flights, I received the Air Force Commendation Medal.

I also started flying as both element lead and flight lead during this time period, gaining necessary experience as the squadron and wing were rapidly losing our most experienced pilots. In spite of the numerous cancellations due to weather and the need to fly some non-counters over Laos, I still managed to complete 11 missions in February for a grand total of 50 – halfway home.

I would be very busy for the next month. I flew every day for the first seven days of March. On the 7th of March 1968, my 57th combat mission, I was awarded an Air Medal for silencing an anti-aircraft site near Tchepone, Laos. On that mission we were assigned the task of simply cutting a road. While we were rolling in on the target a ZPU-4 opened up on our flight. The ZPU-4 was a quadruple anti-aircraft version of the Soviet 14.5 mm machine gun and a fearsome weapon against low-level flights.

I spotted the position of the gun on a hilltop just to the west of our assigned target. I called out that I had the "gomer" in sight and rolled in with two 750-pounders, putting my sight "pipper" directly in the middle of the four barrels that were then directing a sustained, high rate of fire at me. Ignoring the tracers surrounding my Thud, I punched the pickle button and pulled up and left, turning in my seat to watch my bombs falling towards the ZPU. The bombs impacted directly in the revetment surrounding the weapon and I could see pieces of gun barrels, wheels, tires, sandbags, dust, dirt, and gomers blasting skyward. We completed our road cut with no further molestation from the area defenders and returned safely to Takhli.

The fact was that by this time in my tour I had honed my dive-bombing skills to the point I was virtually a human computer and never missed my target. I used the TLAR system or "that looks about right" to determine my release point. Actually I always set my sight to manual, or fixed, using 220 mills of depression and flew with my seat in the full up position to ensure my sight-picture was always the same. As we were no longer using the pod formation dictated by pack six missions the roll-in point was within my control and I utilized a very steep dive angle, minimum of 60 degrees, to minimize the effect variables such as release altitude and airspeed had on the point of bomb impact. The system was very effective and I achieved a certain amount of notoriety and respect within my squadron for my bombing abilities.

The Air Medal is awarded to any person who has distinguished himself by meritorious achievement while participating in aerial flight. An award may be made to recognize single acts of merit or heroism and is primarily intended to recognize those personnel who are on current flying status which requires them to participate in aerial flight on a regular and frequent basis in the performance of their primary duties. The Air Medal is also awarded for meritorious service through completion of a specified number of combat missions. That number would vary in relation to where the flights took place, recognizing the danger inherent in the area, e.g., 10 flights over North Vietnam would earn an Air Medal while 35 flights over Laos or South Vietnam would qualify for an award. I completed my time in Southeast Asia with a total of 21 such medals.

On March 7th, a four-ship composed of invaluable 357th TFS members Jim Light, Gary Olin, Cal Jewett, and Ron Venturini completed their 100th and final missions and departed Takhli. It was a great celebration but I was particularly saddened to see my roommate and some good friends and mentors leave the squadron. Other experienced pilots had also departed the unit via MIA, KIA or POW status, not at all the best ways to leave.

On 10 March Lima Site 85 was overrun by North Vietnamese troops and the site was permanently lost. Lima Site was the name given to landing sites in Laos and such sites were primarily manned by United States Air Force personnel. LS 85 was the location of a TACAN beacon installed to assist strike aircraft in navigating to their assigned targets in Laos and the northwestern portion of North Vietnam (In actuality, to navigate to our targets in North Vietnam, we primarily relied on the Doppler, dead-reckoning and map-reading). It was also the site of one of the skyspot radars and the 357th TFS was given the task in November of flying the first skyspot bombing missions to Yen Bai airfield in pack five, another MiG base, just northwest of Hanoi.

Col Giraudo, the 355th TFW commander and eventually a two-star general, would lead those test missions personally. The "Big Kahuna" was a larger-than-life figure. He was a fighter pilot and a POW in both WW II and Korea. In Korea he was shot down on his 99th mission so he was determined to complete the 100 missions over North Vietnam in the Thud, which he did. As an example of his dedication to his men, after flying the skyspot test missions to Yen Bai, he refused to allow the 355th to fly any more such missions as the QRC-160 pod formations that had been so successful in preventing SAM losses could not be employed in the skyspot flights.

I flew one of those Yen Bai flights with the Big Kahuna and, even as a brand new wingman, I realized the inherent danger of using the skyspot tactic in heavily defended areas. The northeast monsoon had set in and there was a solid underlayer of clouds topping out around 10,000 feet that probably extended down to ground level. Our flights were flying at around 15,000 feet in the clear, straight and level, in a loose fingertip formation. There is no way we could have avoided SAMs as they would not be seen until they had emerged, flying at Mach 2 plus, from the solid layer of clouds immediately below us. Fortunately no SAMs were fired and we returned to base, not knowing whether or not the target had even been hit with our bombs. Skyspots were OK in South Vietnam but they were deadly over North Vietnam.

I would fly a total of three missions with the Big Kahuna before I departed Takhli. The second flight with Col Giraudo was as his wingman on a flight to Laos: the Colonel was flying a two-seater "F" with a one-star general from 7th Air Force in the back seat for an orientation ride. I thought to myself the general should have been taken on a pack six strike if he really wanted to see what combat in the Thud was all about. The flight included a simulation of the pod formation as well as the actual tactics used to attack the assigned target, yet another road cut. We successfully returned to base and the non-counter was relegated to the unremarkable memory pile except for flying with the Big Kahuna – a privilege apparently reserved for the more experienced pilots in the wing.

When I arrived at Takhli there was a KC-135 tanker detachment of five aircraft already deployed to the base under Operation King Cobra to support our fighter operations. In spite of the sometimes intense rivalry between multi-engine drivers and fighter pilots, we at Takhli enjoyed a great relationship with the 135 crews. There was a true mutual admiration shared by our respective groups as the 135s respected us for the dangerous and difficult missions we flew and we respected them for the many high-risk, life-saving flights they undertook to save our behinds.

While sharing a beer or two with us at the club, one of the KC pilots openly lamented the fact they would again become second class citizens to the B-52s as their mission changed. In February those tankers were redeployed to Ching Chang Kuan (CCK) Taiwan to support the increased activity of the B-52 force and to make room at Takhli for the newest guys on the block. In mid-month Takhli received those new and untested residents to replace the departed KC-135s.

The Air Force decided to rush a small detachment of F-111As to Southeast Asia, under the name Combat Lancer, to boost night and all-weather attacks while testing the aircraft's overall combat capability. Six aircraft reached Takhli on the 17th of March.

The first Combat Lancer mission on March 18, 1968 attacked a truck park and storage area in pack one. Shortly thereafter the first combat-related loss happened on March 28, 1968. The target was the same Chao Hao truck park attacked on the 18th. The crew was killed. Another F-111 crashed and was destroyed on March 30, 1968. That crew successfully ejected and was recovered. At month's end, after 55 missions against North Vietnam targets, two aircraft had been lost and two more aircraft arrived as replacements. The loss of a third Combat Lancer aircraft on April 22 halted all F-111A combat operations. Neither the aircraft nor crew was found. The surviving five aircraft finally returned to Nellis on November 22nd ending the initial combat trial run for the "Flying Edsel" (after the ill-fated auto of the same name) as we called the airplane.

It was also during this time period that the North Vietnamese appeared to be constructing another MiG airfield at Vinh, located very close to South Vietnam and within range of our major bases. Someone came up with the brilliant plan to bomb Vinh regardless of the extremely bad weather and the fact it was located in a Navy route pack by having the Thuds use their radars to ease down through the overcast, break out of the clouds at around 1,000 feet or so, then use a high speed run straight and level over the airfield dropping high-drag snake-eye bombs, a bomb that we did not ever carry. This was going to be a "cluster____" of the first order as the idea was to perform this raid one ship at a time in a long, drawn-out, trail formation.

For once being the force commander may not have been such a bad assignment as the first 105 or two may have had the element of surprise resulting in a chance of surviving the air defenses provided they did not crash trying to get down through the clouds. The decision was made to attempt this looming fiasco from the Gulf rather than from the west because of the mountains; impact with cumulus-granite is almost always fatal. As was my fate at this particular time, I was going to be part of the last two flights in and probably one of the last aircraft to break out of the clouds into a hornet's nest of ground fire with all the gunners expecting another sitting duck to pop through the clouds. Some of the best news I have ever had was to be informed the last two flights in the strike were cancelled before the mission ever got underway. The first two flights were aborted while airborne - someone finally made a really good decision.

During the battle for Khe Sanh, many of our flights wound up orbiting in the area, waiting for attack clearance, because of the large number of aircraft diverted under Operation Niagara: Gene Basel's flight was caught in that situation. As they were running low on fuel, they managed to get clearance to join a Misty (F-100) FAC in route pack one at Mu Gia pass. Gene was shot down on his 78th mission, bailed out, and was picked up by a Jolly Green. He ended his tour in the hospital at Korat.

I was becoming one of the "old guys" by now and I was definitely no longer a newbie or an FNG. I was a flight commander and I had led many two and four ship attacks in the lower route packs and Laos. Although I had flown only 16 flights to pack six, I was now the pilot in the 357th with the most pack six missions primarily because of the bad weather over the last few months and the departure of all the guys who had spent extensive time in pack six. As a reward for having survived, I was designated as one of the two 357th strike force commanders: it would now be my turn to lead 16 Thuds into the heartland of North Vietnam. I thought what a change for a former C-130 pilot. I was sitting in a downtown bar one evening when I struck up a conversation with another GI sitting next to me; turns out he was a master sergeant who worked at wing headquarters. When I introduced myself he said, "I know you, I keep track of your daily activities and schedule on Colonel Giraudo's force commander board." I guess I could no longer keep a really low profile, if I ever had one to begin with.

My career as a force commander was brief and very uneventful for which I was exceedingly grateful. My first attempt was a planning nightmare. The target was on the northeast railway but we had no Brown Anchor tanker support over the Gulf. The tankers that were assigned to support the mission were all going to orbit over Thailand and Laos. That meant we had to ingress from the west, fly completely across North Vietnam, strike our target, reverse course, and egress the reverse route.

No matter how many times I calculated the route and the fuel needed, the results all came out the same: I fully expected some of our aircraft would be bingo fuel at roll in, or even worse, just prior to reaching the target. Bingo fuel by some of the Thuds prior to roll in would mean the attack would have to be aborted and the entire force faced with a very difficult reversal in course. Such a maneuver would undoubtedly destroy the integrity of the pod formation, exposing us to SAM radars and to an unacceptable risk from MiG activity that was always heaviest in that region of North Vietnam. I finally managed to identify an acceptable secondary target, closer to the tanker orbits than the primary, and briefed that if any aircraft declared bingo fuel we would attack the secondary on my command. Bingo fuel was computed, and briefed, to be higher than the normal bingo fuel computation.

I spent a sleepless night thinking that my first effort to lead the force was going to be an absolute disaster and one from which I probably would not return. I wondered how I would fare in a North Vietnamese prison if I managed to get through a bailout. I also knew I could not hide among the local population very long with my blonde hair. I reached the briefing room early to check the weather - it was still terrible. Thank heavens I would not get the opportunity to either check into the Hanoi Hilton or to earn a Purple Heart on that day. The target would have to wait for better weather.

My second chance to lead the force was not nearly as bad as far as the planning went. It was to be my old friend Kep Airfield and we had Brown Anchor tankers. The route had been flown many, many times before so flight planning was a breeze. Not only was the planning easy, the weather was so bad that there was little hope for any clearing at all. Sure enough, the strike was cancelled at the briefing and we headed for our Thuds to strike suspected jungle in Laos.

Preflight revealed no discrepancies and I climbed into the cockpit. As I cranked up the airplane, I heard the crew chief exclaim over the intercom, "Sir, you have a bad fire out here!" Of course that immediately caught my attention and I started to shut down the aircraft and run like heck. He then said, "It is going flat, fast." I paused and thought, "How does a fire go flat?" I then realized he must have said "tire" not "fire". I asked him to "say again" and he replied that I did indeed have a flat tire. I thought what an ignominious way to abort a mission but it was the only ground abort I would have in my tour. I flew 20 missions in March to bring my total in counters to 70. I was climbing closer to the ultimate goal.

Although I had already volunteered to extend my time at Takhli I was notified of my next assignment during the month of March. I received orders to report to Williams Air Force Base in Arizona to learn how to fly the F-5 and then to train foreign students in ordnance delivery and fighter tactics. The F-5 was a single-engine, single-seat, fighter version of the T-38 trainer. It was designed to be a foreign military sales (FMS) aircraft for our numerous allies around the world. What a tremendous assignment; from the standpoint of the airplane, the overall mission, and the location of the home base. It would also have entailed trips to places like Norway and other countries interested in procuring United States warplanes. In spite of the numerous perks associated with accepting that assignment I decided that I wanted to be a Sandy pilot (combat search and rescue missions) and fly the closest thing I could get to a WW II fighter, the A-1 Skyraider.

One of the senior officers in the wing learned of my future plans and met me at lunch to try to get me to change my mind. He had been a vice-commander of the United States Aerospace Research Pilot School at Edwards AFB and said I was too valuable to the Air Force to be used as "cannon fodder". He also said with his recommendation, and based on my flight time and experience in the C-130, he could guarantee me a student slot as a multi-engine test pilot at the school. Attendance at the test pilot school was also an opportunity to perhaps get into the US space program. I thought about the possibilities and decided I still wanted to pursue the A-1 assignment. In my mind's view (erroneous as it was), "real" pilots flew combat. After all, the early astronaut positions were filled by monkeys.

The Air Force personnel office surprisingly approved my request and my orders were changed to report to Hurlburt Field in Florida for A-1 training at the end of my tour at Takhli. I remember reading somewhere that "choice, not chance, determines destiny." My choice certainly determined my future destiny in the United States Air Force. The FMS sales of F-5s never materialized as our allies decided they would not settle for anything less than a front line fighter and eventually the countries the US tried to sell F-5s to procured F-16s instead. The F-5s in the Air Force inventory were then used in an "aggressor" squadron to train pilots in dissimilar air combat tactics.

On the 31st of March President Johnson ordered a halt to all bombing of North Vietnam north of the 20th parallel (that included pack six), trying to induce the North Vietnamese to return to the peace negotiating table. The northeast monsoon and that March directive from the President of the United States may have saved me from joining my comrades on the MIA, KIA, POW lists. Purely by circumstance, the commander of the training wing at Nellis who had determined that multi-engine pilots could not possibly survive transition to the Thud may have also had a hand in keeping me unharmed as the shift to class 68B directed by that commander delayed my arrival to the battle zone by a couple of months. That delay, coupled with the bad weather and the bombing halt, kept me from flying the number of pack six missions the pilots from the earlier class (68A) had been required to endure.

BOMBING HALT & IN-FLIGHT REFUELING

April Fools Day was the effective date for the end of bombing north of the 20th parallel as ordered by President Johnson on 31 March. Reflecting the change in missions our ordnance loads started to include two rocket pods, or two CBUs (cluster bomb units), or two more 750s slung on the outboard pylons in lieu of the QRC pods which were of no use in the lower route packs and Laos. During the months of April and May I flew several non-counters in Laos because of the halt ordered by the President.

Although we would no longer be flying to places like Hanoi, Kep, Yen Bai, and Lang Son, the danger had not exactly disappeared as David Coon of our squadron could readily attest. Dave was hit by ground fire during his dive-bomb run on one of the never-ending road-cut missions and discovered his Thud would not pull out of its rapid descent. His hydraulic systems had been damaged and the aircraft was no longer controllable. Dave was just about to violate the guidance contained in a passage from an old Air Force manual that read, "It is generally inadvisable to eject directly over the area you just bombed." He had little time to make a decision as the ground was coming up very fast. Grabbing the ejection handles, he blew himself out of the fatally crippled Thud at an airspeed of around 500 knots. A slight breeze fortunately helped carry his chute just west of the road and across a ridgeline where he was caught in the towering trees typical of the region.

Rescue was alerted and the Sandys and Jolly Greens quickly picked Dave out of his predicament. He was returned to Takhli that evening complaining of a sore back suffered when he fell out of the tree while trying to use a vine to climb down from his lofty perch rather than trusting his nylon let-down device. As you could guess, we quickly started calling him Tarzan much to his chagrin.

In-flight refueling (IFR) was a way of life for us as we always had at least one, usually two, and sometimes three or more rendezvous with our tanker friends per mission. We would join with the tankers almost immediately after takeoff for the pre-strike refueling. That usually occurred just at or shortly after dawn. The tankers would be orbiting in their assigned racetrack pattern over either Thailand or the Gulf and we would be vectored to their position by our GCI (ground controlled intercept) controllers. The tankers would be approaching opposite our flight track and we could spot them around 20 to 21 miles out. Getting closer, the tankers would begin a shallow, left turn to our heading as we closed for the hook-up.

The tankers cruised at 275 knots and our cruise speed was 350 knots: refueling speed was a compromise at 315 knots so the tankers would push it up and we would throttle back to complete the joinup. We normally approached the tanker in our fingertip formation with the element on the right: Lead would close on the boom (or drogue) with two flying on the left wing of the tanker, and three and four flying on the right wing. After topping off lead would move down and behind two as three moved to the boom: three would fill up, and drop behind four as two moved to the boom and so on. This carefully choreographed maneuver would be repeated until the tanker had towed us to the drop off point to continue our mission.

KC-135A Boom Refueling Four F-105s (USAF Photo)

In a strike force mission five tankers would be lined up at staggered altitudes feeding all 20 Thuds at once, which did not take long as fuel was transferred at the rate of about 4,500 pounds per minute. The high tanker would be around 18,000 feet, which was almost the ceiling for a fully loaded Thud flying at 315 knots; this often necessitated refueling in afterburner, a maneuver that always made you sweat just a little more. There was something very disconcerting about stabilizing a few feet behind the boom and then engaging the afterburner to make the final hook up. You had to be cautious accomplishing this task because burner selection caused an immediate decrease in speed as the exhaust petals went to the trail position, followed by a sudden increase in speed from the burner light.

All this activity required rapid compensation to preclude an overrun, sometimes through the use of speed-brakes. You also had to very efficiently accomplish this maneuver as you were burning fuel almost as quickly as it was being replaced. As previously mentioned, combat refueling was done almost in silence once the joinup was accomplished. This was not to maintain radio silence but was a result of the fact the boomers were very experienced as were the Thud drivers and everyone knew what was going to take place. Generally the boomers would simply place their boom in the refuel position and the Thud pilots would deftly put their aircraft on the boom.

Refueling complete, a disconnect would be made and the tanker and receiver would be separated. Although we had the capability to initiate the disconnect through the use of our air refuel disconnect button located on the throttle just below the speed brake switch, the boomers usually made the disconnect which would result in some fuel spray on the windscreen of the Thud and occasionally the cockpit would be filled with eye-stinging JP-4 fumes. (During refueling the temperature control lever was in the ram position allowing outside air to circulate through the cockpit.) We refueled with oxygen masks hooked up, using the 100% oxygen setting on our regulators for this reason. I was quite proud of the fact I never had an unintentional disconnect in over 200 aerial refuelings in my tour.

IFR required proficiency in formation flying and those pilots who suffered from a lack of that proficiency also suffered during refueling while airborne. Boom tankers had markings on the boom as well as receiver lights to assist in maintaining the proper position for refueling. On the KC-135 the receiver lights were directly behind the nose wheel door making them pretty useless for fighters; however, I suppose they were of more benefit to the B-52s. I never even looked at the receiver lights as I was able to judge my proper position simply by flying formation using the tanker as my reference point.

Probe and drogue refueling was quite a different matter as you had to pay very close attention to the drogue while continuing to maintain a good position in relation to the tanker. The drogues did not have markings as did the boom and the boomer had no control and very limited visibility over the drogue so there would be little assistance from him. Whereas the boom was rock steady as it was approached, the drogue was always in some motion. As the drogue (which looked like a cone-shaped basket) was attached to a hose in a 315 knot wind stream it is easy to see how it would be slightly, but continuously, bobbing and weaving.

To connect with a drogue the Thud had to move to the trail position on the tanker stabilizing about 10 feet from the drogue with the extended probe aimed at the 10:30 position on the drogue. The pilot then had to establish a good sight picture of the tanker. When the drogue had stabilized as much as it would the pilot added power to attain about a 2 knot overtake keeping the sight picture of the tanker as the guide. The drogue could not be used as a primary reference as you would simply end up chasing the elusive basket and never making the correct connection. As the Thud moved forward the slipstream over the aircraft caused the drogue to move away: with the proper closure rate and with the probe in the correct position in relation to the basket a good contact could be made. Too slow, or bad position, and the probe would miss as the basket moved away. Too fast, or bad position, and the drogue could end up wrapped around the probe or the external stores on the airplane - a dangerous situation.

Drogue refueling could be very exasperating as sometimes it seemed impossible to get the right closure rate to attain a successful contact. Once that contact was made between probe and drogue the pilot maintained a position in relation to the tanker that put a small curve in the hose attached to the drogue. A disconnect was made by simply easing directly back while maintaining level flight.

On one of our route pack one missions during the month I was part of a four ship that had one of the wing staff pilots flying. Bomb run completed, we returned to our tanker rendezvous point to discover our "boomer" had an air abort and had to be replaced with a drogue tanker. I thought this was going to be fun, something out of the ordinary: a thought not shared by the staff pilot who expressed a sincere desire to try to find another tanker due to his lack of any recent experience on the basket. As there were no other tankers available we continued to join on the drogue tanker. The staff pilot said for the rest of us to refuel first as he did not want to damage anything that could prevent the others from refueling - turned out to be a good decision.

The three of us hooked up with no difficulty and moved out to the wing of the tanker while the staff pilot cautiously approached the basket. He made several attempts to get a connection but all he succeeded in doing was getting the drogue to angrily beat him around the canopy. I could tell the pilot was concentrating on the drogue itself as he appeared to be trying to jump forward and stab it. There was a good reason Thud pilots generally referred to "probe and drogue" refueling as "poke and duck" refueling.

Finally it appeared a successful contact had been made and the Thud was in a normal flight position with a good connection between refueler and receiver. I checked my position on the lead and the tanker and looked back to see how the refueling process was going. I could not believe my eyes: The 105 was in a 90 degree vertical position relative to the tanker with flames erupting from both ends of the aircraft as it was apparently compressor stalling. The Thud continued on to its back, twisting in a left spiraling turn down with the drogue and a lot of hose still attached to the probe. The pilot recovered from his highly unusual attitude and leveled off with some extra baggage and not much fuel. The tanker was also done for the day as he had a lot of fuel but no way to give it to anybody.

Our flight immediately diverted to Udorn Thailand where the three of us followed the damaged Thud and its disconsolate driver down an emergency final approach for landing. The Thud touched down and was rolling out on the centerline of the runway as we did a go-around and headed for Takhli.

On our arrival Colonel Giraudo met us on the ramp and wanted to know what happened on the flight. We responded that there was some difficulty with the drogue tanker and the diversion was necessary. The Big Kahuna was surprised and said he did not know anything about a refueling issue: he wanted to know why the Thud at Udorn had run off the side of the runway on landing. It was our turn to be surprised as we did not see any of that activity. It goes to show that it was never advisable to decorate your aircraft with a basket and 20 feet of hose and then attempt to land.

Weather presented some complications in what was otherwise a very normal routine where IFRs were concerned. Over Southeast Asia it was not at all unusual for the tankers to be hidden by clouds or rainstorms. Many times the tankers and the Thuds had to search for altitudes where there was a break in the cloud cover and refueling between cloud layers was frequently accomplished. At times we would encounter scattered clouds during the refueling process. The visual sight of swirling mists causing the tanker to suddenly disappear and then just as suddenly reappear was not only nerve-racking, it induced feelings of high speeds and vertigo.

Flying in the vicinity of thunderstorms would also occasionally create St. Elmo's fire, a buildup of static electricity that appeared as luminous, blue plasma attaching itself to the leading edges of the wings, tanks, and other stores on the airplane. St Elmo's fire used to appear in the rigging of sailing ships during severe weather and the mariners of that era were mystified and terrified of the phenomenon. Even on our flights, there was nothing quite as discomforting as the sight of St Elmo's fire surrounding the fuzes on the nose of bombs hanging on your wing: especially if one of the arming wires had pulled out and the fuze arming propeller was spinning.

On one such bad weather flight I was leading a four ship and the clouds were so thick we could not find any altitude or area clear enough to make our rendezvous with the tanker. The GCI site finally managed to vector us to a position slightly in trail with our tanker and 2,000 feet lower. Our flight was getting extremely low on fuel and it was imperative that we find that tanker. The GCI operator said he could not get us any closer with his equipment and I had to resort to a radar skin paint of the tanker using the Thud's R-14 radar that is part of the fire control system to complete our rendezvous.

Normally when the flight lead has to start looking at the radar the wingmen have to assume responsibility for maintaining safe separation from other aircraft and to visually acquire the tanker. On that joinup the weather meant the wingmen had to fly close formation and keep visual contact with me. I closed on the tanker until the blip that was the tanker appearing on my radar screen had centered on the scope: we were under the tanker but exactly where under the tanker no one knew. I checked to make sure the tanker and I had exactly the same altimeter setting and started easing up in the thick, swirling clouds. Getting closer and closer to the bottom of the tanker while watching the altitude difference dwindle to less than 100 feet, I finally spotted rivets in the clouds - oh %#*>*. I was too far forward and the boom was behind me.

Wondering how my vertical stabilizer could have possibly missed the tanker and its boom I started easing back on the throttle to compensate for the slight overrun. Miraculously the boom appeared just to the left of my canopy and I was able to make the connection. My wingmen stayed glued to me rather than go to the wing of the tanker as no one could clearly see the tanker itself. I was flying looking at the end of the boom while fighting vertigo and my wingmen were looking at me. We stayed in close formation at the end of that boom using a very tight version of our normal position-shifting choreography until we had all topped off.

On rare occasions we would have a stress-free mission accompanied by clear weather providing the opportunity to demonstrate our formation flying skills. I was returning from such a flight flying on the wing of Captain Tom Peck and we had just completed our post-flight refueling. As we dropped off the tanker Tom called for me to "Go trail" meaning for me to position my Thud behind and slightly below his aircraft. I placed the nose of my 105 directly under the tail of Tom's 105 and Tom called for us to go to afterburner. I wondered what he was planning as we accelerated under the tanker. As we emerged in front of the tanker Tom began a barrel roll. He was very smooth on the controls and I had no difficulty maintaining my close trail position as we barrel-rolled in front of the nose of the KC-135. The tanker crew called on the radio and said, "Beautiful - looks just like the Thunderbirds." I always knew I could fly the slot as Thunderbird Four but that was as close as I would ever come to that possibility.

The arrival of spring brought the consistent bad weather over the area to an end except for the usual thunderstorms and the scattered cumulus clouds that normally occurred during spring and summer. Ceiling was now unlimited but visibility was still a problem. Southeast Asia is primarily an agrarian society and spring meant it was time to burn rice paddies and clear land for planting. As a result the entire area was enveloped with a blanket of smoke that did not disappear until around the 8,000 to 10,000 foot level.

Above the smoke blanket the air was clear and visibility was great. We could find our targets but we had to be directly overhead to see them clearly as slant range visibility was almost non-existent. It seemed that nothing was ever simple and there was always some issue to contend with. Despite the inconveniences I managed to complete 14 more counters in the month of April to reach a total of 84. My goal was now within reach provided President Johnson did not end all bombing of North Vietnam.

KHAM DUC & MU GIA PASS

12 May 1968 dawned over Takhli. I was leading a two-ship flight on a morning mission to attack a suspected truck park in route pack one just north of the DMZ – it was going to be my 87th counter. My wingman was a relative newbie in the Thud but he had been an F-106 driver prior to coming to our squadron so he was well acquainted with fighter aircraft. Our loadout consisted of six 750-pounders on the centerline MER, two 450-gallon drop tanks of fuel, and two 750-pounders on the outboard stations.

We had just joined our tanker for our pre-strike refueling and I was sitting on the boom feeding my Thud when I received a radio call from the airborne battlefield command and control center (ABCC) Hillsboro, a C-130. The mission coordinator said he wanted to divert our flight from our scheduled mission to assist a friendly outpost under heavy attack and about to be overrun. I inquired as to the location of the impending catastrophe and was given a set of coordinates. I immediately recognized that the location was not in our area of authorized attacks and asked Hillsboro if he was aware that he was talking to a flight of Thuds. He responded that he was and that he would assume full responsibility for the diversion. I told Hillsboro that only one person was responsible for where my flight went and that was me; however, I would willingly take responsibility for where we were about to go.

Meanwhile my wingman had little idea of where we were going as he called on the radio and said, "My maps do not even go to that location." I was sure it was in South Vietnam but I asked for a TACAN position to confirm my suspicions. It was indeed in South Vietnam, at a place called Kham Duc, almost due east of Ubon

Thailand and near the conjunction of Laos, Cambodia, and South Vietnam: it was well south of where F-105s were authorized to strike under the rules imposed by Operation Rolling Thunder, although the January assault on Khe Sanh eased those restrictions somewhat.

The limitations imposed on the Air Force during Rolling Thunder made execution of air strikes very complex as not only the White House and Pentagon were involved; coordination was also required with the US ambassadors in Saigon, Vientiane, and Bangkok. Political considerations were paramount and Air Force squadrons based in Thailand could attack targets in Laos and North Vietnam but not South Vietnam. The defense of Khe Sanh in January in which units from Thailand participated seemed to be an exception to the rule as the United States did not want another disaster like the French suffered in 1954 at Dien Bien Phu during the First Indo-China war.

The tanker agreed to escort us south of his assigned track to get us to the target area with sufficient fuel to hold if we needed to and still have enough fuel to then mount an attack. Topping off completed, we dropped off the tanker and headed southeast.

After departing the tanker I called for afterburners to rapidly increase our refueling speed to en route speed. The increase in speed accomplished, I called "burners now" to return to military (mil) power. My burner cut off but I thought I noticed an unexpected decrease in my mil power. My wingman called and said, "Lead, your speed brake petals are still in the trail position." The F-105 has four speed brake "petals" at the engine exhaust outlet. Those petals open partially, approximately 9 degrees, when afterburner is selected and return to the fully closed position when in military power. Although the speed brake malfunction did not create any perceived loss of mil power as engine thrust is controlled by the throttle and engine exhaust nozzle (and the thrust decay system while taxiing) the problem could be the harbinger of other developing problems. I decided to go to burner again to see if I could get a burner light: I could not. Now the malfunction was becoming more severe but I decided the overall system failure was still not sufficient to warrant abandoning the mission under the circumstances.

Kham Duc was situated in the northern section of Quang Tin Province, South Vietnam, in I Corps Tactical zone. It sat beside National Highway 14, which paralleled the international border with

Laos, and it was surrounded by high mountains on all sides. The Special Forces camp was named after the main village located about 800 meters to the northeast, and was constructed about the mid-point of a 6,000-foot asphalt runway. Before his assassination, South Vietnamese President Diem had used Kham Duc as a hunting lodge, so the airstrip was built there for his access.

The Kham Duc Special Forces camp was under the responsibility of the US Army 5th Special Forces Group and functioned as a training center for civilian irregular defense forces personnel, for reconnaissance of enemy movements, and for combat operations. In January 1968 the North Vietnamese tried to capture Da Nang as part of the Tet offensive but the attempt was quickly repulsed. Khe Sanh then came under siege from the end of January to April. Failing there, the North Vietnamese and Viet Cong forces then targeted Kham Duc. On the morning of May 12th the North Vietnamese had surrounded the area and, after overrunning several smaller outposts, they gradually forced friendly forces into the main camp. Kham Duc had to be evacuated and all available Air Force assets were diverted to assist in that action.

Arriving in the target area I contacted the on-scene FAC and told him we were a flight of Thuds with a total of sixteen 750-pounders and 2,000 rounds of 20 mike-mike (mm) at his disposal. The FAC wanted to know where we were as he did not have a visual on us. I told him we were at 15,000 feet and directly over the airfield and that I had him in sight. The FAC had never worked with 105s before and could not understand why we were not down low with him.

The typical close air support (CAS) role required jet aircraft, primarily F-4s and F-100s, to fly at much lower altitudes, deliver their ordnance one bomb at a time, in a very low-angle 20 degree dive delivery. Our tactics were very dissimilar to the CAS role as we delivered our ordnance in one pass, diving from 15,000 feet to a release altitude of 6,500 feet, in a very steep dive angle, minimum of 45 degrees. The difference in delivery tactics was not only dictated by the tactical role, it was also dictated by the formidable air defenses we had to face over the north: we had to encounter MiGs, SAMs, and radar controlled anti-aircraft guns from 37/57mm to 85/100 mm. The aircraft in the CAS role in the south had none of those defenses to worry about.

I explained to the FAC that it would be very hazardous for us to vary our tactics as accuracy would surely suffer; furthermore our centerline ordnance was wired to release in one pass and we could not alter that from the cockpit. He told us that our target was the area just a "click" (a kilometer) from the edge of the south end of the runway and that we were cleared in hot provided we were sure he was out of our way. The FAC was very apprehensive about us descending on him from above as he still had no idea where we were.

I told my wingman to "green-em-up" and announced that I was in hot. The delivery was a piece of cake, as we thought we had no significant air defenses to affect our concentration or aim: we did not have to look for the MiGs, SAMs, or firecan guns we were used to encountering. For once all we had to do was hit the assigned area which was easy for experienced Thud drivers. I rolled in and centered my sight a kilometer from the south end of the runway. The eight 750-pounders impacted right on target and the entire area just south of the end of the airfield erupted in flames, smoke, dust, and dirt, vegetation, and who knew what else. The FAC was ecstatic as the sight of eight 750-pounders exploding together is much more imposing than the sight of the usual CAS delivery of a single 500-pounder whose impact basically disappears in the jungle foliage. The FAC told my wingman to hit my smoke as that is just where he wanted the ordnance.

Following the equally successful pass from my number two, I discovered my radio transmitter had failed and I was unable to talk to anyone although I could still receive radio transmissions. I joined with my wingman and through the appropriate hand signals apprised him of my difficulty. I indicated that he should assume the lead and to contact the FAC to see if he wanted us to strafe. I thought this would be an absolutely wonderful opportunity to make a low level pass straight down the runway with no chance of hitting friendlies. Our usual strafe attacks in the north had to be high angle, short bursts with minimum time to engage, accompanied by intense return fire.

To my disappointment the FAC thanked us for excellent work and said he had way too many aircraft in the area awaiting their turn to bomb to allow for any strafing. The fact we could not strafe was undoubtedly a blessing in disguise as I would eventually discover.

Our flight headed for the tanker and then home. I flew as wingman and encountered no further equipment failures. Mission complete but it had been in South Vietnam, not in North Vietnam and we could not get credit for a counter - I was still sitting on 86 missions with 14 to go.

That afternoon after my return from the combat mission, I flew a functional check flight in one of the wing Thunderchiefs to complete my day. A week or so later, the 355th TFW received a telegram from an Army Lieutenant Colonel in the 46th Infantry Regiment, 198th Battalion, Americal Division, one of the commanders involved in the defense and subsequent evacuation of the camp at Kham Duc. The message specified our flight by name and stated our actions had prevented the enemy from overrunning the base in the morning before the evacuation could be completed.

We had caught the North Vietnamese troops massing just south of the runway, preparing to make a final assault to take the outpost. Our bombs completely stopped that assault in its tracks and disrupted the entire NVN time schedule. As I was later to learn, the FAC was indeed too busy to allow any strafing passes. Tactical airpower flew approximately 140 sorties during the day. Add to that the B-52 strikes, and the transports carrying out the evacuation itself, plus helicopters and FACs, and the skies over Kham Duc were extremely crowded to say the least.

As it turned out, the anti-aircraft defenses we had to face were a little more extreme than I thought at the time. Seven aircraft would be lost at Kham Duc on the 12th; three helicopters, an A-1E, an O-2 (FAC), and two C-130s. Another C-130 was badly damaged on the runway but managed to get airborne and fly to Cam Ranh Bay. The pilot of the O-2 also managed to get his crippled airplane back on the ground at Kham Duc and he continued to direct air strikes until escaping on the last transport out. One of the C-130s was shot up on final approach and crashed on the runway, colliding with one of the destroyed helicopters and veering off onto the dirt. The other C-130 was shot down on departure from Kham Duc and crashed, killing everyone aboard, approximately 150 people including many South Vietnamese irregulars and their wives and children.

By 1630 the camp had been abandoned but a three man combat control team (CCT) had been inadvertently left behind. A C-123 made a touch-and-go landing to try to locate the team but could not stop because of the ground fire. Another C-123, piloted by Lt. Colonel Joe M. Jackson from Newnan, Georgia, made a landing on the hostile airfield, turned around, picked up the CCT, and successfully took off, all the while under the most intense ground fire. That action resulted in the Medal of Honor for Joe Jackson, who had also been diverted from his assigned mission that day. The successful evacuation of Kham Duc entirely by air was the largest such evacuation in history.

    I initially thought my mission on the 12th of May was something less than noteworthy as I did not get the "counter" I had planned on. I later learned the entire story of Kham Duc and heard of the truly heroic actions on that day by other members of our armed forces and realized the mission had been a resounding success. Ironically enough, I would eventually receive the Silver Star for my actions on that day. The citation for the Silver Star reads as follows: "Captain Wayne A. Warner distinguished himself by gallantry in connection with military operations against an opposing armed force in South Vietnam on 12 May 1968. On that date, Captain Warner was diverted from his assigned mission to provide close air support for the emergency evacuation of a Special Forces camp which was under heavy attack. Captain Warner displayed exceptional courage, fortitude, and determination toward mission accomplishment in spite of formidable defenses and known severe aircraft malfunctions. The superb airmanship and professional competence exhibited by Captain Warner, through the devastating accuracy of his ordnance delivery undoubtedly saved many lives. By his gallantry and devotion to duty, Captain Warner has reflected great credit upon himself and the United States Air Force." (Sometimes, even a blind squirrel finds an acorn.)

    After the mission to Kham Duc it looked like it was going to be difficult to get any counters in May as more and more flights were sent to Laos and we could not get Hillsboro to clear us in to North Vietnam to hunt targets of opportunity. I was flying a mission with Parks Rea as his wingman during this time period to drop some dumb bombs for the umpteenth time on the interdiction point at Tchepone. Our call sign was Wildcat Flight. The tanker had escorted us very close to our target and we arrived on scene with a heavy fuel load. Parks rolled in and I followed: we both completely covered the target with our 750s.

By this time I was quite used to being the lead aircraft rather than the wingman and my practice was to brief the ordnance delivery sequence at the pre-flight briefing. I did not give any further instructions in the air concerning ordnance delivery except to "green-em-up" - I assumed (incorrectly as it turned out) that Parks would do the same to limit radio chatter. As I pulled off my dive bomb pass I felt as if the aircraft was much heavier than it should have been even considering the excess fuel load. That indicated a real possibility of a hung bomb. I did not want to make multiple passes over the same area so, as I was still over the target, I cycled my ordnance switches and hit the pickle button again.

While I was engaged in the process of getting rid of a perceived bit of hung ordnance Parks was in contact with a Misty FAC in North Vietnam at Mu Gia pass. Misty was the call sign given to F-100 fast FACs that were used over route pack one. Misty had cornered a truck just off the road in the pass and wanted to know if we had any ordnance suitable for a truck kill. Parks replied that we had a total of four pods of 2.75 inch rockets and 2,000 rounds of 20 mike-mike. Misty said that was great and to join him post haste.

Parks departed the area knowing I would catch him en route. As we had encountered no ground fire Parks figured there was no need to look each other over for possible damage. All this was transpiring as I was pulling up from my bomb run playing with my ordnance switches. The last radio call Parks made was to say, "Set 'em up for rockets, two." I instinctively followed instructions, setting my weapons select switch on the armament control panel to rockets and punched in the station select buttons then hit the pickle button again trying to rid myself of the bomb I thought I still had. I heard the "swoosh" of 2.75 inch rockets firing instead of the "thunk" of bombs releasing and immediately realized my error, quickly releasing the pickle button - shades of the mission to Kep several months earlier.

My next thought was, "Where was Parks?", as my nose was pointed up firing rockets and I feared he may have been in front of me. Thank goodness, he was well out of the area and I spotted him several miles northeast heading to Mu Gia. I then took stock of what ordnance I had left since Misty was expecting a rocket pass out of me. The rocket pods we were carrying were LAU-3A, 19 tube launchers, meaning each pod carried 19 of the 2.75-inch high-velocity aircraft rockets (HVARs). I looked at my left pod and it was empty with the frangible nose cone gone: the right pod was somewhat better as it still had one rocket. I would at least be able to make a rocket pass for Misty and salvage some of my pride.

I caught up with Parks just as we were getting close to Mu Gia. Misty called to warn us of heavy and accurate 37/57 mm anti-aircraft fire in the pass. That was entirely expected as Mu Gia had been claiming aircraft for years: it was a place to be avoided unless you had a really good reason to be there. Misty rolled in for a smoke mark and relayed instructions to Park who rolled in, fired his rockets (all 38 of them of course) and pulled off, evading the ugly clouds of flak that were now blanketing the area. Misty called and said the rockets fired by Wildcat 1 had not impacted exactly where the truck was located and asked me if I had the truck spotted.

I did - Misty cleared me in and I started my rocket pass in the middle of a lot of flak bursts and angry tracers. The tracers streaked past my cockpit in brilliant red streams: the flak bursts were so thick they would momentarily obscure my vision of the target. I thought, "Man, this gunner is good but not quite good enough: if only I had enough rockets to save a few for that gun crew." I took careful bead on the truck that was only partially hidden in the trees and fired my rocket – note the use of the singular version of the noun. The rocket streaked towards the truck, leaving a pretty puny trail of exhaust smoke. Success! The rocket scored a direct hit on the truck resulting in a very large secondary explosion - that gomer was not hauling rice.

Misty was absolutely ecstatic, yelling "Fantastic shooting, Wildcat 2" on the radio: he could not believe I hit the truck with a single rocket. As I pulled off, Misty said he had another target for me and the rest of my inventory of rockets. I thought, "Yea right, I already have another target in mind if I had any rockets left", but I calmly replied that I had shot all the rockets I had on that one pass. There was a stunned silence on the radio finally broken when Misty said he was sure I had only fired one rocket. I said, "Nope: that was all I had."

We volunteered to use our guns but Misty said the anti-aircraft fire was way too heavy to risk any gun passes so we returned to our post-strike tanker and then home. That evening in the club as we celebrated another successful flight and one that was a counter, an intel officer sought me out to ask a question. He said that was an unbelievable rocket shot on the truck but he wanted to know what in the world I was shooting at on my first rocket pass. He said the gun camera film showed nothing but sky and clouds. I did not claim to be shooting through a fog-bank on the ground as I figured those cameras really do not lie.

I thought my opportunity to get another shot at a MiG had finally arrived as on a pack one mission I spotted what appeared to be two MiG-21s disappearing in the distance behind some large cumulus clouds. This time I was going to be ready. I called to my wingman and said to "set-em-up for some air-to-air." I switched my sights to enable an aerial gun pass, and instructed my wingman to assume a fighting wing. I said I had spotted possible black bandits just northeast of Mu Gia. I wondered why there had been no MiG calls from Ethan and noted the GCI sites were also silent but I was taking no chances. I knew I could not possibly try to dog-fight with the MiGs but I hoped I could make a high speed pass from an advantageous position.

The cumulus clouds were quite thick and I tried to guess where the MiGs would emerge next. I again spotted the two semi-delta winged aircraft dodging between two towering masses of clouds and gave chase. As we were maneuvering into what I hoped would be a tail shot, the two aircraft apparently had spotted us and they emerged from a cloud column heading towards us. At that point we were close enough that I could see they were Navy or Marine A-4s. We closed head-on and, as we passed each other, I rocked my wings in recognition and the lead A-4 replied in kind. I wondered why the Navy was flying in our route pack. We returned to our task of armed road reconnaissance and chalked another episode up to experience.

I seemed to be spending more time flying with command staff at this point and flew a mission with Colonel Larry Pickett, Wing Vice Commander, aptly described in "PAK SIX" as grey-haired and dignified. He was also an absolutely super individual and devoted to his pilots. Colonel Pickett had just celebrated his 50th birthday in May making him one of the oldest fighter pilots to fly a mission over

North Vietnam. The Colonel and I were scheduled into pack one and the weather was atrocious in spite of it being late spring. The Colonel was flying as my wingman and we had difficulty in locating our target because of the cloud cover. We finally managed to deliver our bomb load but we were getting very low on fuel. Our tanker had aborted for some reason and we had no choice but to divert to Da Nang to pick up some gas for our trip home. We decided because of the deteriorating weather and the fact I was very comfortable in formation flying that Colonel Pickett would take the lead on our return journey to Takhli. We made it safely home after flying through some really bad thunderstorms and almost constant cloud cover. I had to stay tucked in very close to Colonel Pickett to keep him in sight. The Colonel's influence on the United States Air Force is well known as he was one of the founding fathers of the Red River Rats Association and directly responsible for the continuation of the organization's activities back in the United States after the conflict was over.

On another occasion, I reported in to our flight shack to brief a two-ship to pack one. I was expecting to see one of my squadron compadres at the briefing but to my surprise, my wingman for the day was none other than the Big Kahuna. Colonel Giraudo had led a flight the day before and he was extremely unhappy with the assistance he had received from the GCI site at Da Nang, call sign "Waterboy". He signed on as my number two as he did not want the Waterboy personnel to recognize his voice, enabling him to properly assess the competence of the personnel at that site.

I was somewhat ill at ease briefing and then leading the wing commander who was known for his skill and leadership qualities as a fighter pilot in WW II, Korea and now Vietnam. Thankfully the mission went as planned with absolutely no problems. The Colonel was pleased with the flight and I could say the Big Kahuna actually flew on my wing. Although I flew 20 times during the month, one was an FCF flight and 11 were non-counters. I did manage to log 8 more counters bringing the total to 92: my biggest concern was if I could reach the magic number and earn the coveted 100-mission patch, a red, white and blue shield identifying the achievement, before the rules of engagement were changed again.

100 MISSIONS NORTH

The squadron was well aware of my proximity to achieving the right to wear that red, white and blue badge and provided maximum assistance in scheduling my flying duties. Between the 13th of May and the 9th of June I flew 22 missions in 27 days, gaining 13 counters. On 10 June 1968 I flew my last F-105 combat mission, #100, to route pack one in North Vietnam ending up with a grand total of 121 combat missions in the Thud.

The last flight was somewhat anti-climatic as the luster of completing 100 missions had dulled with the bombing pause and the lack of activity in pack six. There were three other pilots from our sister squadrons who also completed their 100 missions on the same day. The tradition was well established that the pilot who managed to escape death or capture by achieving the magic number would celebrate by holding an open bar for everyone at the officers club. The four of us decided to have a combined celebration starting with the time the first of the group landed (which was early in the afternoon) until no one could drink anymore that night. I was the last of the four to be scheduled for takeoff and my flight did not land until late in the day. By that time the party was well underway and everyone was at the club when I turned on initial approach. My already somewhat-inebriated squadron mates heard the arrival of my two-ship and headed for the ramp to greet us.

I have to thank my wingman, Art Hood, for getting the counter as we were fragged for a Laos strike - Art was my roommate after Cal left. (For us "fragged" was short for "scheduled pursuant to the fragmentation order." The term had a very different meaning for the ground troops in Vietnam. There it meant the killing, usually by the use of a fragmentation grenade, of an unpopular officer or senior enlisted guy by members of his own unit.) I contacted Hillsboro to see if we could get in to pack one and Hillsboro said there was nothing for us to do and did not grant my request. Art spoke up and told Hillsboro that he knew his lead would not say anything but that if he got in, it would be his 100th. Hillsboro said, "Congratulations, you are cleared for a road recce, hunting targets of opportunity." (Recce was short for reconnaissance.) We did not find anything worthwhile but, as was my standard practice, we shot up suspected truck parks and other areas of road and jungle. I did not believe in carrying ordnance home and tried to always find something authorized by the rules of engagement to shoot at.

Art and I did a mild fly-by with Art landing and then I got to beat the field up a little with some high-speed, low-level passes, slow-speed pass with gear and flaps down and probe extended, followed by a steep afterburner climb, and a pitch out for landing. We were prohibited from doing any victory rolls as they were considered too dangerous.

I landed and proceeded to be de-armed, returning as dusk settled in to the revetment where I was enthusiastically greeted by my squadron. Unlike prior 100-mission celebrations there was no escort by fire trucks spraying water and, much to my disappointment, there was no photographer present to record the event. I did feel the lack of exorbitant display of joy and relief was somewhat understandable as I had completed only 16 pack six missions during my tour compared with the tremendous feat of earlier Thud pilots who had survived 30 to 50 such missions. I was, however, one of the last Thud pilots to spend any time in the Hanoi area pursuant to Operation Rolling Thunder and I was one of the last Thud pilots to complete a 100-mission combat tour as aircrew members arriving in Southeast Asia after 1 July 1968 had to fly a one-year tour regardless of where they flew their missions. (The prohibition against bombing north of the 20th parallel basically evened the playing field between flights over Laos, SVN and NVN as far as the risk of completing the mission was concerned.) Above all, I was alive and I had reached the goal which many of my comrades had not.

Although the celebration at the flight line was somewhat abbreviated, we more than made up for it at the club. For 100-

mission parties the club charged five cents for a beer and ten cents for a mixed drink. The four of us who completed our 100th on the 12th had agreed to just split the bar bill: my share of the total bill came to $150.

As the evening wore on, a bunch of us decided we needed some fried rice from one of the local establishments and we took the Dodge Ram to the front gate where it was abandoned. Obviously someone eventually picked it up and returned it to our hooch. Those of us who made it to the front gate, still in our flight suits, clambered onto one of the local buses that ran up and down the road to town. I do not really remember eating any fried rice but I do remember carrying a bottle of Jack Daniels in my hand as I walked through the gate. The bottle was part of my bar bill.

At some time in the wee hours of the morning, I awoke to find myself in bed and I thought, "Oh good, someone took me home." I later woke up for good, nursing an excruciating hangover. As I sat up, shielding my eyes from the bright sunlight streaming through the cracks in the walls of the shack I was in, I came to the slow realization that, "No, I am not in my hooch." I was still in my flight suit and boots clutching the now empty bottle of Black Jack in one hand and my "go-to hell" hat with its last precious mark in the other. I slowly got up and walked through the bar/restaurant in front of the shack where I had been sleeping (passed out is actually more accurate) and stepped into the dusty streets of Nakhon Sawan.

I flagged down the local bus to get a ride back to the base. Riding the bus was a common occurrence during the evenings and at night for all of us but it was one of the few times I caught the bus in mid-morning. The bus was packed so I rode standing, clutching one of the support poles and marveling at the number of farm animals that were on the bus with me. I said to myself, "Does a chicken, pig or goat need a ticket?" The bus driver somehow knew exactly where I would be getting off and he stopped at the main gate where I disembarked: guess he recognized the flight suit, boots, and hat.

As I approached the gate, the two air policemen on duty greeted me with, "Good morning Captain Warner, we heard you finished up yesterday." They called and got me a ride back to my hooch where I headed for the shower. I spent the 11th recuperating from the previous evening and on the 12th I started the remainder of my year at Takhli as a functional check-flight pilot.

A Loaded F-105D and My "Go-to-Hell" Hat with 100 Missions Marked (USAF Photo)

FUNCTIONAL CHECK FLIGHTS

I flew my first FCF on the 12th as a 355th Wing flight-check officer although I remained attached to the 357th TFS. The wing flight-check office had an EB-66 pilot and two F-105 pilots assigned. We also had a single NCOIC (non-commissioned officer-in-charge) assigned to the office to take care of the scheduling and paper work.

Check flights were absolutely great to fly: there was no pre-flight planning to have to worry about and no briefing to attend. If there was an aircraft ready for a flight, we were given a tail number and parking spot and given a ride to the airplane after donning our flight gear. There was no weather briefing to contend with as we were always VFR (visual flight rules) requiring no clearances: if the weather was good we flew, if it wasn't, we didn't. It was that simple. We had a set routine to fly to check out all the systems on the aircraft and when we were done with that we could fly around Thailand checking out the scenery.

One of my favorite places to go was to see if I could catch a train running north of Takhli. The railroad track was straight as an arrow for miles and miles and it was elevated on an earthen berm above the surrounding rice paddies. I could drop down to 20 to 30 feet above the rice paddies and wave at the train passengers as I flashed past at almost the same elevation as the train itself.

Shortly after that first FCF flight for the wing I was tasked to fly another Thud to Tainan, Taiwan for IRAN. Remembering the last minor fiasco of the return Thud not being available as scheduled, I asked that the readiness of my ride home be absolutely ascertained. I was assured that it was indeed ready and waiting.

As there were no other 105s scheduled for IRAN, a "buddy" from Cam Ranh Bay in South Vietnam was selected for my flight to Clark and then to Tainan: that buddy would be an F-4 Phantom. I departed Takhli and flew around the south end of Thailand to set course for Cam Ranh Bay. I had flown in and out of Cam Ranh many times in the C-130 and well remembered the aluminum matting runway. The mats had a tendency to shift under the wear and tear of multiple landings and the uneven surface made the C-130 register from negative one to positive two Gs on takeoff and landing. I wondered how the Thud would react and hoped for dry weather as the aluminum mats were also very slick in a rainstorm.

As I approached Cam Ranh, the weather was splendid and I contacted the tower for landing instructions advising them that I was indeed a Thunderchief and not another Phantom. I decided to intentionally make a no-chute landing as I thought the transient maintenance troops at Cam Ranh had probably never seen a Thud and I did not want to have to repack the drag chute myself. The final approach speed in the Thud was 180 knots compared to the final approach speed of the Phantom of 120 knots. As I touched down, using maximum aerodynamic braking to prevent any hot brake issues, the tower said, "Cookie, you looked extremely hot on final." I responded that I was right on my required final approach speed and taxied to the end of the runway. It was a good thing I did not have to stop to de-arm as the ground troops at Cam Ranh were preparing to spike my tires to prevent a hot brake explosion. Ground control called and told me to shut down to have my tires spiked and I replied, "Not on your life." If they had spiked those tires I would have been stuck at Cam Ranh for months.

I taxied in and finally convinced transient maintenance that a Thud landed at a much higher airspeed than did a Phantom and they left my tires alone. I asked for a full load of fuel including all three external tanks and a cartridge for a cart start. For ferry flights or extended overwater flights we carried two 450-gallon tanks on the inboards and the 650-gallon tank on the centerline, resulting in a total fuel load of 3,100 gallons or over 18,000 pounds of JP-4.

The Thud had two different methods of starting the engine: an air cart could be used to provide a continuous blast of air to turn the engine over, or a cartridge, similar to a 20mm shell, could be inserted into a breech where the explosive force of the ignited shell turned the engine over.

I left my Thud in the hands of F-4 maintenance guys who I feared had no idea how to tend to my airplane. As it would turn out, my fears were absolutely well founded.

I checked in with base operations at Cam Ranh to meet my buddy and do some flight planning for the trip to Clark. The F-4 crew was a Major in the front seat and a First Lieutenant GIB (guy in the back). As the F-4 aircraft commander was a Major, I deferred to him as flight lead; I also felt I could probably fly better formation on the F-4 wing than an F-4 pilot could fly on my wing.

That issue settled we started doing some flight planning where it would not be long before we all realized the difference in flight characteristics of our aircraft. The F-4 guys wanted to cruise around 26,000 feet to Clark. I told them that regardless of the advertised service ceiling of 48,000 feet for the Thud, I doubted I could get any higher than 18,000 feet in the full fuel load configuration. They both registered looks of astonishment and I had to remind them their aircraft was designed for high altitude air-to-air combat while my Thud was designed to deliver a nuclear weapon fast and low.

We completed our planning, agreeing that I would try to climb to 22,000 feet for cruise. We set a start engine time that should have given us enough leeway to get to our aircraft, complete the necessary walk-around check, and get strapped in. As I approached my airplane, I immediately noticed the ground crew had the caps off the external fuel tanks filling them individually with hoses. I said, "What are you doing? The Thud has single point refueling capability and all you have to do is plug in the hose." Their feeble response was, "We tried that but we could not get the airplane to accept any fuel." I then asked if they had turned on the battery switch, to which they responded. "Oh." Already knowing the answer, I asked if they had put a cartridge in the starting breech. As expected their reply was that they did not have any but that they would use an air cart. Thank heavens I had not used my chute as it would have been lying on the ground waiting for me to pack it.

As I was standing in the revetment waiting impatiently for the JP-4 to fill the tanks, the start engine time had come and gone and there was no way for me to communicate with the F-4. The

Phantom taxied up in front of my Thud with the crew looking at me like, "What are you doing?" I strapped in while the refueling was being completed, praying that the ground crew would properly seat the tank caps, and motioned for them to plug in the air cart for engine start. Another problem: the J-79 twin engines on the Phantom were smaller engines than the J-75 used on the Thud. The J-75 developed 26,000 pounds of thrust with afterburner compared to the J-79's 17,000 pounds of thrust with afterburner.

The air cart that was attached to my engine was not up to the task of turning the bigger J-75 engine over and the ground crew had it cranked as fast as it would run, roaring, shaking and belching out a huge cloud of exhaust smoke. I crossed my fingers and engaged the throttle knowing the engine was not spinning as fast as it should to prevent a hot start. A hot start would necessitate an engine shut-down and I anxiously watched the temperature gauge climb, and climb some more. It was pegged at the maximum allowable and then, much to my profound relief began to return to normal.

Finally I was able to taxi and motioned for the ground crew to pull the chocks. We taxied out, took the runway and ran up the engines. The F-4 rolled and I waited for my 20-second spacing. The F-4 was about 10 feet in front of me so I waited some more. I did not begin my roll until 45 seconds had passed and I wished I had waited some more: I was overtaking the Phantom so quickly on the runway I thought I may overrun him. I thought, "What a dog that airplane is on takeoff." We broke ground just as I was joining on the wing of the F-4 and the GIB looked surprised to see me so soon. He later wanted to know why I had released brakes so soon after the Phantom rolled and I told him I had waited more than two times our normal spacing.

We remained in afterburner, climbing to 22,000 feet and leveled off. As I was already on his wing, the Phantom pilot called over the UHF to cut the burners off. I immediately fell out of the sky dropping in a hurry to (you guessed it) 18,000 feet. The Phantom requested clearance for us to fly at 18,000 feet and he dropped down to my altitude.

I slid out into a relaxed route or spread formation and we headed for Clark. I was having trouble maintaining my position on lead as I would drift out in front, throttle back, drop behind and throttle up, repeating this process over and over. I noted we were flying exactly at an indicated 350 knots so I asked lead to push his airspeed up a knot saying I would explain on the ground. The F-105 flew in a nose up attitude at speeds below 350 knots and a level attitude above 350 knots - similar to a boat getting on plane. Not only was the Thud more maneuverable at speeds in excess of 350, the fuel flow difference was 3,000 pounds an hour more at 349 knots (9,000 pounds an hour) than it was at 351 knots (6,000 pounds an hour). As a result I arrived at high station at Clark after the 1,000 mile journey using 4,000 pounds less fuel on the trip than did the F-4. We landed and headed for the officers club to eat and then to the VOQ to spend the night.

That evening at dinner the F-4 GIB started questioning why F-105 pilots had only to finish 100 missions while the fighter pilots in South Vietnam had to spend a year, usually accumulating in excess of 200 missions. I asked the GIB, "How many times have you been shot at by radar controlled 37/57 mm anti-aircraft guns?" He said he had seen ZPU heavy machine guns multiple times. I then asked, "How many times have you been shot at by 85/100 mm anti-aircraft guns?" He said he had not been fired at by such weapons as they were not found in South Vietnam. I asked, "How many times have you dodged SA-2s while inbound to a target?" Again he had to reply he had never taken such evasive action. I then asked, "How many times have you been engaged with MiGs and had to evade their missile or gun fire?" He was now starting to adopt a more silent approach to answering my inquiries by merely shrugging his shoulders. I delivered the coup-de-grace by asking how many of his comrades had become residents of the Hanoi Hilton. Discussion was over; score another one for Thud drivers. That evening we also met another 105 pilot from Korat who was delivering an aircraft to Tainan and we all agreed to fly a three ship for the remainder of the journey.

Upon arrival the following day at Tainan, I walked into the operations shack to pick up my return ride. Guess what, I should have known it would not be ready and the maintenance folks had no idea when it would be ready. Once again I contacted Takhli notifying the 355th of the situation and once again I was instructed to get a travel voucher to fly home commercially. This time there would be no loss of flight gear, however, as I had no civilian clothes with me and my flight gear would also ride home commercially.

Again I caught the Chinese Civil Air Transport C-46 from Tainan to Taipei where I attempted to get a room at my favorite hotel. Unfortunately the manager I knew had taken a few days off and I was told the hotel was booked solid. There were a couple of GIs standing at the registration desk and they overheard the conversation. Turns out they were a flight engineer and a loadmaster from Operation Ranch Hand, the C-123 aircraft that delivered Agent Orange in South Vietnam and they immediately volunteered to double up in a room to make a room available for me. They said, "There was no way they would let a Thud driver go without a room."

The F-105 patches commanded tremendous respect wherever we went, even F-4 pilots had to grudgingly demonstrate respect and admiration for the way the Thud drivers accomplished the mission assigned to them. Although it may be a dubious mark of distinction in some quarters, the F-105D is the only aircraft in the history of the United States Air Force that eventually had to be withdrawn from combat because of the tremendous losses they suffered (335 single-seat Ds out of 610 Ds produced) - losses that were the direct result of the mission flown with the ordnance available at the time and not because of any shortcomings in the aircraft or crews. The two-seat Wild Weasel variants continued to be used until retired in 1984.

I checked in at the Taipei International Airport to claim my ride back to Bangkok aboard Pan Am dressed in my Sunday best: a sweat-stained flight suit, flight boots, g-suit with survival knife and pen gun flares, survival vest with survival radios, day-night flares, medical kit, 100 rounds of 38 ammunition, a 38 S&W, my helmet and oxygen mask, my backpack parachute, my gloves with missing fingers and my go-to-hell hat. I unloaded the 38 and hid it in my helmet bag with my helmet. I did not think about the survival knife sewn to the back of one of the legs on my g-suit and it remained in the usual location.

I was not about to check the parachute as baggage, knowing the ripcord would undoubtedly be pulled, spilling the chute all over the baggage compartment. I asked one of the stewardesses where I could safely store my chute. She had a weird expression on her face and asked, "What is it?" While thinking what a ridiculous question I simply replied, "It is a parachute." I later had a good friend point out that I had missed a golden opportunity as my response should have been, "Why, it is a parachute. I never fly Pan Am without one."

Surprisingly enough no one ever questioned my "hand-carried" items or my unusual travel attire and, after a brief stop in Saigon, I arrived in Bangkok where I hopped on the old standby, the Thailand shuttle, to reach my final destination.

The F-111As at Takhli had a less-than-stellar trial run at combat and the Air Force did not know exactly what was causing some of the losses of aircraft and crews. After the Flying Edsels were removed from combat, attempts were made to identify potential issues and the 111s were permitted to fly daylight training missions: some of those missions were flown with an F-105 flying chase.

On the 26th of June, I flew one of those chase flights in a two-seater "F" carrying an F-111 crew member, a Major, in the back seat. As we taxied out for takeoff, I got irritated at the disparaging remarks my back seat passenger was making about the antiquated equipment in the 105 and reminded him that the reason he was in my airplane was because his airplane had the undesirable habit of getting lost and crashing for no apparent reason.

When the Edsels first arrived at Takhli, they were greeted with great fanfare and hordes of reporters and news media. While they were enjoying the limelight, the tired, dirty, old Thunderchiefs were busy taxiing past to deliver another blow to the North Vietnamese. As we taxied past the throngs admiring the Edsels, most of the Thuds would extend the refueling probe on the side of the aircraft, an appendage Thud drivers referred to as the "dog-pecker", in a less than complimentary "salute" to our new tenants.

On the 29th of June I climbed aboard the base C-47, Gooney Bird, to ride to Da Nang to retrieve a battle-damaged Thud that had been unable to make it home. I had a tail number of the bird I was to rescue and slept most of the way to South Vietnam. As I jumped out of the Gooney at Da Nang I looked around the ramp to locate my 105. There was a Thunderchief on the ramp but it was a different tail number. I checked in with transient maintenance and discovered that the 105 I spotted was indeed the one I was to fly to Takhli. I was told there were two damaged Thuds at Da Nang and one was considered unsalvageable but it had a good aft section. The entire tail section, or aft section, of the 105 would unbolt just behind the wings and separate from the fuselage exposing the engine. The airplane I was to retrieve needed a good tail section so the maintenance guys put the tail section of the totaled bird on the rear of my airplane.

Of course they said they were not sure how well the airplane would trim as they did not have all the necessary jigs, etc. to make the swap but they felt there should be no real problems in flight. I asked about other damage and was told, "The airplane has no navigational systems operative; the sight and radar are destroyed; the landing gear was damaged but they were able to jack the airplane up and repair most of the damage to the point the gear would retract; only one radio is working; there is no water injection; there are numerous temporary patches on the skin of the fuselage and wings; the gun is disconnected; and last, but not least, the engine has been changed; however, there was no time or place to run the new engine as is normal after an engine change." OK, what is the bad news, I thought.

I deliberated over the news for a moment and concluded: "Well, I do not need nav equipment as I know where Takhli is even if it is several hundred miles away (522 to be exact); I will not require a sight or radar; they said the landing gear worked; I only need one radio; patches are not that uncommon on our airplanes; water injection is only needed for heavy weight take offs; I do not need a gun to fly home; and I can run the engine at the end of the runway prior to takeoff to see if it is developing full power." No sweat GI, let's go home.

I strapped in and fired up the engine. I taxied to the arming area where I could position myself for the necessary engine run. While I was running the engine at full military power, a twin-engine C-123 Provider built by Fairchild Aircraft taxied in front of me and called the tower for clearance. The 123, which resembled a small C-130, was told he would be number two in line for takeoff behind me. The 123 then asked the tower just how long they would have to wait on the "Thud". I did not like the way the 123 co-pilot pronounced Thud: it sounded to me like he used it as a dirty word and certainly not with the amount of respect the aircraft deserved.

I completed my engine run noting the exhaust pressure ratio gauge did not exactly reach the minimums required. No sweat: I thought, "I have plenty of runway and I will just abort if the engine thrust does not develop as it should." Engine run complete, I obtained clearance from the tower, and taxied in front of the 123 to take the runway. As I rolled past the 123 I could not help myself and I punched the mike button saying, "By the way *trash hauler*; that is **"Thunderchief"** for you." As I took the active the tower radioed with great enthusiasm, "The **Thunderchief** is cleared for takeoff." I could hear nothing but laughter in the controller's voice and even more in the background noise from the tower. I guess my transmission made the controller's day a little lighter.

The trash hauler almost had the last laugh though, as my aircraft with the new tail section was not exactly trimmed to fly a straight line. As was typical of a lightweight 105 with no external stores it accelerated like the speed of light. The faster I went, the more the airplane crabbed to the left. I found myself looking at the side of the runway rather than the end. I was all a--holes and elbows keeping the airplane on the concrete. I had already given up trying to keep it on the centerline. I was so occupied with keeping the aircraft off the grass I forgot all about any attempt to abort. With a lot of rudder and aileron I finally managed to get the seriously ill Thud into the air where it continued to fly in that very distinct crab.

I flew in a very unconventional attitude back across South Vietnam, Laos, and into Thailand where I landed at Takhli. I opted for a GCA approach rather than the normal pitch-out to take advantage of the lengthy final leg on the GCA. That would give me the opportunity to figure out the appropriate amount of rudder and aileron to compensate for the crab on landing. It would also give me plenty of time to lower the landing gear and ascertain how that would affect the handling of the aircraft.

On touchdown I managed to keep the Thud headed in the right direction with a welcome assist from the drag chute and taxied to my parking spot. I was rather proud of my feat in getting the worn out Thud home but that feeling was quickly squashed by the old Master Sergeant from maintenance who met me on the ramp and said, "Captain, why did you bring that piece of s--- back here?" The badly beat-up bird was towed to the end of the ramp to become a source of usable spare parts although there were not many such parts left on her.

THE END OF MY AFFAIR WITH THE THUD

Mach number is scientifically defined as the speed of an object thru a medium such as air, divided by the speed of sound under the same conditions: in brief an aircraft traveling at the speed of sound is traveling Mach 1. Because the speed of sound varies with temperature and as altitude increases the temperature generally decreases, the speed of sound is reached at a lower indicated airspeed at higher altitudes. At sea level Mach 1 is roughly 650 knots and it was not at all uncommon for the Thud to surpass the speed of sound exiting a target in North Vietnam.

The 105 had a service ceiling of 48,000 feet and was classified as a Mach 2 aircraft. I was curious to see how close I could get to the advertised specifications of the Thud and used my "extra" flight time during an FCF to attempt to reach those limits. I climbed to 46,000 feet on one check flight in a "D", spotting a cell of three B-52s around 30,000 feet returning to U-Tapao, Thailand from an Arc Light mission bombing someplace in Laos or South Vietnam. I attempted to join on the 52s in a very loose formation but I could not maintain position with the Buffs as I had to hold a higher airspeed than they were flying to maintain my altitude.

Giving up on this effort, I then nosed over, lighting the burner in a power dive to see how fast the Thud could really go. I was able to attain Mach 1.68 as I passed through 20,000 feet but that was all I could coax out of the airplane. The advertised specifications are obtained using factory-fresh aircraft with no external stores and no modifications such as camera blisters, added cooling air ducts or camouflage paint. I satisfied my curiosity and concluded that aircraft actually used in combat are, in most cases, probably not able to match the operating limits reached by earlier prototype aircraft.

In July I flew 41 FCF flights, followed by another 25 in August. The last week in August I took leave to participate in my brother's wedding back home in Indiana. I took a taxi to Bangkok to enjoy the scenery in Thailand. In the States taking a taxi for a 130-mile ride would have been prohibitively expensive but this was the Far East and a dollar went a lot further. The taxi driver wanted to stop for lunch at a roadside thatched hut and I readily agreed, letting him order for me as the locals had seen very few foreigners and we had difficulty communicating. The first dish was some kind of rice in an opaque liquid: it was cold to the touch so I incorrectly assumed it would not be as spicy as most Thai food. Wrong - I think I destroyed most of my taste buds on the first bite so I cannot say I really enjoyed the remainder of the lunch, especially considering I had no idea what I was eating.

On the trip we met several 10-wheel tanker trucks loaded with jet fuel negotiating the narrow two-lane blacktop road at breakneck speeds. We also saw one turned upside down in the ditch by the road. To satisfy the enormous fuel needs of the aircraft at Takhli approximately 200 truck loads of JP-4 were delivered daily by such trucks and wrecks were very commonplace on that highway.

After spending the night in Bangkok I took another taxi to U-Tapao airfield where the B-52s and KC-135s were stationed, hoping to hop a ride on one of the 135s headed east. I was in luck and managed to catch a flight going to Okinawa the very same day. We arrived on Okinawa in the midst of a typhoon evacuation and Kadena Airbase was in a frenzy of activity trying to get aircraft off the island and out of harm's way. I immediately found a seat on another tanker that was headed to Guam, the right direction to get back to Indiana. The aircraft had spare engines aboard, numerous maintenance personnel, other spare parts and tool kits, and I wondered just how close to being overloaded we were. Takeoff roll on the big guys is measured not only in feet but in minutes and seconds. I think it took us over two minutes from the time brakes were released until we were safely airborne and I had my fingers crossed the entire time.

On arrival at Guam, the flight crew took me aside and said, "Not everybody aboard is going to be back on this airplane when we depart because there will be time to accurately calculate the load considering the fuel needed to get to the west coast. We will add your name to our crew list and we will pick you up by the crew gate as we go to the airplane." Once again the Thud patches on my flight suit paid handsomely in dividends.

I arrived at Travis Air Force Base where I checked in with the passenger terminal to see what I could do to facilitate a return ride to somewhere close to Thailand. If I was able to get anyplace close I knew I could find a ride the rest of the way. The Sergeant at the terminal said the only way to get a hop for the Far East was to place your name on the waiting list and then sit in the terminal area waiting for your name to be called. If your name was called and you were not present, your name was removed from the list and you had to start the process all over. He said the waiting time was running three to four days and by the time I got back to Travis from Indiana, my name should be at the top of the list. Again my identifying patches saved the day as the Sergeant added, "For a Thud driver I will ensure your name remains on the top of the list even if you are not here."

I then changed into my blues from my flight suit and headed to San Francisco International to catch a commercial flight home. I was seated in the terminal awaiting my flight when an Air Force Colonel noticed me: I had my feet propped up on my B-4 bag exposing my unauthorized footwear. Rather than wearing the standard low-quarter black dress shoes I always wore zippered, plain toe, black boots with my blues. I also still had my very striking (at least in my mind) handlebar moustache as I was not quite ready to shave it off even though my combat tour was officially over as I had completed my 100 missions. I was still at Takhli flying dangerous missions in the F-105, right?

My guess is the Colonel had just read the Air Force regulations concerning proper wear of the uniform and the necessity to be properly trimmed and shaven. He approached and I could tell by his demeanor that it was not going to be a friendly conversation. The Colonel said, "Captain, are those boots authorized?" I replied, in a matter-of-fact but quite agreeable tone, "Why no, Colonel, they are not." He then asked, "Captain, does that moustache meet Air Force regulations?" Of course my response was, "Why no, Colonel, I do not believe it does." Seeing some kind of theme arising from our brief discourse, the Colonel then demanded to know what unit I belonged to. I responded with an obvious amount of pride that I belonged to "The Bridge Busting Professionals of the 355th Tactical Fighter Wing and the Dragons of the 357th Tactical Fighter Squadron, flying the pride of the Air Force, the F-105 Thunderchief." I guess my response convinced the Colonel that I was undoubtedly incorrigible because he abruptly turned around and walked away without any further conversation. I arrived in Indiana just in time to participate in all the wedding festivities.

The Wedding

With the successful completion of the wedding mission, I returned to Travis to discover my name was indeed at the top of the waiting list as promised and I left Travis after about a six-hour wait in the passenger terminal. As I boarded the contract carrier, World Airways, I received a warmer than usual greeting from two really cute stewardesses that were on board. One asked what the "little turtles" meant on some of my ribbons. (The "little turtles" were the oak leaf clusters given for multiple awards of the same medal.) After takeoff for what would be a long overnight flight, one of the young ladies came to my seat and said, "Why don't you join us at our jump-seat and we can talk about those turtles." The stewardesses placed a blanket on the floor in front of the jump-seat for me to sit on as there wasn't room for the three of us on the small fold-down seat and I found myself sitting in front of two very short skirts directly at my eye-level. Although it was going to be difficult to maintain proper eye contact, I knew that sitting on the floor in that situation was definitely going to be more fun than sitting in my assigned seat between two Army troops bound for Southeast Asia. The conversation and the company certainly helped turn what would have been a very tedious and boring flight into a pleasant interlude and the time passed quickly. Upon my return to Takhli, I flew another 23 FCF flights during the remainder of September.

There was no requirement for a "bear" to be in the back seat of the "F" on a check flight and by regulation the back seat was to be unoccupied unless the flight surgeon needed to log his flying time. Rarely did "Ma" Smith find the need (or urge) to fly and I would take deserving crew chiefs along for the ride. It was a form of an incentive flight to reward those troops for the long hours of intense labor they put in to keeping our birds airborne.

I figured that was also a way to repay some of the crew chiefs for the extra attention they gave the pilots in carrying out our missions. They always assisted us in strapping into the aircraft and in disembarking after a flight. After all strike force missions, the crew chiefs would scramble up the ladder to take our helmets and hand us an ice cold beer and an ice-water-soaked towel to wrap around our feverishly heated heads and necks. I was never a beer drinker but I came to look forward to that ice-cold can of beer after a sweat-draining, hair-raising flight over North Vietnam. Most of the crew chiefs continued that tradition even after we stopped flying into pack six.

Silver F-105 Carrying Full Bomb Load:
234 was Shot Down over Laos in December 1968. (USAF Photo)

Death was still a part of our everyday activity and on 12 September 1968 our squadron was again reminded of that fact. Sam Maxwell was shot down in his F-105D over Laos and listed as MIA. Sam had a premonition that something was going to interrupt his tour in the Thud but he persevered in carrying out his duty to the end.

Near the end of September the entire squadron took a down-day to take a trip on the base Gooney Bird to visit Korat and our sister wing of Thuds. The big event was the appearance at Korat of a USO show named the Ladybirds; we found it an odd coincidence that President Johnson had earlier visited Korat and his wife was nicknamed Lady Bird. The big draw for the show was that the Ladybirds were an all-girl topless band.

We arrived over Korat, made a low-level pass over the base, and rolled the officers club with dozens of rolls of toilet paper we threw out the open troop door of the C-47. After landing, we all entered the club en masse where some of us sat on the bar to get a better view of the show. Almost immediately one of the bartenders informed us that the wing commander at Korat had a rule against sitting on the bar and that we should obtain seats on the barstools. You can probably guess that the result of receiving this bit of information was for everyone in the squadron to try to get a seat on the bar.

Finally the Ladybirds appeared, the entire squadron watched intently to see how an accordion player could possibly play that instrument topless. The mystery was soon solved when we discovered the accordion player did not remove her top: that was undoubtedly a very smart move on her part but we still wondered if she had learned that the hard way.

The show was over and we returned to the Gooney Bird where the flight time back to Takhli was logged as one pilot and 24 co-pilots. I have often thought of the disastrous consequences if that C-47 had crashed - an entire F-105 squadron would have been lost at the same time.

Somewhat sadly, my time with the Thud was growing very short and on the second of October, 1968 I flew my last FCF flight in the F-105 in a "D". I had now flown 121 combat missions, 100 over

North Vietnam, and 125 functional check flights in that marvelous aircraft.

Oddly enough, my last combat flight at Takhli took place the following day. I logged 3.3 hours as a first pilot aboard an EB-66C on a jamming mission over northern Laos. I was strapped in a web seat with no outside visibility except for a small six-inch square window well above my head when seated. We started receiving warnings from Ethan about MiG activity in our immediate area and I started considering the real possibility I would be shot down when I had absolutely no control or say-so in the entire episode.

We safely completed the mission without any MiG attacks and I started clearing the base at that point. I was pleasantly and completely surprised by my squadron with an unexpected going-away dinner at one of the restaurants in Nakhon Sawan. I tried to quietly leave Takhli with little fanfare as I hated saying "goodbye" but that last get-together was special. I then departed Takhli by taxi as I found my previous cab ride to Bangkok definitely beat sitting in the rear of another C-130 on the Thailand shuttle.

At the end of the month Operation Rolling Thunder came to an end with a complete halt to the bombing of North Vietnam. Sadly, the operation had been a tremendous strategic failure as it cost the United States far more than the value of the damage inflicted on North Vietnam. Around 900 aircraft were lost during its execution with about 80 percent of those losses resulting from anti-aircraft fire.

Out of 833 F-105s produced, two were prototype F-105As, 78 were F-105Bs, 610 were F-105Ds, and 143 were F-105Fs. The B series aircraft were never sent to Vietnam and saw duty in reserve units and the training role so the inventory of Ds and Fs available for combat totaled 753 (including the units not stationed in Southeast Asia). Of that number 382 were lost, including 62 operational losses (non-combat-related). The Thud served admirably, delivering 75% of the bombs dropped on North Vietnam during Rolling Thunder in spite of the fact that it was not designed for that role.

A-1 TRAINING: THE SKYRAIDER

Upon arriving at Travis Air Force Base I contacted the long-term storage facility that had kept my Dodge while I was at Takhli. When I reached the pick-up point at the front gate I spotted my car sitting in front of their office with the engine idling: it appeared ready to make a trip across country to Indiana and home for leave before going to Florida.

First I decided to drive to Los Angeles for a little hot-rod work on the hemi. There I had a roller cam installed by Racer Brown and a custom exhaust system designed and welded by Doug's Headers. The people of Los Angeles certainly did not provide any kind of a welcome back to the United States and it had nothing to do with Vietnam. I could not get any place to cash a check and credit cards were still a thing of the future so I finally went to a bank and talked to the manager explaining I needed some cash. The bank cashed a check for me only after the manager contacted my bank in Colorado Springs to obtain assurance the Colorado bank would honor the check even if my account did not have sufficient funds.

I must have been in the wrong part of town because that evening, in a bar not far from my motel, I was told I would not be served and that I should leave the premises as my blonde hair was not welcome. (I noted the staff and patrons all had a definite Hispanic appearance.) From the malevolent looks I was getting I did not have to be told twice and I returned to the relative safety of my room, making sure the door was securely locked and bolted. Thankful to leave the so-called City of Angels, I was on the road home for a short leave before beginning training in yet another airplane that was entirely different from what I had been flying.

I reported to the 4410th Combat Crew Training Wing at Hurlburt near the end of November 1968 in Class 69-5 with twelve other wannabe Skyraider drivers. Hurlburt began as an auxiliary training field for Eglin Field during WW II. It was initially designated Eglin Auxiliary Field No. 9, and later as Eglin AFB Auxiliary Field 9/Hurlburt Field, before being administratively separated from the rest of the Eglin AFB complex in the 1950s.

In preparation for their carrier-borne mission to Tokyo in WW II, Jimmy Doolittle and his Raiders practiced short runway takeoffs with their B-25 bombers using a short cross-field runway near the southern end of Hurlburt Field's main runway. The field was closed following WW II but was reopened in 1955. In the early 60s the 4410th was activated to provide combat training in several piston-engine aircraft including the Skyraider.

The Skyraider was conceived near the end of WW II to meet requirements for a carrier-borne, single-seat, long-range, high-performance dive bomber. Designed and built by the Douglas Aircraft Company, deliveries of the aircraft began in December 1946 with the designation AD-1 and the Skyraider saw widespread use in Korea.

The Skyraider went through several versions with the AD-5 being significantly widened, allowing two crewmembers to sit side-by-side. The AD-6 was a single seat attack version with improved low-level bombing equipment, and the final production version of the aircraft was designated the AD-7. Skyraider production ended in 1957 with a total of 3,180 built. In 1962, for Air Force use, the existing AD-5 Skyraiders were re-designated A-1E and the existing AD-6s and 7s re-designated A-1Hs and A-1Js, respectively.

The A-1 was large for a single piston-engine aircraft with a wingspan of 50 feet and a length of 39 feet; it had an empty weight of 12,000 pounds and a max takeoff weight of 25,000 pounds. The aircraft we flew were powered by the Wright R-3350-26WD radial engine. The engine was rated at 2,700 horsepower for takeoff and was the largest, most powerful engine ever put in a single-engine airplane.

The rated maximum speed of the airplane was 322 miles per hour with a cruise speed of 198 miles per hour and service ceiling was specified to be 28,000 feet. The side-by-side-seating series A-1E, A-1E-5, and A-1G airplanes had a large middle compartment that could be equipped with passenger seats, could carry litter patients, or could carry cargo; however, I never saw one put to such use.

All aircraft were fitted with four 20mm wing-mounted cannon and could carry up to 8,000 pounds of ordnance or external stores on fifteen hard points or mounting stations. The Navy used Skyraiders extensively in Vietnam as did the Air Force. Affectionately called the flying dump truck or the SPAD (for Single Place Attack, Douglas), the airplane performed its job in Vietnam well especially in the search and rescue role. During the conflict the Skyraider would suffer 256 total losses with 198 of those losses in combat.

Our class had six Lieutenants, two Captains, four Majors, and one Colonel. Of that group two of the Majors would not return from their tour in Southeast Asia. Major James B. "JB" East was killed in action in Laos on April 26th of 1969 and Major Franklin W. Picking was killed in action in South Vietnam three months later on July 23rd. Lieutenant Richard Craft and I would share an instructor's time and effort and the three of us got along extremely well making for an enjoyable training tour. Although they may not have realized it, all of us in 69-5 had great respect for JB East and Major Ed Bulka and they became the unofficial elder statesmen and leaders for our class. Ed went to the 6th Special Operations Squadron stationed at Pleiku, South Vietnam after completing A-1 training.

A-1 Class 69-5 at Hurlburt. I am kneeling fourth from the left between Rich Craft and JB East. Ed Bulka is standing third from the right. (USAF Photo)

The bachelor officers quarters at Hurlburt were newer than those I had at Sewart AFB and thus a little better but the facilities were still not entirely to my liking. I decided to check on possible living arrangements in Fort Walton Beach even though I would have to bear the added expense. I was still single, expected to live in the BOQ, and no quarters allowance would be forthcoming. I found a motel on the beach, the Carousel on Okaloosa Island, that had winter rates and agreed to rent a room for the two months I would be in town.

Fort Walton Beach was a great place to live and, to my knowledge, all of us in the class enjoyed our brief stay in the area. The beaches were almost deserted as it was winter but the weather was always great and we could find lots to do to keep ourselves entertained in our down times. Bacons-by-the-Sea was the best bar and restaurant in the area and we spent quite a bit of time frequenting that establishment. I was sitting at their bar in my flight suit having a beer one day after flying when two Air Police appeared in the doorway: several ladies I did not know immediately surrounded me to hide what I was wearing from the APs as flight suits were not authorized to be worn off base. The APs departed and I bought a round of drinks for my unknown benefactors.

Smitty, the other Captain and I were eating dinner at the Sea Gull one evening where Smitty made the mistake of ordering fried chicken in a seafood restaurant. He tried a few bites but left the majority of the chicken untouched. Our waitress was an elderly lady, a grandmotherly type, and she asked Smitty what was wrong with the chicken. Smitty politely replied he just wasn't hungry but the waitress insisted on the real answer. Smitty said the chicken tasted like fish. Our waitress reached over Smitty, picked up a chicken leg and took a bite. She then returned the leg to his plate and said, "There is nothing wrong with that chicken, you eat it." I immediately thought of Nip and the ice cream at Takhli but Nip had not tasted the ice cream. I wondered what Smitty was going to do and, just as I had done at Takhli, he complied with the orders of the waitress although he did not eat the leg.

On the 6th of December in 1968 I flew my first training flight in an A-1E. It was quite an adjustment from the Thud. Everything happened so quickly in the 105 that you had to be mentally well ahead of the airplane to keep from killing yourself. The A-1 seemed to operate in slow motion to me and I had to readjust my entire thought process. For example, a turn to initial approach required two to three miles for the Thud as it flew initial at 350 knots, twice as fast as the A-1.

Not only that, the Skyraider turned on a dime and the first time I tried to approach the field for landing I started my turn to initial way too early. I made the turn and the airplane was definitely not lined up on the runway. I literally had to fly the airplane to the exact spot I wanted to turn and then turn: there was little lead time or extra space required. I initially encountered the same difficulty in formation flying as I was used to creating at least a 100-knot overtake on the aircraft I was joining on, opening the speed brakes and throwing up the wing closest to the lead aircraft to kill off overtake speed, and deftly sliding into position.

With the A-1 there was very little overtake to be had in aircraft speed and you had to carefully rely on the cut-off angle, driving the airplane into position with little throttle movement. If you tried to kill off airspeed or facilitate the rejoin by turning the nose or throwing up a wing you would turn inside the lead aircraft and eventually have to chase him in trail to finally reach his wing. I quickly overcame that issue simply through the experience of a couple of flights and by continually reminding myself I was no longer in a supersonic, century-series aircraft.

For the first time in four years I was able to spend Christmas with part of my family. My brother was stationed at Keesler Air Force Base in Biloxi, Mississippi, just 160 miles away and I managed to go celebrate the holiday with him on the 24th and 25th. I learned a valuable lesson at that time - It is not wise to try to Christmas shop on Christmas Eve as the store shelves in smaller towns are absolutely empty at that late date. December went by very quickly as I flew fifteen times during the month including flights on the 23rd and the 26th.

The Hurlburt Officers Open Mess was an old, white frame building on the water that allegedly had been used as a storage facility for Al Capone's bootleg whiskey operation during the 1920s but I never actually read anything that could support the legend. It did have a good bar and oysters on the half shell were available during Friday evening happy hour for fifty cents a dozen. I was eating lunch at the club one day when the wing safety officer came over and said he needed to talk to me. He had also been the wing safety officer at Craig Air Force Base when Tom Pierson was killed and remembered me from that time. An edict had been issued by the Air Force that there would be no more third tours in Vietnam for pilots. I was told that I certainly did not have to return if I did not want to and there was some concern as to whether I could return. I assured him that I did want to go back to Southeast Asia and that the official records would show my C-130 tour was in Okinawa, not Vietnam. He was satisfied and nothing more was said about my upcoming third trip to the combat zone. In hindsight the reasoning behind the rule prohibiting three tours was well justified: perhaps I should have listened.

A few days later I was in the bar waiting for some friends to join me when I got into a conversation with a Lieutenant Colonel who discovered I was a USAF Academy graduate. He explained that he was an Air Officer Commanding (AOC) for one of the cadet squadrons at the time I was still in school and said one of the funniest things he heard about during his assignment was that one of the cadets had attended the Commandant's Ball in the fall of 1962 dressed as a girl. I asked if he would like to meet her as I knew exactly where she was at that precise moment. He immediately knew he was talking to Wendy Brown.

The absolute best part of flying the A-1 was the engine start; I never got tired of hearing those eighteen cylinders come to life accompanied by a cloud of smoke and very noticeable airframe vibration. I would always stop what I was doing to listen to an engine start if I was anywhere within hearing range.

The throttle was opened about an inch, the mixture control lever was set to idle, the propeller control lever was set to full increase, external power was used or the battery-generator switch was set to "on", fuel booster was turned on and the starter button was depressed and held. We counted sixteen blades as the prop turned to ensure oil was in the nose case and to get rid of any unburned fuel in the cylinders. Sometimes in hot, humid air that unburned fuel would fire and the engine would spin a little quicker. After any leftover fuel was cleared and the engine was turning on starter only, the primer pushbutton was held down simultaneously with the starter button until the engine was running. The pilot's instruction manual clearly stated that intermittent priming (pickling) would result in erratic fuel flow causing an engine backfire.

A tradition in squadrons flying reciprocating aircraft was that a backfire required the purchase of a case of beer for the outfit. During my first few days of training I asked to ride with the squadron commander on a test hop to increase my learning time in the aircraft. He granted permission but, by his attitude, I do not think he was too thrilled about my riding along. He noticed that I watched him pickle the prime button on start and he tersely said, "You do what you are taught to do and do not pay any attention to what I am doing." I followed the written instructions (and his advice about ignoring his actions) and never had a backfire during my time at Hurlburt.

After fifteen flights in the two seat A-1E I was scheduled to fly the single seat A-1H. The A-1H had a bubble canopy instead of the big greenhouse that readily identified the E series. As a result you could see outside both sides of the airplane instead of just being able to see out the left side. In addition to the more confined cockpit area in the single-seater the "H" had a much shorter control stick and you had to be careful not to let your strap-on knee pad (where maps, flight data etc. were carried) interfere with control movements. That first flight was a treat and I always enjoyed flying the much more svelte "H" series.

On one of my January flights I had a lapse in concentration on landing and almost had an absolute catastrophe. Maximum crosswind for the A-1 was only 20 knots and I had some crosswind on that flight. The A-1 also used a lot of rudder for control because of the torque created by the huge propeller and the tremendous horsepower of the engine. The takeoff run always demanded a lot of right rudder, especially in a loaded A-1, and close attention to rudder placement was required as takeoff speed increased. (Cutting power on a takeoff required rapid control reversals to counteract a sudden roll.) The F-105 had required very little rudder movement because of the centerline thrust and I was used to relaxing rudder pressure almost as soon as the touchdown was made. The Thud's drag chute also acted to keep the aircraft on a straight roll out.

On the day referenced I touched down and immediately released all rudder control: the aircraft made almost a 90 degree turn to the right and I was looking at the side of the runway. I frantically applied full left rudder, left aileron, and stood on the left brake. The airplane snapped back to the proper heading, aided by the locking tailwheel, and I breathed a huge sigh of relief as I rolled out. Mobile control naturally notified the squadron of the horribly botched landing and I was appropriately chastised back at the flight shack. I had made a mistake, but I was able to recover with rapid corrective action.

On the 13th of January I was flying solo in an A-1E in the number two position following my instructor and a student in another A-1E: we were on a cross country to Cairns Army Airfield at Fort Rucker, Alabama. The lead aircraft developed an engine malfunction and started losing oil pressure. An emergency was declared and a straight-in approach to runway 36 at Cairns was authorized. I followed lead down final in close formation until he started his flare for landing and I applied full power and went around.

The tower called and wanted to know if I had any problem with making a right turn to runway 24 and landing on that runway. I said "Not an issue" and rolled out on a base leg looking at the runway. Runway 36/18 was 5,000 feet long and runway 6/24 was only 4,500 feet long. Hurlburt had a 9,600-foot runway and Nellis and Takhli had 10,000-foot runways. After landing on those long runways for the past two and one half years that runway at Cairns looked awfully short: true, I made landings on 3,000-foot runways in the C-130 but that had been a long time ago. I wondered if I had made the best decision but as I approached final the momentary lack of confidence subsided and I touched down with no problem.

I flew nineteen times in the month of January and nine of those flights were in the single seat "H" series. I generally got along well with our instructors at Hurlburt as most of them recognized my skill as an aviator and accepted (or at least tolerated) my somewhat cocky attitude but I also knew there were one or two of the older, risk-averse pilots closing out their careers as instructors who viewed me as somewhat of a wild child, prone to being overly aggressive in my flying. My guess is those guys took the old adage to heart, "There are old pilots and there are bold pilots, but there are no old and bold pilots." One of the instructors not stricken with the singular goal to retire at a ripe old age actually taught me how to do a complete loop in the A-1, starting from level flight, gaining no more than 500 feet in elevation by coordinating stick, throttle and flaps, and returning to level flight at the entry altitude. He said not to let anyone know what we had done as that maneuver was definitely not in the training manual.

The last week of the month I decided to get an early start on the mandatory Southeast Asia moustache and started letting it grow. At the time NFL star quarterback Joe Namath was offered a handsome sum for some charitable reason to shave half his moustache off. I was at the sign-in log as this issue was being discussed by several of the instructors when the squadron commander abruptly asked in a mocking tone how much I thought my moustache was worth. I replied, "Not much, I am sure." He said he didn't think so either and then curtly ordered me to shave it off. I looked around the room at the instructors, many of whom were sporting large bushy moustaches, and the previously noisy room turned absolutely quiet. I simply smiled and said, "OK." I saw no need for any unnecessary confrontation with the commander as I knew I would be in the training squadron for only a few more days and I thought I would have the whole next year to let my moustache grow.

On the 30th of January I flew my last A-1 training flight in an "H". We celebrated the completion of our training at the now defunct Hunter's Lodge in Fort Walton Beach and graduation took place on the 4th of February. I then departed for Indiana in my hemi. My next stop would be to once again attend the PACAF jungle survival school before reporting to the 56th Special Operations Wing at Nakhon Phanom, Thailand.

NAKHON PHANOM: FIREFLY & SANDY

Following graduation I spent a very short time at home before I again departed by commercial air for San Francisco and ultimately for the Far East. I executed a power of attorney for my father to sell my hemi convertible as I hated to let it sit for another year as it had while I was at Takhli. (I now hate to think about what the car would be worth today if I had kept it.)

Naturally I was scheduled to attend PACAF jungle survival training as the pipeline for replacement pilots assumed it would be my first visit to Vietnam. I arrived in the Philippines in mid-February and reported to the school. I began to wonder if someone in personnel would notice my extensive time attending survival training and decide I should be transferred to that specialty code for future assignments. When I checked in the non-commissioned officer-in-charge of the school recognized me and said, "You have been here before; haven't you?" I said I had and the sergeant decided there was no reason for me to have to again sit in the jungle for an unpleasant few days. He said, "Attend classes for a refresher and when we go to the field, you can stay behind and enjoy yourself for that time period." I needed no additional urging and did exactly that, lounging by the hotel pool and spending my money on exotic food and booze while my classmates endured the heat, humidity and critters of the Philippine jungle.

I arrived in Bangkok on the 20th and headed for my old resting place, the Federal Hotel, to spend the night. On the following day I could not find a taxi at the hotel so I walked down the street to look for a cab into downtown Bangkok.

While walking I was approached by a young (20-something) Thai of the male variety who engaged me in conversation. I assumed he was practicing his English skills as he did not appear to be a street hustler; he was dressed in a button-up silk shirt and casual slacks. After exchanging the usual pleasantries he casually mentioned that he knew I would be leaving Thailand in less than a month. I thought, "He thinks I am one of the thousands of GIs that have been lucky enough to visit Bangkok for R&R just before the end of their tour." I laughed and said, "Not unless the war ends very suddenly as I am just starting a tour." He smiled and replied, "I know, but the truth is; you will leave Thailand in less than a month and you will be back in the states in less than three months." I looked at him to try to judge just what his motive was and he laughed and said, "Not to worry. Something is going to happen and you will think it is very bad when it does, but over time it will turn out to be a good thing." We shook hands and I started to leave when he handed me a small, plastic, red and black object that looked like a kid's secret code stamp saying, "Keep this to remember me by. If we meet again you can pay me whatever you think my prediction was worth."

That evening I moved to the government contract hotel, the Chao Phya, in order to use their landline to Nakhon Phanom. I knew that I had not necessarily been assigned to a squadron and I wanted to be in the 602nd. I telephoned the 602nd explaining that I was a new pilot assigned to the 56th SOW and that I wanted to be placed in the Sandy outfit.

The voice on the other end wanted to know if I was the F-105 jock that was scheduled to report. When I replied in the affirmative the voice said, "We will pick you up when you land." The following morning I hopped on the old standby, the Thailand shuttle, and landed at NKP where a pilot from the 602nd was waiting in a jeep to pick me up. We went to the Sandy hooch where I was given a room to toss my B-4 bag in and we went to the Sandy Box to meet some of the other guys I would hopefully be flying with, including Lieutenant Colonel Walter Steuck, the squadron commander.

Nakhon Phanom looked like a WW II base with wooden hooches dotting the red dirt landscape of northeast Thailand: the asphalt runway we used was destined to be a future taxiway for the permanent concrete runway that was under construction. The remaining taxiways and ramp were made of pierced steel planking (PSP). I first landed at NKP in 1965 in my C-130 when the PSP taxiway was the runway. The aircraft lining the ramp all had propellers and there was not a jet to be seen.

The threat of communist insurgents entering Thailand from neighboring Laos during the 1960s prompted the United States and the Thai government to enter into an agreement to establish Nakhon Phanom Air Base (NKP). The base would be located in northeastern Thailand just a stone's throw from the Mekong River that separated Laos and Thailand. It was also just barely 60 miles from the border of North Vietnam and 230 miles from Hanoi. The proximity of the base to Laos resulted in the erection of a high fence with guard towers and searchlights that surrounded the airfield. That perimeter was also patrolled by Air Police sentries accompanied by guard dogs.

The first American military personnel to arrive at NKP in 1962 were part of a Navy construction battalion known as Seabees who undertook the task of constructing runways and raising the first buildings at the new base. The first USAF unit assigned to the base in June 1964 was a very small detachment of rescue helicopters. On 2 February 1966 the Thai government approved the establishment of a United States Air Force Air Commando unit in Thailand, using the existing USAF facilities at NKP to give the appearance that the United States was not introducing another unit into Thailand.

The 56th Air Commando Wing was formed on 8 April 1967. Nearly one year later on 1 August 1968 the 56th ACW designation was changed to 56th Special Operations Wing. At the time of my brief stay at NKP the following units were assigned to the 56th SOW: The 1st Special Operations Squadron flying A-1s, call sign "Hobo"; The 21st Special Operations Squadron flying CH-3s and CH-53s call signs "Dusty" & "Knife"; the 22nd Special Operations Squadron flying night missions in the A-1, call sign "Zorro"; the 606th Special Operations Squadron flying C-123 flareships, call sign, "Candlesticks"; the 609th Special Operations Squadron flying A-26Ks, call sign "Nimrod"; Detachment 1 of the 40th ARRS flying the HH-3, call sign "Jolly Green"; and, the 602nd Fighter Squadron, call signs "Firefly" and "Sandy". Firefly was used for strike, reconnaissance, and escort missions while Sandy was used for search and rescue missions.

On the 23rd of February Colonel Steuck accompanied me to see the wing commander, Colonel Edwin White, who would make the decision as to which unit I would spend the next year in. Colonel Steuck advised me to speak up during the interview and let Colonel White know my feelings if I wanted to be a Sandy pilot.
Colonel White noted I was an experienced pilot and that experience could be very valuable to the Zorros: the A-1 squadron that flew the night interdiction missions. I said, "Colonel, the only reason I volunteered for this tour was because of the tremendous respect I have for the Sandy pilots who rescued many of my former comrades. I want to be a Sandy pilot. Besides, I figure I have already done my fair share of night flying in this region and my experience can also be put to good use in the 602nd." Colonel White replied, "Then a Sandy pilot you shall be." The meeting was over and I made my way to the Sandy hooch where I was able to claim the room temporarily provided to me as my own - or at least half of that room, as "JB" East would become my roommate.

Our quarters at NKP were reminiscent of the quarters at Craig AFB: it was a single-story wooden building with a porch running the full length of the structure. We were assigned two to a room and the furnishings were sparse to say the least: two single beds and two desks. The rooms were dark with heavy window dressing to preserve night vision and kept cool by a continuously running air conditioning unit. Our shower room and latrine was located in the middle of the hooch and the first room was designated the Sandy Box.
Rather than being used as a bedroom, that was the place we all congregated to exchange war stories and sing songs accompanied by Gene McCormack on his guitar. Gene tried his best to get us to sing with less rowdy enthusiasm and with some effort at achieving harmony but it was a losing battle. There was a refrigerator in the Sandy Box that was well stocked with beer but some of us started drinking tequila, using a squeeze bottle of lemon extract and a salt shaker from the club. The air in the Sandy Box was thick with cigarette smoke, the walls were decorated with wise bits of advice,

humorous and brief anecdotes, and notable quotes, and it was always noisy with laughter and boisterous conversation.

The very next day, 24 February 1969, I flew my first combat flight in an A-1G. As was standard procedure my first five flights would be with an experienced A-1 driver in the right seat. On that first flight I quickly learned a fully loaded A-1 was not exactly the easiest beast to herd around the sky. At those heavy weights the aircraft was very slow to respond and you had to be very conscious of critical things like stall speed. Takeoff roll seemed to take forever and the use of rapid power application required tremendous right rudder as you bounced and waddled across the uneven asphalt.

The secret to good dive bombing remained as it had been in the Thud: a good roll in and a steep dive angle. On my first roll in I could not believe how difficult it was to get the heavily loaded Skyraider to enter the roll and my old technique of pulling back on the stick while rolling left to an inverted position and then pushing the nose down did not work well in the A-1. I wound up pointing the nose well away from my intended target with precious little time to correct. The FAC graciously said that my ordnance was not exactly where he wanted it: a fact I was already well aware of. I quickly adapted to a technique that worked well in the Skyraider and that resulted in no further problems with accuracy.

602nd Fighter Squadron at NKP

My next four flights were flown on the 25th, 26th, 27th and 28th. At the beginning of February I had not yet graduated from A-1 training in Florida and by the end of February I had completed my first five combat missions in the Skyraider over Laos. My flight on the 28th was a check ride to see if I was combat ready: it was with George Marrett, experienced A-1 driver and heroic Sandy Lead, extraordinary test pilot, and presently accomplished author including "Cheating Death: Combat Air Rescues in Vietnam and Laos." We had an uneventful flight over northern Laos as described beginning on page 182 in "Cheating Death" and George declared me to be qualified to fly combat sorties at the conclusion of the mission.

I must have been destined to become a Skyraider pilot as George also relates in his book it was a custom for the squadron pilots to visit the zoo in Bangkok and have their picture taken with a boa constrictor wrapped around their body. The snake actually belonged to an independent vendor located near the entrance to the zoo and was not part of the zoo itself. I was not in the 602nd long enough to learn of that particular custom but I actually made the zoo trip and had my picture taken with the snake many months earlier while I was still flying the C-130.

On his first R&R trip to Bangkok George decided to visit the zoo and hold that boa which he described as looking big and hungry. In spite of consuming a couple of Singha beers at a nearby beer garden, George eventually decided he was too valuable an asset to the United States Air Force and the taxpayers who paid for his training to risk being a snake snack. He concluded he did not really need a photo with a boa constrictor wrapped around his body and, to this day, he admits he still does not have one. George completed his

217

tour in April, 1969 after flying 188 missions in the Skyraider and resigned from the Air Force to pursue his career as an author and civilian test pilot for Hughes Aircraft Company.

    I flew my sixth mission on the first of March and was scheduled to fly a local area flight in an A-1H on the second to reacquaint myself with the single seater. I would fly the squadron commander's airplane, "Maggie's Orange Blossom Special III." The airplane had just had an FCF flight by Captain Jerry Jenkinson and was cleared to resume flying combat sorties. Colonel Steuck flew combat in WW II, Korea and Vietnam: in each conflict he had named an airplane after his wife hence the III on Maggie's Special.

    I reached 15,000 feet southwest of the airfield when I heard a distinct backfire from the engine. I quickly checked over my engine instruments and the previously normal readings started becoming erratic. I immediately headed back toward the airpatch in a descent and the big radial engine literally started coming apart. I declared an emergency and notified the tower of my difficulty. The backfires were becoming increasingly violent and more frequent no matter what throttle, prop, or mixture settings I tried. I turned north paralleling the runway just to the east side of the air base with flames pouring out of the engine, trying to set myself up for a dead-stick landing. With each revolution of the engine I felt the airframe shudder from those explosive backfires: the cowling started separating from the airframe and bits and pieces of sparkplugs, wiring, and assorted engine parts started peppering the front of my windscreen. Suddenly the noise ceased and was replaced with stunning silence - I became a flaming glider.

    I continued on my northerly heading electing to spend my rapidly diminishing flight time trying to restart the engine rather than trying to position myself for a landing with no power. The sad fact was, I simply did not have enough of an engine left to start and I watched the ground rapidly approaching. I called the tower to verify I was headed for an unpopulated area in preparation for a bailout.

    I always had an understanding with my airplanes: as long as they did what they were supposed to do we would remain companions, but the minute they did not perform as expected, I would rapidly leave their company with no hesitation. Regardless of that understanding I did not comply with my own advice and I did hesitate, almost too long. I decided that I would punch out of the stricken A-1H at 2,000 feet above the ground as chances of a successful bailout decrease dramatically below that altitude. What I failed to take into consideration was the ground elevation of roughly 500 feet in northeastern Thailand or the tree height of another 100 feet or so. As I read 2,000 feet on the altimeter (above sea level) I reached for the handle on the seat to engage the extraction system that would pull me out of the airplane.

The A-1 did not have an ejection seat: instead it used the Stanley Aviation "Yankee crew escape system." To use the system the pilot pulled the extraction control handle located on the seat front between the pilot's legs. A half second later a cartridge in a launcher tube expelled the extraction-rocket that then fired, pulling ten foot pendant lines attached to the shoulder harness of the pilot. The extraction force pulled the pilot up while the seat pan folded down. The pilot's seat belt and shoulder straps were automatically released and the pilot was separated from the seat that remained in the airplane. Just prior to extraction-rocket burn-out the pendant lines were severed from the rocket which continued on its path. The parachute was then automatically deployed by another charge that expelled the chute from its pack and the extraction from the aircraft was completed. The system could be used at any airspeed and any altitude, including ground level, on the "fat-face" A-1E and "G", but there was a minimum airspeed requirement of 80 knots for the single seat "H" and "J".

As I reached for the handle, I asked myself if I had everything hooked up for a successful extraction. My reaction was to check my harness to see if I was ready when I reminded myself that I simply did not have any time to check anything; it was either hooked up properly or it wasn't. By this time my altimeter read 1,500 feet and I was only about 800 to 900 feet above the tree tops considering ground elevation and tree height. I assumed the proper seating position and pulled the handle.

I was startled when the canopy was separated from the airplane by the explosive charge and I looked to my left. Bad move, when the extraction pendants deployed one of them caught the side of my helmet twisting the helmet down over my eyes blocking all my vision. That pendant also pulled my left arm up and away from my body where the 120-knot slipstream stripped my tightly fitting glove completely off my hand. The repositioning of the helmet also created another problem as the chin strap was now strangling me. The chute opened and my knees slammed hard into my chest. I was blindly swinging back and forth in the chute, oscillating badly, which could present more serious problems if I contacted the ground in a swinging motion.

I was struggling trying to loosen the chin strap and straighten up the helmet when I finally got the helmet off my head, clutching the helmet tightly in my hand. Great, I could at least breathe again. As I removed the helmet my sunglasses (non-prescription as I had "lost" the prescription glasses at the beginning of my Thud tour) were blown off and I tried in vain to catch them. I realized the oscillation had stopped without any effort on my part and I watched the Skyraider level off in front of me until its airspeed reached the stall point. The A-1 rolled onto its back, did a split S into the ground, and erupted into a huge fireball. I took a deep breath and thought, "I am sure glad I am not still in the cockpit."

It was March and the fields and rice paddies below me were dusty and dry. I could see several split rail fences dividing those fields and they became the next immediate concern. I knew I was going to miss the tree line but landing on one of those fences was not going to be a pleasant ending to my parachute ride. I crossed my legs as well as my fingers and I put my helmet back on and hooked up the oxygen mask to protect my face.

As I drew closer to the ground, thanks to a slight breeze, I could see that I would not land on any of the fences. I prepared for the landing wondering how hard that would be as I already felt like I had been run over by a truck, and a big one at that. I reached up to grasp the risers of the chute, assumed the proper leg and body position, focused my eyes on the horizon, and waited for the impact. I hit the ground and did a great parachute landing fall, absorbing the landing with my legs and rolling onto my back. I felt like I had finally done something right and happily lay on the ground for a few moments listening to the birds singing their springtime songs. In a perfect world a pilot always tries to have an equal number of takeoffs and landings: I had just violated that maxim as landing without the airplane attached to your butt does not count.

I did not take long to rest and I started gathering my chute as I figured a Jolly Green would be after me real quick. I saw movement in the trees and bushes off to my right and looked to see several tribesmen approaching my location. As was their usual attire they were dressed in loin cloths and they were all carrying machetes. The local population chewed beetlenuts that stained their lips, gums and teeth a dark red prompting me to think of cannibals. I said to myself "I hope they are friendlies" as the northeastern section of Thailand was infiltrated with tribes supportive of the communist insurgents in Laos. At least they were not carrying weapons and I correctly surmised they were simply local farmers checking out the commotion.

They approached cautiously and one of them came trotting over to say, "You, number one." The Thais judged everything on a rating scale from one to ten with one being the best and ten being the worst. I immediately knew they were indeed friendly by his greeting and I thanked him in Thai for his kind remark.

I heard the Jolly Green approaching and I attempted to establish radio communication with my survival radio. I told the Jolly to have the door gunner wave if they read my transmission and the gunner started waving. The HH-3 circled to head into the wind and sat down in the dry rice paddy to pick me up blowing dust and dirt in every direction. In the meantime my new-found Thai friend was concerned about a cut I had over my left eye that was bleeding rather profusely.

The PJ from the Jolly ran to my position, grabbed me by the shoulders and literally picked me up to look into my eyes to determine if I was suffering from shock. (Pararescue Jumpers, or PJs, are the only members of the military whose primary duty is to conduct personnel recovery operations in hostile areas.) Shock was a common occurrence in bailout situations. While the PJ was asking me if I was OK, the Thai started pounding him on his arm, pointing at my eye and the blood and saying, "Look: come out, come out: you fix, you fix." It was a rather ludicrous sight as the PJ was around 6'4" and 240 pounds while my Thai friend was around 4'6" and 110 pounds. I had to admit I was very impressed with the little guy's genuine concern and I wish I had left him some memento of our chance encounter.

The PJ hustled me aboard the chopper and pushed me to the front of the aircraft behind the pilots. I had no intercom capability and the PJ had to let me know what he wanted by pushing me into the jump seat. The Jolly lifted into the air and we flew over the site where Maggie's Special III was still burning.

A-1H of the 6th SOS in Flight (USAF Photo)

We landed at NKP where I was greeted by several of my squadron mates and a female intelligence officer. She had a fond spot in her heart for the 602nd in spite of the fact she was almost seriously injured in a jeep under the control of Clyde Campbell in an incident that happened weeks before my arrival in February. (Clyde plus the female intel officer and several other Sandys had had a little too much to drink and Clyde turned the jeep over near the Sandy hooch.)

I was taken to the base dispensary where I was examined by a flight surgeon who decided that there was nothing wrong with me other than the cut over my eye, a cut behind my left ear, and a bruise that covered every square inch of me from shoulders to knees. There was a watered-down version of a rescue celebration at the club that evening as my recovery was just minutes away from NKP and in a non-hostile environment. I watched from the sidelines as I knew I had yet to take part in a real rescue mission and had not earned the privilege of participation.

Several of us went back to the Sandy Box where we continued our party and I added a comment to the walls of wisdom. While I was being treated by the flight surgeon that afternoon he asked what I was flying. When I responded the A-1 he observed that, "If you only have one engine and it quits, you are in trouble, aren't you?" That astute observation was deservingly immortalized in the Sandy Box.

I jokingly harassed Jerry Jenkinson about releasing an obviously faulty airplane from the FCF he had just flown. Captain Jim Jamerson, a classmate of mine from the Class of 63 at the Academy, had been in the squadron for almost a year and he knew the pilots much better than I did: Jim quietly informed me that Jerry felt extremely bad about the incident and had assumed some measure of personal responsibility for my misfortune. Nothing could have been farther from the truth of course as no FCF pilot has a crystal ball. I attempted to ease Jerry's concerns as I had no wish to cause him any additional grief.

The 602nd came close to having three 1963 Academy graduates in the squadron at the same time but Captain Joe Pirruccello was killed in action on December 8, 1968. Jim and Jerry both successfully completed their tour with the squadron and Jim went on to become a four-star general in the Air Force. Jerry was not as fortunate and returned to the states to be an instructor in UPT at Webb AFB in Texas where he was killed in an aircraft training accident on December 17, 1969.

I did not fly for three days to give my injuries time to heal, especially the cut behind my ear that painfully interfered with wearing my helmet. On the 3rd I was invited to ride along in the chopper with a team to examine the site of the crash. One of the team members was a ground officer who carried a lot of Thai money to pay the locals for the return of aircraft parts they had confiscated.

The crash site was absolutely amazing: there was a small hole created in the jungle foliage where the aircraft had hit the ground. The surrounding vegetation bore scorch and burn marks from the fire and there was a large crater in the middle of the clearing. The only sign of the A-1 was the four breech blocks of the M-3 20mm cannon (the back ends) protruding about six inches from the ground and the four bent tips of the propeller surrounding the engine which was deeply buried in the dirt. There was no other sign of the Skyraider as the wreckage had been carted off during the night by the local population. The cannon were buried too deep in the ground to dig out and the engine was too big to attempt to remove it. We spent a very short time on the ground at the site and departed leaving the money carrier and a couple of escorts sitting at a small table in the clearing waiting to buy back A-1 parts. Unhappily, the 3rd was not a good day for the squadron as Captain Clyde Campbell was killed when his A-1 crashed for unknown reasons in Laos while on a bombing run.

I decided to make good use of my down time to check in with the base personnel office as I realized I had not actually signed in with anybody who kept track of paperwork. The personnel officer, a Major, was absolutely incensed that I had already been flying combat missions and no one in personnel even knew I was on base. He said, "What if you had been shot down: officially you are not even supposed to be here at NKP." I did not tell him why I wasn't flying that particular day as I figured he may have had a stroke. That evening I went into the town of Nakhon Phanom. I soon learned why the guys at NKP did not frequent the local restaurants and bars as often as the guys at Takhli and Ubon did - a trip into town required a forty-five minute one-way ride by taxi across a dark, deserted road that was under construction through the wilderness and the town resembled an old, wild-west movie set.

I flew my next six combat missions as a Firefly wingman on the 6th, 7th, 8th, 9th, 11th and 12th of March. Two flights were in a "J", two were in an "H" and two were in an "E". During those flights I gained badly needed experience in combat operations in the Skyraider. On one of the missions I flew on Captain Rich Hall's wing. As we approached our target area I spotted two trucks on a road in broad daylight. In 38 months of combat I had never seen a sight like that: the trucks were usually caught at night or hiding in the trees during daylight hours. I excitedly called out the target to Rich as the trucks tried to seek cover from what they knew was about to happen. The trucks managed to get under the trees before Rich could spot them and he cleared me to make the first bomb pass as I knew where the trucks had hidden.

I rolled in, dropped a 250-pound bomb on the hiding spot, and then pulled up to avoid any ground fire. We received some scattered 37mm flak as I was trying to gain altitude. The A-1 had a very low rate of climb, especially when heavily loaded, and it normally required several minutes to regain lost altitude. In fact, on departure from NKP it could take up to 45 minutes or more to climb to 10,000 feet.

Just as I started my pull, to my chagrin, the engine died and I started to settle into a dive. I had already learned a few days earlier I did not care for silence when I expected to hear the comforting sound of the big radial. I suddenly realized that in my excitement over the trucks I had failed to switch from my external fuel tank to my internal tank. The fuel carried in the 150-gallon stub tank lasted just about the same time it took to fly to the northern sector of Laos where we located the trucks. I thought I was about to land on the same road I had just bombed - never a good thing to attempt. Switching on the boost pumps and saying a little prayer, I turned the main fuel selector to the internal position. The engine immediately caught and I started the slow climb for another pass. I could not say for certain we actually destroyed those trucks as we created no secondary explosions but I know for sure we at least scared the devil out of their drivers.

On another flight I was following Lieutenant Jon Ewing when we encountered some pretty severe weather. In order to keep Jon in sight my formation was so tight I had to pay close attention not to clip his wing with my prop. Jon was a really good pilot and close friend. He had to land his A-1 gear-up at Ubon Air Base at Christmas in 1968 after taking a 37mm hit in his left gear-well, almost taking the left wing off the airplane. The good news was he then actually participated in the Bob Hope show at the base (a show he was afraid he was going to miss) meeting one of the dancers ironically named "Sandy."

The weather cleared during our flight and on the way home we saw Ethan orbiting nearby. (As you probably recall from my Thud episodes, Ethan was one of the four-engine EC-121s that provided MiG warnings to aircraft in the area.) Jon said, "Let's go fly some formation with the big guy." We started a slight climb to Ethan's altitude and approached him from his right side. As we moved into position on Ethan's right wing we could see the co-pilot look up from his charts or whatever he was reading and Ethan abruptly went into a steep dive.

The EC-121 crew thought they were about to have a mid-air collision and took evasive action. After they realized what was actually happening, the pilot angrily made a radio call saying we had caused him to tumble all his gyros and radars: he was absolutely livid and threatened to report the incident. Jon apologized over the radio and we decided it was really time to go home. A few minutes later Jon called me and said, "Do you think I am in big trouble?" I responded that I doubted Ethan would bother to make a call to the squadron and, even if he did, all we would get was a good chewing out. I figured it was as much Ethan's fault as ours as he did not even know we were in the area.

Flying the A-1 was not necessarily difficult but it was another matter to really fly it well: that would only come with experience, provided you survived long enough to gain that experience. The 602nd lost a lot of airplanes and pilots because of lack of time in the airplane. I, for one, can readily testify to the truth of that observation. Ordnance delivery was complicated by the number of stations or hardpoints on the airplane that carried ordnance and the wide variety of ordnance that was carried. The F-105 had five points to carry weapons, fuel, and other external stores where the A-1 had fifteen stations. In the Thud over pack six the rule was one pass and haul ass. On the other hand the A-1 made pass after pass, changing ordnance and stations on each of those passes, and the armament control panel for the Skyraider had multiple switches to set before making each armed pass. A typical load for an A-1 was a 300-gallon fuel tank on the center station, a mini-gun pod on the left stub, a 250-pound white phosphorous bomb on the right stub, and a mix of cluster bomb units and rockets on the twelve wing stations. The four 20mm cannon carried 200 rounds of ammunition per gun in the wing storage compartments.

The pilot also had to be careful not to get into an asymmetrical wing loading situation that would cause a loss of control: the left inboard wing load could not weigh over 540 pounds more than the right inboard wing load while the right inboard wing load could not weigh over 1,300 pounds more than the left inboard wing load. The outboard stations had a 270-pound and 650-pound maximum differential. To simplify matters ordnance was usually released in pairs simultaneously from each wing. One exception was that the inboard stations usually carried a fuel tank on one stub and a bomb on the other stub.

On one of my missions, during my preflight cockpit check, I noticed the left inboard switch seemed to be in the bomb position even though the stub had a fuel tank hanging from it. The mounting was twisted and did not line up with the remaining mounts and I figured the switch must have simply been out of alignment. I thought the crew chief would not have left the switch in the bomb position and I elected not to try to reposition it. I had been warned about the distinct possibility of bombing off a fuel tank and should have checked the switch by actually toggling it. As I pulled out of my bomb run to drop the right inboard station load I heard my lead call, "Hey two, you just bombed off your fuel tank." The crew chief was not a happy camper when I taxied in to my parking spot. I am sure his maintenance request for another fuel tank probably contained a reference to a "dumbs---" pilot.

Our normal Firefly missions lasted around three to three and a half hours but my flight on the 8th lasted only about an hour. Not long after I crossed the Mekong River into Laos I started noticing fluctuations in my oil pressure gauge. The pressure started dropping and oil started leaking, or I should say pouring, from the engine cowling and covering my windscreen. I called lead and said I needed to return to base as quickly as possible. Firefly lead checked me over, confirming that I was losing a lot of oil and we proceeded to immediately head for NKP. I once again had my fingers crossed as I approached home base knowing my oil supply was rapidly being depleted. The leak was getting worse and the A-1 was now drenched in oil. I had difficulty seeing anything in front of me as my vision was severely limited by that oil blanketing the windscreen. I turned on final for a straight-in approach, slid open the canopy and used a lot of rudder and aileron to side-slip the aircraft in order to see around the windscreen and find the runway. I was praying the engine would not seize, as it could have at any moment, and the tension created by the situation was worsening by the second.

I finally safely touched down, breathed a tremendous sigh of relief, and carefully taxied off the runway shutting the engine down on the taxiway to preclude running the engine absolutely dry of oil. The A-1 had an oil capacity of thirty seven and a half gallons and I later discovered I had about a gallon and a half left. As I climbed out of the cockpit I tried in vain to find some foothold on the oil-covered wing and fuselage but I slipped anyway and fell flat on my back on the ground. It was a fittingly inglorious way to end that flight.

I flew combat mission number twelve on twelve March: it was in an A-1H. On my flight home, after expending our ordnance on yet another patch of jungle with no apparent results, I had an epiphany. I was hot, sweaty, dirty, tired, and slid open the canopy of the "H" to obtain some measure of relief from the heat and humidity in the cockpit. I listened to the monotonous explosive roar as each of the eighteen cylinders fired through its short exhaust stack and I asked myself, "What am I doing still here in Southeast Asia? I have flown over this same area with people trying very hard to kill me in 1965, 1966, 1967, 1968, and, now in 1969. Nothing has changed except I am looking at a different airplane on my left wing. The war is going to go on and on and I have not made a bit of difference. Have I, in fact, made one trip too many?"

I received Sandy briefings on the 13th and sat on Sandy ground alert on the 14th. I was scheduled to fly my first airborne alert Sandy mission on Saturday morning the 15th as Sandy 4. As I recall, Major John Shacklock would be Sandy 3. Saturday morning dawned hot and humid and I was in a reflective mood: it was the Ides of March (remember Julius Caesar) and March had not necessarily been a good month during my brief Air Force career. I thought of Tom and the 13th of March five years earlier as I suited up for the day. I thought of the Navy A-4s colliding under my flare light on a Friday the 13th. I also thought bad things always happen in threes: I had bailed out on the second; I almost had to repeat that activity on the 8th and now it was the 15th. Even more foreboding, it would be my thirteenth combat mission in the A-1.

I walked out to my airplane: it was an A-1H, Navy serial number 134562 transferred to The United States Air Force as serial number 52-134562 according to the official U.S. Navy and U.S. Marine Corps BuNos-Third Series. The airplane bore the name Fightin' Polish Eagle given to it by Ron Furtak, one of the designated instructor pilots in the 602nd.

I went through my prefight and strapped myself into the airplane. Engine start accomplished, I taxied to the end of the makeshift asphalt runway where I lined up by Sandy 3 and ran the engine to full power for the standard checks. Bad news: while I checked magnetos the engine started backfiring, reminding me of Maggie's Special. I returned to the ramp and stayed strapped in the airplane while the crew chief and engine mechanics worked feverishly on the engine. Maintenance completed, I again taxied out running my engine up while taxiing as I did not want to delay our flight any more than was absolutely necessary. I hoped the ground crew had properly fastened the engine panels they had removed during the magneto work. Everything appeared normal, engine instruments were in the green, and I notified Sandy 3 that I was ready to roll. I watched as Sandy 3 roared down the runway to get airborne and I started my takeoff run.

Two A-1Hs in Takeoff Position (USAF Photo)

I released brakes and quickly applied full throttle while shoving the right rudder pedal forward and using a little right aileron to counteract the tremendous torque from the engine. As I gained speed I released some of the rudder and aileron pressure to keep the Skyraider aligned in the middle of the runway. It seemed the aircraft did not accelerate quite as fast as normal and I started becoming somewhat apprehensive. At 50 knots I released the back pressure on the control stick and allowed the tail to fly. I continued bouncing and waddling across the rough asphalt as the heavily laden A-1 struggled to attain a flying speed of 117 knots. At 80 knots I checked the engine instruments rapidly to ascertain everything was still good to go. I again checked my airspeed and the dial had not moved remaining on 80 knots. My limited experience said not to worry as the Skyraider seemed to always stagnate in the 80-knot region before continuing to climb to takeoff speed.

By now the end of the 7,800-foot runway was appearing in my vision and I started to become concerned over the possible failure of the engine to develop full power considering the magneto difficulties already encountered. The manifold pressure read the required 56 inches and engine instruments were in the green but the airspeed still read 80 knots. I suspected some kind of instrument failure and decided to try to fly the bird off the ground. Unfortunately I tried that maneuver just a few knots too soon. I was well over 80 knots but not quite to the needed 117 knots. When I applied back pressure on the control stick the slight change in angle of attack killed off my acceleration and the A-1 skipped and floated without getting airborne.

Now things were getting desperate and I analyzed my alternatives as my remaining runway was disappearing way too fast. I could fly the airplane at 80 knots if it was not loaded but I could not risk jettisoning my ordnance and external fuel because I was too close to the squadrons of A-1s and helicopters lining the ramp just off my wingtip. I could elect to use the extraction system as I had the minimum 80 knots needed by the "H" but that alternative did not appear too inviting as there was a chance of something malfunctioning in the extraction system and I would simply blow myself out of the cockpit and into the ground with no chute. My remaining choice was to abort the takeoff, take the arresting barrier, and take my chances. I could not believe it: after well over one thousand takeoffs in my flying career I finally had an airplane that was not going to get airborne.

I called "Sandy 4 aborting" and pulled the throttle to idle, quickly reversing my rudder and applying aileron to counteract the sudden wing rise. I heard the tower ominously exclaim over an open mike, "Somebody get the crash trucks quick!" I dropped the tailhook preparing to engage the barrier as I left the runway but there was no barrier to engage on the makeshift runway. As I headed into the cleared area south of the runway I attempted to collapse my landing gear in accordance with established procedures for tail draggers as they tended to flip upside down in rough terrain. The Skyraider was bouncing so badly I could not grasp the landing gear handle.

That turned out to be a good thing because there was a ditch just off the end of the runway I would have to cross. If I had managed to collapse the landing gear I would have probably gone nose-low into the ditch creating an abrupt halt to aircraft movement. I probably would not have survived that impact and the certain resulting explosion. As it was, I hit the ditch in the nose-high attitude typical of the tail-dragging A-1 and the ditch sheared the landing gear from the airplane. I skidded to a halt on the belly of the Fightin' Polish Eagle in a cloud of dust and dirt while scattering my ordnance load all over the ground: for the moment I was safe and uninjured.

All right, I had survived the crash but now I had to escape from the airplane. I quickly checked to see if I had any injuries from the unexpected ride through the dirt and knew I was OK. I thought I would not immediately blow the canopy as it could possibly provide some protection from an external fire but I realized I had to stand up after actuating the emergency single point release of the lap belt, shoulder restraint straps, and pendant line connections.

In the simulator the secondary escape system, also known as the ground egress system, was used so many times it operated with the slightest pull of the handle. I grabbed the handle and pulled but nothing happened. I pulled again with as much force as I could muster, almost bending the handle, but the system was hopelessly jammed. I could see the first flames licking around the left wing root and I knew I had to get out fast. I went ahead and blew the canopy off the airplane and I reached up to manually disconnect the four Koch fittings that secured me to the airplane, starting with the left shoulder fitting.

As I was working to release that fitting the aviation gas seeping from the ruptured lines connecting the squashed 300-gallon belly tank reached the hot engine. The result was a huge explosion that forced flames to erupt under the instrument panel, filling the cockpit and hitting me in the chest and face. I had my helmet and sunglasses on with the helmet visor pulled down: my nose and face were also protected by my oxygen mask and I shielded my face with my right arm in reaction to the explosion. As I looked back up I could see the flames burn away the sleeve on my right arm.

I looked down to watch the legs burn off my flight suit and I realized I was screaming in pain and frustration. It was as if my mind and body were two separate entities and I thought to myself, "Wayne, you're screaming." I could push myself back in the seat to get my face and chest out of the fire and I did so while still attempting to release my harness fittings. I got the left shoulder disconnected and started on the right shoulder fitting.

In the meantime a thousand thoughts were filtering through my mind. I thought, "Now I know how Joan of Arc felt." I managed to get the right shoulder fitting undone while listening to the sound of my blood sizzling on the hot floor pan. Two more quick thoughts passed through my brain: "I wonder if the fire-fighting foam the Air Force uses will be cold on my arms and legs," and "I will never eat steak again." Now I was struggling to release the two fittings on my leg straps. I had to force my hands into the flames to get to those fittings and that took every ounce of will power I had left.

I noticed two guys in t-shirts and sweat pants standing well off to the left of my burning aircraft and I cursed them saying, "I hope you SOBs are enjoying watching me burn to death." I started to wonder where the rescue trucks or helicopter were and soon realized that no one was coming after me. I said, "Wayne, you are going to have to get yourself out of this cockpit if you want to live. No one else is going to help." I was still struggling with the lap belt and leg strap fittings but my strength was rapidly fading. Adrenaline alone could not pull me out of the airplane.

Suddenly I heard the distinct sound of powerful rotors over me: a Jolly Green was there to my rescue. I was indeed fortunate that a Jolly Green HH-3 piloted by Major Stuart Silver was preparing to launch on a test hop and was sitting on the ramp waiting for me to take off. Major Silver immediately recognized my predicament and lifted off to hover over me using the rotor wash to beat down the flames that were eating me alive. I thought, "Just like an angel." With a renewed vigor I again attacked the stubborn leg straps managing to get the right one released.

My strength was fading fast and my mental faculties were finally starting to be affected. I kept telling myself to get out of the airplane; you have to get out of the airplane. I was starting to stiffen up, my legs did not want to move and my hands and arms were drawing into the classic burn pose known as the pugilistic position. I tried to get my legs to move me to a standing position but the left leg strap was still fastened. I managed to get my right foot up to the edge of the windscreen and canopy sill where I could push off to get myself out of the cockpit. With a mighty push I propelled myself over the left canopy rail and ended up snarled in the remaining leg strap, hanging upside down against the side of the burning A-1. I thought, "I am so tired I think I will rest for a moment before continuing this fight. At least I am out of the airplane." In reality I was not in a much better spot as the airplane was still burning, its ordnance was still going off and I was still caught in my seat and chute harness.

My luck had not yet completely run out. My EC-121 formation flying buddy, Jon Ewing was in the Sandy alert shack standing ground alert and he heard the ruckus. He went to the front porch to see a Skyraider burning in the field near the shack. At first glance the two Sandy pilots on alert thought the burning A-1 was a Zorro as the tail carrying the identifying TT was already blackened to the point it could have been a TS. Jon watched for a minute and he realized the burning A-1 was a Sandy. He also immediately knew it had to be me as I would have been the last A-1 scheduled to take off during that time period.

He ran across the field and climbed on the wing of the burning airplane, ignoring the exploding ordnance that prompted the evacuation of the south end of the airfield. I was revived by the sudden appearance of Jon and told him I was really, really glad to see him. Immediately after Jon arrived on the scene one of the two guys I had earlier been cursing also put in a welcome appearance to help. Grady Allen was a PJ and he was asleep in his hooch when I ran off the runway. The noise woke him up and he proceeded to the scene in sweat pants, T-shirt, and barefoot. Jon pulled my parachute knife from its pocket on my flight suit and cut the strap that had refused to let me escape. We ran from the burning airplane but I only made it a few feet before I momentarily lapsed into unconsciousness and fell face-first in the dirt. My comrades picked me up and Jon said to run, "We are not out of it yet!"

We dove into the ditch that had sheared the gear from the aircraft where I almost collided head-to-head with my flight commander who had also come to assist in my rescue. Grady and another PJ then cut the smoldering and smoking emergency flares from my survival vest. They also removed my 38 S&W and the 100 rounds of ammunition I carried. Meanwhile members of the group flagged down the Jolly and Major Silver landed in the field where I was loaded into the chopper for a ride to the front door of the dispensary. I was loaded face first on the floor and then into a web seat where I twisted around to lay on my back. I then passed out again and came to in the dispensary to the sound of the flight surgeon cutting and pulling on the remainder of my gloves trying to remove them.

I complained to the flight surgeon telling him to cut more and pull less and he patted me on the chest saying, "Why aren't you asleep; I have given you enough morphine to knock out a horse." The doctor continued to cut away clothing and boots and began wrapping me in bandages. I once again lapsed into a semi-conscious state as the medical staff continued to prep me for immediate transport to Clark Air Base where the closest large hospital was located.

Jon Ewing returned to the alert shack to discover no one there: he did not know the area had been evacuated because of my exploding ordnance. The HH-3 Jolly piloted by Major Silver took several hits from the 20mm shells in my wings cooking off. Shortly after all of us had left the scene of the crash, the 250-pound white phosphorus bomb on my right inboard stub detonated. By the time the fires subsided almost nothing was left of the Polish Eagle except for the wingtips, part of the tail, and the armor plate behind the pilot's seat. The best part of the information found in the U.S. Navy and U.S. Marine Corps BuNos –Third Series describing A-1H serial number 52-134562 is in the last two words: "…aborted takeoff at Nakhon Phanom Royal Thai Air Base, exploded and burned Mar 15, 1969. Pilot survived."

Jon left the empty alert shack and came to the dispensary to check on me where the flight surgeon told him, "If you want to see

Wayne again, you had better see him now." I never really knew exactly what that statement meant as it could have related to the fact I was leaving right away for Clark or it could have had a much more ominous intent. I drifted into consciousness again to find Jon standing next to the gurney I was lying on.

He looked extremely distraught and said, "It should have been anybody but you. It should not have been you: anybody but you." I tried to ease the pain and anguish suffered by both of us by saying very optimistically, if unrealistically, "Hey, it is OK. I will be back flying with you in a couple of weeks." That certainly did not turn out to be the case. Jon was awarded the Airmen's Medal, the highest non-combat award given, for his role in saving my life. Grady Allen and Stuart Silver certainly deserved recognition for their efforts but, to my knowledge, they were not appropriately rewarded.

The next time I regained consciousness I was being wheeled out of the dispensary accompanied by my squadron mates and the female intelligence officer. I told her we really needed to stop meeting that way: the fact is I never did know her name. As I was being wheeled down a hallway to take me to a waiting C-130, a base chaplain approached me in an obvious hurry as he was out of breath saying, "Captain Warner, do I have your permission to pray for you?" I said, "That might be a good idea." Just like I thought at Takhli on the verge of leaving for a combat mission in the Thud, a good word to the right place from the right source never hurt anybody.

I was loaded on the Thailand shuttle for the last time: not as a pilot or a passenger but as a litter patient. The C-130 departed NKP and landed at Korat where I was transferred to a waiting C-141 for the remainder of the trip to Clark. The engines on both aircraft were running and the transfer rapidly took place with my stretcher being carried from the rear ramp of the 130 to the rear ramp of the 141. I later felt somewhat privileged to have all those resources dedicated to my care. As had been predicted earlier on the street in Bangkok, I departed Thailand in less than a month after I had arrived. I ended my brief Sandy career never taking part in a rescue except for the two episodes where I was the party being rescued. I did achieve the honor of using the call sign Sandy once; even if it was just to say, "Sandy 4, aborting."

The Fightin' Polish Eagle Burning (USAF Photo)

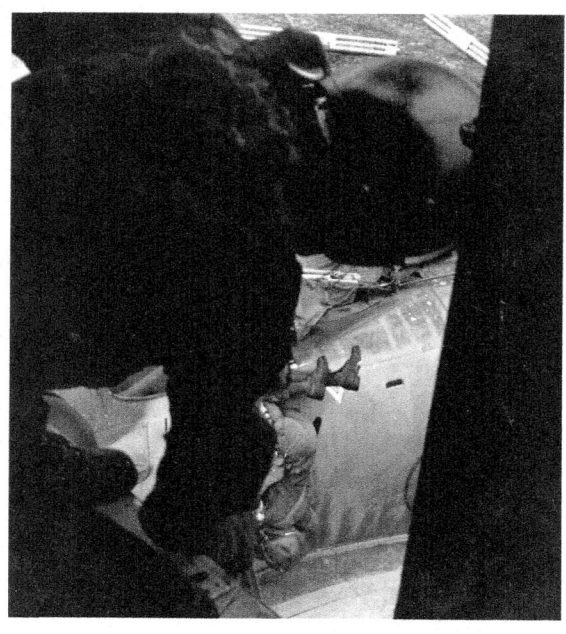

Photograph taken from the Jolly Green. PJ is standing in the door. I am hanging upside down trapped by my harness. (USAF Photo)

PJ Grady Allen in his T-Shirt Removing my Flares/Ammo (USAF Photo)

Remains of the Polish Eagle (USAF Photo)

HOSPITALS

CLARK AB; 106th GENERAL HOSPITAL; BROOKE ARMY MEDICAL CENTER; WRIGHT-PATTERSON AFB

I regained consciousness for a brief period as I was carried from the C-141 to an ambulance at Clark AB: the ambulance was one of the hearse-type vehicles used during the 60s painted Air Force blue. I do not remember anything after that until I came to in my new quarters. I was surprised to see I was in a two-bed semi-private room with no roommate. I expected to be in a ward and said to the nurse, "My condition is not catching." She replied that they were concerned about me catching something rather than the other way around. I did not know burn patients are highly susceptible to infections.

The Red Cross sent a young guy to my room to write a letter home for me. I dictated and he wrote - that would be the only letter my parents received from me for the next few weeks although the Air Force did provide a telegram delivered by a taxi letting them know about the accident, where I was, and that I was listed in critical condition.

In one of my lucid moments I carefully examined my burns trying to see what had happened to me. The right arm and hand were grotesquely swollen: the fingers had expanded to the point they looked like sausages. The arm was the size of a leg and ranged in splotchy hues from black to brown to wax-colored white. It was hard as a rock to the touch. My left hand and arm were also burned but not nearly as badly as the right arm. Both legs were burned from just above the knees to above the ankles where my boots had been.

The right side of my face and neck was burned between where my oxygen mask had been to where the edge of the helmet protected me. The right half of the eyebrow over my right eye was gone and the skin surrounding that eye was burned although the eye seemed OK. Records indicated I suffered approximately 40% burns with 30% being third degree.

I again looked at the arm and decided it would have to be amputated as I saw no way it could be saved. The following day the doctor came to my bed and told me they were going to have to work on the arm. I thought, "This is it; this is where I lose the arm for good." I weighed the alternatives, considering all that had happened, and came to the conclusion that an arm for a life was a good deal and I accepted that trade-off with no second thoughts. To this day, I am amused at TV and movie scenes where an injured character yells he would rather die than lose a limb. Believe me, that is not a wise choice.

The doctor returned to the room with two nurses and a small operating table holding various scalpels and other tools of the medical profession. As they busied themselves for the forthcoming procedure I decided that, although I accepted the loss of the arm, I was not going to watch them remove it. I turned my head towards the wall and grasped the lower bed rail with my left hand in spite of the pain in that hand.

I could feel them lifting the right arm and pulling and tugging on it. I could also tell they were working at the shoulder area and I thought there will not be enough arm left for even a prosthetic hook. The operation was over and the doctor and nurses left the room. I do not have any idea how much time passed before I finally decided I needed to see what I looked like without an arm. I was lying on my back and as I straightened up my head I caught a glimpse of my swollen forearm at my side. My immediate reaction was, "I can't believe this: they cut the damned arm off and left it in bed with me!" After that alarming thought, it occurred to me that maybe they had not amputated the arm after all. I said to myself, "See if it moves: try to lift the arm." I raised the arm to discover the doctor had made two deep, full length incisions from shoulder to wrist on each side of the arm. The arm now looked like a sausage that had ruptured while being cooked.

As I was pondering the rationale behind this procedure the doctor happened to be walking past the room and noticed what I was doing. He quickly entered the room and asked if I knew what they had done. I said I thought they were going to remove the arm as it could not be saved. The doctor was profusely apologetic and told me that they would never under any circumstance perform an amputation without the full knowledge of the patient. He also was amazed that I still had the mental capacity, in spite of the morphine, to grasp some of what was going on. The doctor then explained that they had performed an escharotomy which is a surgical procedure used to treat full thickness, third-degree, circumferential burns. Full thickness burns are characterized by the skin becoming tough and leathery, while the underlying fatty tissue expands thus the procedure is used primarily to combat gangrene. Shortly after the escharotomy I was prepped for air transport to the U.S. Army 106th General Hospital in Yokohama, Japan, also known as the Far East Burn Center or Kishine Barracks. Clark AB simply did not have the facilities to care for the extensive burns I had suffered.

I arrived at Yokota Air Base aboard a C-141 on 21 March and then was strapped in an Army med-evac helicopter for the remainder of the trip to the 106th. A severe late-winter storm prevented the chopper from an immediate departure from Yokota and I had to wait and wait while strapped on a litter. I started hallucinating and became absolutely convinced that my hands were clasped across my stomach and that my fingers were twisting themselves around each other, like snakes, until they would be hopelessly tangled. I became so insistent that a corpsman eventually had to un-wrap me so I could see my arms were actually at my sides and my fingers were not getting twisted together. I thought, "Am I losing my mind?"

The 106th was established in 1965 to handle casualties from Vietnam and the large number of burn patients created by the conflict required the creation of a burn unit at the hospital in 1967. The decision was eventually made that the facility was neither equipped nor staffed to provide long term care for seriously burned patients and an agreement was reached with the Surgical Research Unit, Brooke General Hospital, Fort Sam Houston, San Antonio, Texas to accept those patients. A regularly scheduled air evacuation flight was established to transport the seriously burned directly from

Yokota to Kelly Air Force Base in San Antonio. I would be on one of those flights.

Thank heavens I did not have to spend more than ten days at the 106th. I received tremendous care at Clark AB but my memories of the 106th are nothing but nightmares. I was placed in the intensive care unit after my admission where the patients surrounding me died soon after my arrival. As I was being admitted I could hear the two corpsmen prepping me discussing my hair. One wanted to know why I had so much hair and the other responded that they had an Air Force Captain as a patient. The two then laughingly said I shouldn't mind if they shaved that hair off as I really did not need it. After my head was shaved I was wheeled into the ICU where I was placed in a corner between several open windows with no blankets or covering. It was Japan in March and the temperature was below freezing: I thought I had been placed in a corner to die without disturbing the other patients and I shivered miserably throughout the night. I later discovered that was necessary to try and get my abnormally high body temperature under control but no one bothered to explain that to me at the time. I do not recall ever meeting anyone in my entire stay that identified himself as a doctor and the corpsmen were a mean-spirited bunch that could have cared less about their patients.

After a few days in the ICU, due to a lack of space, I was moved to a bed in a ward where the other patients were ambulatory. Every morning the corpsmen would come through early demanding everybody get up without checking to see that I was neither able nor supposed to get out of bed. One of them smacked me on the soles of my bare feet with a clipboard to wake me up, causing my legs to spasm violently and I angrily cursed him, telling him to look at the notes on my patient record.

Just before I departed the 106th, I was in the salt water tank soaking my burns when the decision was made it was time to remove the thick eschar from my right arm: that arm was peeled like a banana after they cut through the tissue between the escharotomy incisions. Again no one explained what they were doing, or why, and I loudly protested exclaiming, "Stop! Stop! You are pulling off my skin."

The only pleasant memory I have of my stay in Japan was the numerous cards and letters I received from my friends. I especially treasured the card from Parks Rea and the 357th TFS at Takhli, and the card from Ed Bulka reminding me that to be an ace, you had to destroy five *enemy* aircraft. As could be expected, those treasures were lost and probably destroyed at the 106th as they never accompanied me to the states.

I do not know what the problem was at the 106th, whether the corpsmen were all disgruntled draftees or the doctors were cast-offs from normal medical society or both, but the care at that facility was absolutely disgraceful. It was painfully obvious to me that the facility definitely was neither equipped nor staffed to provide for any patient, much less the seriously injured patients. At long last I was air-evacuated to Yokota for the trip to Brooke; I was greatly relieved to know I had not only survived my crash but I had also survived the 106th General Hospital.

The C-141 I was on landed to refuel at Travis AFB in California en route to San Antonio. It was 31 March 1969 and the California weather was gorgeous. As the C-141 was packed with litter patients it was not unloaded for the refueling stop and our aircraft met the fuel trucks on a taxiway well away from the terminal and other buildings. For safety reasons fire trucks were standing by and all the doors and ramps on the 141 were opened. I could smell the fresh air and could see the beautiful sky as I thought, "Thank Heavens, I am home. If I die, at least I will die in the United States." The thought of just being back in our country tremendously buoyed my spirits. Although I did not realize it at the time in my semi-conscious state, the prediction by the Thai on the street in Bangkok that I would return to the United States in less than three months had also come true.

Brooke General Hospital was everything the 106th was not - the doctors, nurses, and corpsmen were professional, courteous, and caring. I was introduced to my doctor soon after arrival: he explained in detail what I was going to have to endure over the next several weeks and months. He also said there were two ways for a patient to cope with the pain of recovery; one was for the doctor to administer copious quantities of pain killers, including morphine, which invariably led to serious drug rehabilitation issues, and the other way was for the patient to simply endure that pain resulting in a much shorter total recovery period. My doctor did not like the drug addiction approach and I was eventually quite thankful for that as I observed the addicts created from pain-killing drug therapy suffering intense withdrawal pains long after their burns had healed.

The first step in the long process toward my rehabilitation had started in Japan: the debridement process. Debridement is the medical removal of burned, dead, damaged or infected tissue to improve the healing potential of the remaining tissue. Removing the worst eschar tissue on my right arm was the beginning of my debridement. Each day I would be placed in a large stainless steel tank filled with salt water where the doctor and corpsmen would take razor blades, scissors, wire brushes, and scalpels to snip, scrape, and cut bits and pieces of my burned flesh from my arms and legs. Salt water was used because the military discovered in WW II that sailors who were burned and spent time in sea water recovered more quickly than ground troops who were burned. To counteract the pain I was given a single Darvon tablet before entering the tank. I was also treated with a topical ointment known as sulfamylon to prevent infection and help the second and first degree burns heal.

As Brooke was a research center, large numbers of visiting doctors and nurses from other countries as well as US medical personnel seemed to always be present when I was being sliced and diced. I asked why I always had an audience and the answer was that I made less noise than most of the other badly burned patients. For years afterward I could not stand the sound of scissors cutting anything.

The skin regulates body temperature and the loss of skin results in feeling cold even though body temperature is elevated: shivering is a way for the body to try to warm itself and I had been shivering non-stop for weeks in spite of the fact my body temperature hovered around 103 degrees. Every muscle in my body ached and all I wanted to do was stop shivering for just an hour or two.

The debridement process was over - now I needed new skin. A person's body will not permanently accept another person's skin as replacement skin which means the source of skin for grafts must come from one's own body (an autograft): the more burn coverage a person has, the less skin is available for grafts. To ensure that my body would accept an autograft, heterografts (also known as xenografts) and homografts (also known as allografts) were first used on my wounds. Homografts use skin harvested from cadavers and heterografts use skin harvested from animals, primarily pigs and dogs. Homografts and heterografts provided only temporary covering as the patient's immune system would reject the foreign skin, usually within seven days. Those grafts were then replaced with an autograft.

Skin grafts were used in several thicknesses. A split-thickness skin graft involved the epidermis and a little of the underlying dermis; the donor site usually healed within several days. I had several full-thickness skin grafts that were necessary for severe burn injuries. Those grafts involved both layers of the skin and the donor site required more time to heal. My full-thickness grafts were perforated with multiple small holes and then stretched to cover more debrided area. To harvest the donor skin a grafting machine was applied to the donor area, and the skin removed. The best way to describe the way the donor area felt is to say it felt like a huge floor-burn.

After the graft was stitched to the recipient area, it was covered with non-adherent gauze and a layer of surgical gauze was held in place with sutures. A sterile non-adherent dressing was also applied to the raw donor area for several days to protect it from infection. As the donor area scabbed over, the dressing would gradually be removed. The bandages used to wrap the grafted areas had salt water poured on them every few hours to keep them moist and prevent them from sticking to the new skin.

The grafting operations were done under anesthesia; I underwent eight such procedures including four homografts, two heterografts, and two autografts. I returned from my first heterograft operation and awoke to the smell of wet dog. I looked at my hands and arms and my appearance was very much like a werewolf. I had wire frames that extended from hand grips in my palms past the end of the fingers, and clips on my fingernails. Rubber bands ran from the clips to the wire frames to keep my fingers from curling or drawing. My fingernails had grown long and were black and curled like claws and my hands and arms were covered in dog skin, hair and all. My doctor said all they had to do was keep me away from fire hydrants.

After the grafts using cadaver and animal skin, which my body rejected in a few days as expected, the doctor was ready to attempt the first autograft using my body as the skin source. My donor areas were my upper left arm, my chest, and the unburned areas of my thighs. The last autograft took place on the 25th of April. My autografts were successful and my face had almost healed by this point. I gave up any thoughts of looking like Captain Ahab from Moby Dick or having a hook for a hand. Due to my progress I was moved from the third-floor ward holding the more severely burned patients to the second floor ward holding the guys who were rapidly healing. We referred to ourselves as crispy critters. To pass the time we had television available and my favorite show was the Lawrence Welk show although I never watched it again after I left the hospital. My favorite song was Doug Kershaw's "Louisiana Man" and I later had the opportunity to tell him so at a Y2K celebration in the Sheraton Hotel in the French Quarter of New Orleans.

My recovery progress hit a huge stumbling block within days after my transition to the second floor: I suddenly started having severe breathing problems and could only take very shallow, painful breaths. After suffering for a day or so, I finally casually mentioned it to one of the nurses; the reaction of the medical personnel was immediate and greatly concerned. I had suffered a completely collapsed right lung or spontaneous pneumothorax which is a common secondary effect from serious burns.

I was quickly transferred to the intensive care unit and a thoracic surgeon was summoned to my aid. The surgeon immediately pushed a scalpel through my chest and rib cage and inserted a tube to try to re-inflate the lung. That was done without the benefit of anesthesia of any kind and the doctor had to kneel on the bed using both hands to force the scalpel through the chest muscle. As he strained to penetrate the chest wall he commented that I was a lot tougher than I looked. The operation was successful: the tube quickly filled with bloody fluid and my breathing improved. During the next several days the location of the tube was moved four different times, each time using the same painful procedure. On the positive side, I learned what it feels like to lose a knife fight without actually engaging in one. Although the possibility of removal of the lung, or at least a portion of it, was considered, the surgeon told me he decided such extreme surgery was out of the question as he feared I would not survive the operation.

As part of the thoracic treatment a large hypodermic needle was daily inserted into my back at the base of the lung cavity to draw fluid from the lung space. The needle was so large a scalpel had to be used to make a small incision for the needle to enter. I felt like a pin cushion as I was also given multiple shots of antibiotics and blood was drawn from my femoral arteries on a daily basis. I was not only required to "donate" blood, I was also the recipient of thirteen pints of rare B-negative whole blood during my stay at Brooke.

One day just before lunch, the surgeon entered the ICU and said he needed to perform a bronchoscopy: a medical procedure for viewing the inside of the lungs. He explained a bronchoscope consisting of a rigid metal tube with an attached lighting device would be inserted through my mouth into my lungs to allow the surgeon to examine my airways for any abnormalities such as foreign bodies, bleeding or tumors. He told me he would place three shots in my neck and throat to help deaden the pain but that the procedure would be done with me sitting on the edge of my bed while I was conscious. The surgeon then looked at his watch and said, "Oh look, it is almost lunchtime so we will do this after you have eaten." He left and I thought, "Who in the heck wants to eat now?"

Shortly after the lunch serving-trays had been cleared, the surgeon returned to perform the procedure: no shots were administered to my neck or throat and I sat on the edge of the bed while a corpsman braced his knee against my back and grasped my forehead with his right hand, pulling my head rearward and straightening my throat for the tube to be inserted. With the placement of the tube, I felt as if I were suffocating and gasped for air while clutching the corpsman's left hand as if it were an aircraft throttle. Once again, looking on the positive side, I now knew what it must feel like to be an apprentice sword swallower.

Meals were never an event to look forward to. In spite of having absolutely no desire to eat, we were forced to consume copious quantities of calorie-laden protein to enable the body to regenerate itself. The rule was, "You had to eat your way out of the hospital." I developed such a gag reflex to meat that a dozen scrambled eggs at a time took the place of the meat on my tray. The nurses and corpsmen would carefully examine our trays at the end of the meal to make sure we did not try to hide food in empty drink containers or under a plate. In spite of the large amount of food I consumed on a daily basis my weight dropped from 150 pounds to 106 pounds. I could not say I was all skin and bones; however, as I had very little skin left on those bones - unless you also counted what did not actually belong to me during the homografts and heterografts.

I had now been in the ICU for over a month and growing more and more depressed each day. Patients kept coming in the ICU and patients kept leaving the ICU but not one left alive. I was becoming convinced that my last days would be spent in that room where everyone was covered in sterile gowns and face masks and I wondered what the people who cared for me on an around-the-clock basis looked like. Some of the nurses told me the only way to combat that depression was to contact my parents and let them know what was happening. They said that if I did not, then they would. I made the telephone call and my parents made a very quick all-night trip to San Antonio from Indiana to bolster my will to live.

Finally one patient's misfortune turned into my good fortune. The patient in the bed next to mine had been in the ICU for three long years and he suffered heart failure. The ICU staff immediately tried to revive him with open heart surgery taking place inches from my bed. The doctor frantically trying to save the guy yelled at the corpsmen, "Get Warner out of here, he does not need to watch this." I was wheeled around the corner and after a while the doctor came and said, "If we have to assign someone to sit by your bed full time, you are getting out of this room." Within minutes I was happily moved from the ICU back to the third floor ward with all my chest tubes, collection bottles, and my own personal attendant.

After escaping the dungeon of death and having the most-welcome company of my parents and brother, my overall condition improved rapidly and I soon started walking about the ward for exercise. I tried going for a walk in the rose garden outside the hospital but the summer heat in San Antonio quickly persuaded me to return to the air conditioned comfort inside.

My doctor was married to a Thai and he took me to a party at his home where his wife had prepared a Thai dinner. Ironically enough, he met his wife while working in a clinic in Laos before the Pathet Lao created the need for me to have been in that part of the world. I knew I was getting better when I finally noticed that many of my nurses were really attractive; especially Linda, who worked in the ICU where her face had always been hidden. Several of the nurses slipped me out of the ward one evening and took me to a party where I discovered I did not have the hand strength to open a twist-off cap on a beer bottle. The nurses asked why my hair had been shaved at the 106th as they said there was absolutely no medical reason for that to have been done. They were absolutely appalled at my memories of that hospital.

On another evening several of us were taken by members of the hospital staff to the Riverwalk in San Antonio for a Mexican dinner which was quite a welcome change from the meals we were used to eating. It was always great to get away from the sounds and smells of the burn wards for even a short period of time.

The war was still part of my life as it was sometime during the month of May that my mother hesitatingly informed me my last Air Force roommate, JB East, had been shot down by ground fire over Laos and was missing (declared KIA several weeks later). JB was flying George Marrett's A-1 named "Sock It To 'Em" on that mission. JB's remains were recovered in 1994 and he was buried in Fort Sam Houston Military Cemetery not far from Brooke. I was also informed during April or May the accident investigation board concluded the official cause of my 15 March crash was material failure (airspeed indicator) and airfield facilities (no barrier and the ditch at the end of the runway). That welcome news was delivered to me by Rich Hall who took the time and effort to pay me a most appreciated visit. Rich also presented me with the photos of the aborted takeoff that are included in this book. (The picture of me on the ground was given to me by Grady Allen years later when we finally met.) After three long, painful months at Brooke I was transferred on 26 June 1969 by an Air Force med-evac flight from the care of the United States Army to the care of the United States Air Force at the Wright-Patterson AFB hospital in Ohio. Almost one month later, on 20 July 1969, Apollo 11 astronauts Neil Armstrong and Edwin "Buzz" Aldrin landed on the moon. To be honest, that historic event did not get my full attention as I was much more interested in recovering from my injuries and worrying about the fate of my comrades still flying in Southeast Asia.

In August I was released from the hospital for three days to make a visit home. I flew commercially and the stewardess noticed I had trouble getting into my seat; my legs would not bend at the knees from the burns and my right elbow and wrist were frozen in position. She then invited me to ride in the first class section where I had room to stretch out my legs and make myself as comfortable as possible considering my overall medical condition.

I returned to Wright-Patterson to meet my medical evaluation board in late August where I was told I would not fly again and that I would be retired with a 100% disability rating. My Air Force career started at Wright-Patterson on 29 April 1959 with the physical examination for admission to the United States Air Force Academy and that career ended in retirement on 9 September 1969 from the results of another medical exam at the same Air Force Base.

My separation from the United States Air Force was definitely without fanfare as was typical for Vietnam returnees. There were three people besides me at my retirement ceremony, a two-star general, a colonel, and the photographer. I was simply another of the thousands of patients in military hospitals at the time.

Retirement Ceremony (USAF Photo)

Once again I boarded a commercial flight to Louisville, Kentucky. I was 28 years old and retired. I always knew I would retire from the Air Force one day; I just did not expect it to be quite so soon. What would I do with the rest of my life? While I was pondering the answer to that question the two stewardesses aboard sat down beside me and started inquiring about my ribbons and my injuries. I decided there was no immediate need to try to determine my entire future course of action and I wondered if their lay-over would give them time to go with me to the Kentucky State Fair. Wishful thinking soon returned to reality as I knew I could barely walk, much less stand up for any period of time, and getting excess sun on the newly grafted areas would have sent me right back to the hospital. That prospect was definitely not in my future plans and I bade the two ladies good-bye when I departed the aircraft.

About two months after I returned to my hometown, which is right across the Ohio River from Louisville, a surprise package was delivered to the apartment where I lived - it was my B-4 bag containing the uniforms, flight suits and civilian clothes I had taken to NKP with me almost a year earlier. Someone hurriedly packed my belongings while I was being treated at the NKP dispensary and the bag was placed on the C-130 as I left the base.

Thanks to the people handling me, the bag managed to stay with me until I reached the 106th General Hospital where it remained when I was transported to the States. I guess someone was tasked with cleaning out storage rooms at the hospital and the bag was identified and finally shipped to my home address. It came as no big surprise that my belongings were "lost" at the 106th.

The bag was encrusted with mold and dirt and I had to struggle to get the zippers to work. As I was wrestling the bag to open it, the biggest zipper broke and the contents, including a brief case, spilled onto the floor. The impact from the fall broke open the briefcase but the only object to actually roll out of the case and slowly settle on the floor in plain view was the little red and black object given to me by the young Thai on the street in Bangkok.

EPILOGUE

In my five and one half years in the cockpit I accumulated a total of 2,365 flying hours with 952 of those hours (40%) in combat. In my 38 months in Southeast Asia I flew 637 missions, including 374 combat flights, with 170 of those over North Vietnam. For contributions to the United States effort in Vietnam the units I belonged to received the following awards and decorations for the time periods in which I was a member of the unit: the 355th TFW was awarded two Presidential Unit Citations and the Air Force Outstanding Unit Award with V device (for valor); the 56th SOW was awarded a Presidential Unit Citation; and both the 355th TFW and the 56th SOW were awarded the Vietnam Gallantry Cross unit award with Palm.

In 1970 I was presented the Colonel James Jabara Award for airmanship from the United States Air Force Academy for my efforts in Southeast Asia and the mission at Kham Duc. The award is presented annually to the graduate whose accomplishments demonstrate superior performance in fields directly involved with aerospace vehicles. I was privileged to join a rather distinctive fraternity in receiving that recognition but I knew I had not really done anything other than what I was being paid to do.

After my retirement from the United States Air Force, and while trying to acclimate myself to the civilian world again, I started thinking in earnest about how to begin the next part of my life. Although by the fall of 1969 I was physically recovering, my time in a hospital was not yet completely over and I had various reconstructive surgeries performed over the next three years at the Veterans Hospital in Louisville, Kentucky. Mentally however I was just beginning the recovery process. In the first two months of 1969 I was a member of an elite fraternity; I was a combat-seasoned fighter pilot – at the top of the pyramid in our minds. I had been an aircraft commander and mission commander in multi-engine aircraft, a flight lead and force commander in fighter aircraft, and I was being prepped to lead combat search and rescue missions. I had the responsibility of making life or death decisions on a routine basis that impacted lots of other peoples' lives. I had a long-term job I loved and I was supremely confident in my abilities to perform that job – a confidence that I recognize some people viewed as bordering on arrogance. My future was bright as my officer effectiveness reports recommended early promotion and attendance at any advanced military schools I selected. Unfortunately, my life-long plans literally crashed along with my airplane that previous spring. That fall, upon being thrust back into the civilian world, where service in Vietnam was treated indifferently by most and reviled with open hostility by some, I suddenly felt I was a "nobody". I had no worthwhile individual identity and no sense of belonging to a specific group. I did not have a job, much less a career; I was generally ill-at-ease with members of the opposite sex and, at times, very self-conscious of my badly-scarred appearance. I was unable to perform the simplest of physical tasks and I faced an uncertain future - a completely new condition for someone who had always had a life-long desire to fly for the military.

Over the next year I found a temporary measure of solace in NHRA drag racing where I drove a 1970 426 hemi-powered Dodge Challenger SS/DA with some limited success at mid-western racetracks. That car was a special-order "demo" as I had started working part time as a salesman for the local Dodge dealer to keep myself occupied. The dealer had already sold me a 1970 hemi-powered Dodge Charger that became my tow car. The arrangement was made with the owner of the dealership that I could order any car I wanted as a demonstrator as long as I would buy the car when I stopped working there. I was able to escape the realities of the world, at least for a short period of time on the weekends, by encasing myself in a bright-red 3,000-pound steel cocoon and thundering down a narrow asphalt strip in a civilized version of head-to-head combat. In spite of the adrenaline of occasionally winning at the drag strip, by the spring of 1971 I recognized I still needed something of a permanent nature to do to prepare for the future and restore my badly damaged self-esteem.

The burns I incurred with the resulting lack of mobility limited my job opportunities in the future and I decided to go to law school as I thought there are a lot of different things one can do with a law degree. I confess I never had a great desire to be an attorney but they seemed to do OK as far as income potential went and the profession certainly does not require any outstanding physical attributes. At any rate, that course would immediately establish a couple of short-term goals, with the potential for creating a long-term career.

I approached the Veterans Administration to inquire about the Vocational Rehabilitation Bill and informed the VA I wanted to go to law school. The counselor suggested law school could prove to be very boring to me as their tests indicated I was a little more adventuresome in nature than most attorneys. He described it as being off the scale in my desire for adrenaline-producing vocations. Instead the VA wanted to send me to school to become an osteopath and specialize in performing surgery. I failed to see much difference between being a doctor or a lawyer and the amount of schooling involved. At any rate, I was not overly enamored with the prospects of attending medical school and suggested to him that I could probably still fly if I had the manual dexterity to perform any surgery. While displaying my hands with their splints and bandages, I asked the counselor if he wanted me to operate on him. He replied, "I see your point." The decision was made to send me to law school.

My father knew the comptroller for the University of Louisville and arranged for me to meet him in an effort to entice me to remain in the Louisville area as I wanted to attend school in Florida. After meeting the comptroller, he arranged for me to meet the Dean of the Brandeis School of Law at U of L. The Dean said, based on my graduate record exam scores, which were excellent, and my Academy transcript, which was mediocre (placing me comfortably in the middle of my class) but from an acclaimed institution, he would recommend my admittance to the school and to suggest the admittance board waive the requirement for me to take the Law School Aptitude Test (LSAT) as he called it "essentially a writing exercise." The Dean even graciously offered the suggestion that writing assistance could be provided if my hands did not heal quickly enough. I was not about to look a gift-horse in the mouth and readily agreed to accept that generous offer.

I began classes in the fall of 1971 and graduated in the spring of 1974 without requiring any assistance in writing. In the early spring of 1972 I accepted a part-time job working as a clerk for the Judge of the Superior Court (family court) in Clark County, Indiana. My future wife, Vickie, was attending Indiana University and worked part-time in the Juvenile Division of the Court. I managed to get her telephone number in the two days our jobs overlapped and we were married in June 1973. She laughingly informed me at the time that regardless of where I lived she wanted to live in Florida, a condition to which I readily agreed.

The spring of 1974, just before graduation for both of us, I learned the United States Air Force hired civilian attorneys for certain duties. Wright-Patterson Air Force Base advertised for positions in the base legal office and in the Office of the Staff Judge Advocate for the Air Force Logistics Command (AFLC) performing weapon systems and aircraft acquisition. I interviewed for the positions in April 1974. While I was in Ohio it snowed both days and I decided I was not ready for cold weather regardless of the fact I did not have a job waiting for me on departing law school. I arrived home in Indiana on a Friday night and told Vickie we would probably have several days before having to make a final decision if I was offered a job. We agreed that I would not accept the job in the base legal office but that I would consider the acquisition job with AFLC. On the following Monday morning at 0800 I received a telephone call telling me I had the job in acquisitions. I was the last applicant interviewed and the attorney selection board had been holding off making a decision until they talked to me because of my Air Force background.

I asked if I could take a day or two to consider the offer and the response was in the affirmative. As Vickie and I wanted to live in Florida, I then contacted Eglin AFB to see if they had any acquisition attorneys. At the time Eglin only had one civilian attorney position and it was for an experienced attorney; however, the personnel office informed me there was a movement underway to expand the Eglin mission and civilian attorney slots would be available in the future. The personnel office also told me to take the Wright-Patterson job as it was a beginning level position and it was much easier to transfer locations once one was in the civil service work force.

I accepted the job at WPAFB with the covert intent of transferring from Ohio to Florida at the earliest opportunity. I began work at WPAFB in August as a law clerk as I had not yet received the results of the bar exam taken in Indianapolis, Indiana in June. In October I was notified I had passed "the bar" and my position title was changed to "attorney". The truth was I had never passed a "bar" before - not when I could go in - when I was a fighter pilot. (I must confess I stole that line from my *jefe* and good friend, William Landsberg Esq., who used it at my civil service retirement ceremony. Bill is a story in himself: Valley Forge Military Academy, Harvard at 16, Cornell Law School, entered into active duty as an Air Force Judge Advocate March 15, 1969 on the same day I was roasting myself.)

I received the desired transfer to Eglin AFB in November of 1976 and Vickie and I moved to the Fort Walton Beach area where we still reside today. In 1979 our daughter, Allison, was born. She graduated from Florida State University in 2001 and The University of Georgia School of Law in 2004. In 2008 Allison married John Vann, a Green Beret with the United States Army, Fifth Special Forces, who served in Iraq and other locations in the Middle East. John just completed his masters in project management. They currently live in Atlanta, Georgia where Allison is a litigation attorney, well-experienced in the courtroom.

Time doesn't stand still for any of us and the passing years and other events brought my active duty Air Force career and that of many of my friends to an end. In 1977 I was sent TDY to attend a continuing legal education course at Lowry Air Force Base in Denver, Colorado. For some reason I was walking through the Headquarters building at Lowry and stopped to look at the photographs of the Command Staff for The United States Air Force Technical Training Center at Lowry: the Deputy Commander was none other than Tom Kirk. I asked his secretary if he was in and told her I had been in his 105 squadron. She immediately ushered me into Tom's office where we enjoyed a brief reunion and I was able to say, "Welcome back, Colonel." Tom retired in 1978 and currently resides in Colorado. Johnnie Hall survived his stint as a Jolly Green pilot in Vietnam and retired from the Air Force as a colonel in 1990. He now lives in Cookeville, Tennessee. Bob Storms retired from the Air Force in 1983 and went to work for Hughes Aircraft Company. He currently resides in Albuquerque, New Mexico. Norm Pfeifer retired as a colonel at the end of 1989 and went to work for Flight Safety International. He lives in San Antonio, Texas. Steve Sutton never did get his fighter assignment and resigned from the Air Force on January 31, 1970 in pursuit of other opportunities in life with Raytheon. He now lives in Brandon, Mississippi. Gary Olin retired from the Air Force at George AFB, California in 1985 after flying the F-4G Wild Weasel. He then flew an F-106 and the B-1 for Rockwell for ten years. He now resides in Apple Valley, California. Gary also told me Cal Jewett became a test pilot for Northrop flying the B-2 after his Air Force career. The Big Kahuna, John Giraudo, was promoted to Major General and retired on 1 November 1977. He died on 17 June 1996. Colonel Lawrence "Larry" Pickett passed away in Las Cruces, New Mexico in 2007. Jon Ewing became a T-38 Instructor Pilot at Holloman AFB after he completed his combat tour at NKP. He then flew F-4s in Germany and at Homestead AFB in Florida where he retired after 21 years in the Air Force. Jon then flew commercially for Pan Am and Atlas, hauling cargo in Boeing 747s. He is currently a safety inspector for the FAA and lives in Miami, Florida. In March 1969 I did not know Grady Allen but I finally got to meet Grady in 2008 when he called me on the telephone after locating me by reading George Marrett's book. Strangely enough Grady has a cousin whom I knew from working at Eglin AFB but we never made any connection through that set of circumstances. Grady also retired from the Air Force after his career as a PJ and lives in South Carolina. George Marrett retired from Hughes Aircraft in 1989 and lives in Atascadero, California where he still flies his vintage 1945 Stinson L-5. Ed Bulka finished his one year tour at Pleiku and then served in several command positions including a tour as the base commander of Lackland Air Force Base in San Antonio. His last assignment in the Air Force was at Maxwell AFB in Montgomery, Alabama where he retired. He still lives in Montgomery today. Rich Hall, like George, is still flying – a cropduster in South Dakota. I can say, with absolutely no reservation, what an honor it has been to have known and flown with a band of brothers like I had the privilege to meet in my brief Air Force flying career.

As an Air Force acquisition attorney, I specialized in research and development contracting and weapon systems acquisition. I supported and worked on many smart weapon programs that were and are being used with great success in Operation Desert Storm and the conflicts in Bosnia, Iraq, and Afghanistan. I spent countless hours in defending a multitude of protests over the years from disappointed bidders and offerors and even more hours in the source selection process for hundreds of programs. I also acted as a liaison attorney on several contract disputes before the Armed Services Board of Contract Appeals.

In 1989 I successfully completed the Patent Bar examination and received my five digit identification number as a patent attorney, registered to practice before the United States Patent and Trademark Office. I was named the outstanding civilian attorney in Air Force Systems Command in 1978 and again in 1985. I received the Meritorious Civilian Service Award in 1979 for my work in Research and Development contracting. I was named the outstanding civilian attorney in Air Force Material Command in 1994 and also received the Wrightson Award as the outstanding civilian attorney in the Air Force for the same year. That award is presented for demonstrated excellence, initiative, and devotion to duty. Finally, I received the Outstanding Civilian Career Service Award on my retirement from civil service in January 2004.

My goals as an Air Force attorney, reinforced by my experience in the cockpit and combat, were always to see that the war-fighter got the best weapon possible and to ensure the taxpayer received the maximum benefit from each tax dollar expended on such weapons. My verbal and written combat on behalf of the Air Force and the taxpayer from 1974 to 2004 is material for another story to be told sometime in the future. By the way, thank you for wondering. To answer your question, my eyesight remains 20/30, right on that border, and I still do not have to wear glasses - but that will undoubtedly also change in the not-to-distant future.

SOURCES

The United States Air Force in Southeast Asia, 1961-1973: Carl Berger, editor, Office of Air Force History, Washington, D.C. 1977.

Cheating Death: Combat Air Rescues in Vietnam and Laos by George J. Marrett: Smithsonian Books. 2003.

Aircraft in Profile, Volume 11: Charles W. Cain, editor, Doubleday & Company, Garden City, New York. 1972.

Republic F-105 Thunderchief by David Anderton: Osprey Publishing Limited, London. 1983.

F-105 Phase Manual, Course 111506E, 4520th Combat Crew Training Wing, Nellis AFB, Nevada. 1965.

T.O. 1T-37B-1, USAF Series T-37B, Flight Manual. 1961.

T.O. 1T-33A-1, USAF Series T-33A, Flight Manual. 1963.

T.O. 1F-105D-1, USAF Series F-105D & F-105F, Flight Manual. 1965.

T.O. 1A-1E-1, USAF Series A-1E/A-1E-5, Flight Manual. 1968.

Register of Graduates of the United States Air Force Academy, 2010 edition, published by the Association of Graduates of the United States Air Force Academy.

Board of Investigation, Record of Proceedings, Inquiry into Attack upon USCGC Point Welcome on 11 August 1966, Ordered on 13 August 1966.

Undergraduate Pilot Training Yearbook; Class 65-B, publisher unknown.

Polaris, 1963 Yearbook of the United States Air Force Academy, published by Walsworth Publishing Co. Marceline, Missouri.

Wikipedia: http://www.wikipedia.org

Wikimedia: http://commons.wikimedia.org/wiki/Main_Page

Vietnam Command Files, Operational Archives Branch, Naval Historical Center, Washington D.C.

Cockpit map showing tanker refueling tracks, TACAN channel locations, distances and headings: carried on all my F-105 missions.

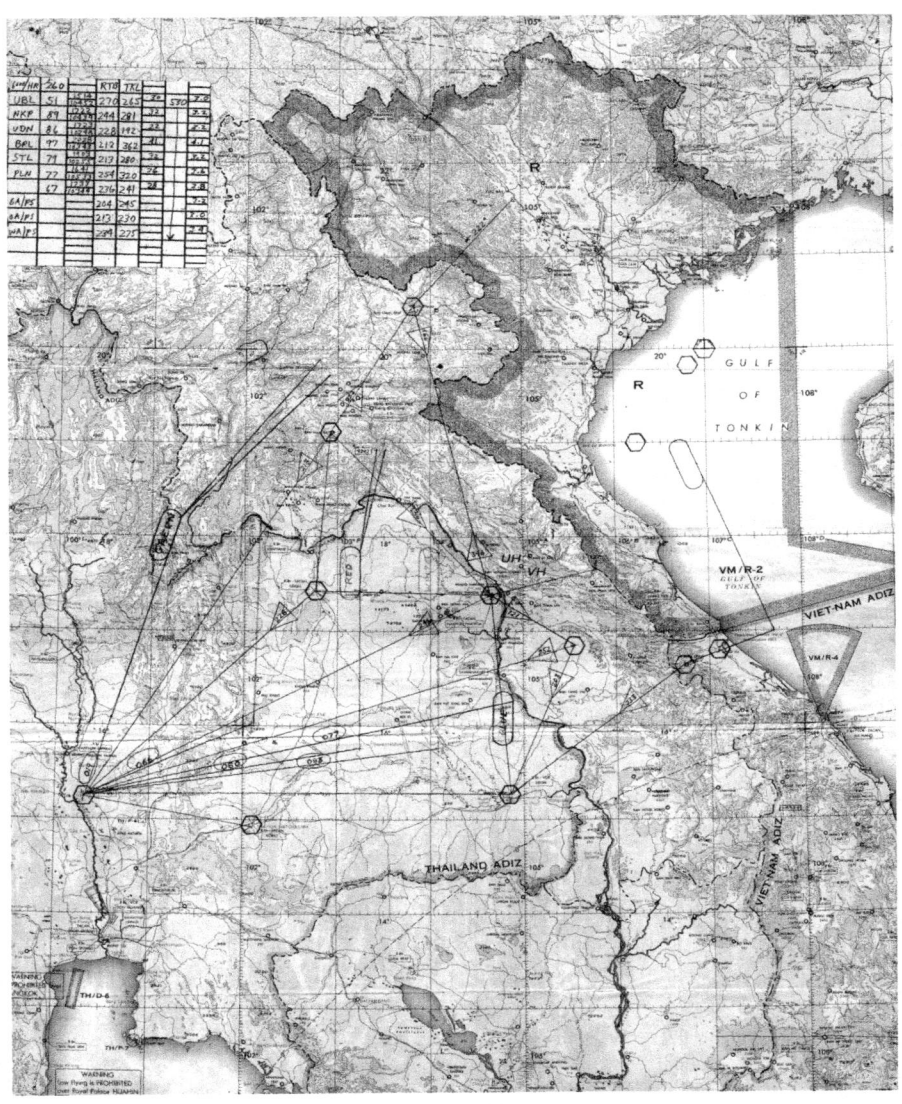

Made in the USA
Middletown, DE
03 November 2022